KU-680-925

The Essence of Services Marketing

Adrian Payne

Cranfield School of Management

FINANCIAL TIMES

Prentice Hall

An imprint of Pearson Education

Harlow, England · London · New York · Reading, Massachusetts · San Francisco
Toronto · Don Mills, Ontario · Sydney · Tokyo · Singapore · Hong Kong · Seoul
Taipei · Cape Town · Madrid · Mexico City · Amsterdam · Munich · Paris · Milan

Pearson Education Limited
Edinburgh Gate
Harlow
Essex CM20 2JE
England

and Associated Companies throughout the world

Visit us on the World Wide Web at:
htpp://www.pearsoneduc.com

© Prentice Hall Europe, 1993

All right reserved; no part of this publication may be reproduced, stored
in a retrieval system, or transmitted in any form or by any means, electronic,
mechanical, photocopying, recording, or otherwise without either the prior
written permission of the Publishers or a licence permitting restricted copying
in the United Kingdom issued by the Copying Licensing Agency Ltd.,
90 Tottenham Court Road, London W1P 0LP.

Typeset in 10/12 pt Palatino
by Keyset Composition, Colchester

Printed and bound in Great Britain by
T. J. International Ltd.

Library of Congress Cataloging-in-Publication Data

Payne, Adrian.
    The essence of services marketing / Adrian Payne.
      p. cm. –– (The Essence of management series)
    Includes bibliographical references and index.
    ISBN 0-13-284852-X
    1. Service industries––Marketing. I. Title. II. Series.
  HD9980.5.P34   1993
  658.8––dc20   92-33438
                                              CIP

British Library Cataloguing in Publication Data

A catalogue record for this book is available from
the British Library

ISBN 0-13-284852-X

---

15 14 13 12 11
06 05 04 03 02

Contents

To my friends
Ron, Dod, David and Peggie

Preface

The service sector has increased dramatically in importance over the last decade, both internationally and in the UK, where it now accounts for nearly two-thirds of the economy by income and jobs.

Deregulation of services, growing competition, fluctuations in demand, and the application of new technologies are presenting a considerable challenge to service companies, which the unification of Europe is intensifying. Banks, building societies, insurance companies, airlines, retailers and telecommunications companies, as well as professional service firms such as accountants and lawyers, need new approaches to address the challenge. The non-profit sector, government and newly privatized utilities are also becoming increasingly aware of the need to improve their performance. In addition, the importance of services as a source of competitive advantage in manufacturing has increased greatly in the last five years.

The text provides an introduction to services marketing and is aimed primarily at managers on short courses and students on MBA, undergraduate and diploma courses. The book does not assume a specialist knowledge of marketing. There are many longer and more complex texts on services marketing and management; however, a short book offering a foundation on the application of marketing for service businesses from a managerial perspective is noticeably absent. It is the purpose of this book to fill the gap. Having read this book, readers may wish to move to more advanced texts, details of which are given in the reading list at the end of the book.

In a short book such as this some decisions inevitably need to be made on which elements of marketing should be discussed in detail and which should be only briefly reviewed. In determining this several issues were considered. Firstly, to what extent are the elements especially important or crucial in service businesses? Secondly, to what degree are the elements different, either substantively or in application, for service businesses? Thirdly, is a good general treatment of the elements available in most marketing texts? Emphasis is placed here on a number of topics which are not discussed adequately in many of the texts on services marketing. The book adopts a managerial rather than a tactical focus, and presents those strategic elements and issues considered relevant to service marketers.

The intention of the book is to provide a managerial framework of services marketing for managers and students with an interest in the services sector. Its focus is primarily on services business but much of it is relevant to services in manufacturing businesses. In keeping with the concept of The Essence series, academic footnotes are kept to a minimum.

Chapters 1 and 2 begin by exploring the nature of services and key concepts in services marketing and relationship marketing. Chapters 3 to 5 examine some specific key tasks in services marketing including development of effective mission statements, market segmentation and service positioning. Chapter 6 involves a review of assembling the services marketing mix. Chapters 7 and 8 are concerned with a detailed discussion of two key challenges to the services marketer – the creation of integrated marketing plans and the development of a customer-focused services culture.

Most of the ideas contained in this book have been used with many managers both at Cranfield School of Management and within service firms. I am particularly grateful to the insights offered and the intellectual curiosity displayed by MBA students and practising managers attending courses at Cranfield, and my colleagues researching and working in the services sector. Sections of this book are based on a number of articles and monographs used at Cranfield on services courses and are included with the copyright holders' permission.

Special thanks are due to Pennie Frow for all her help and support and to Robert Stanley, a pioneer services marketer, for getting me started. I am especially indebted to Anna Newman-Brown for typing this manuscript.

Adrian Payne

1

The nature of services marketing

Introduction

Western Europe is becoming a predominantly service-based economy. Explosive yet erratic growth in this area, coupled with decline in traditional manufacturing, means that whether measured by income or numbers employed, more than 60 per cent of most Western economies are now in the services sector. Intense competition, encouraged by deregulation in both the financial and professional markets as well as the application of new technology, has fuelled this growth. Within all sectors of the economy there has been a growing trend towards specialization leading to greater reliance on external specialist service providers. When the EC dropped its internal trade barriers at the end of 1992, opening up the entire continent of more than 320 million people as a home market, this trend intensified.

Services marketing has increased in importance over the last decade with the advent of competition. Ten years ago competition was relatively less important to firms in service businesses. However, competitiveness has escalated at an alarming rate in most service sectors.

We are frequently asked the following question: 'Is the marketing of services, and consumer or industrial products, similar or different?' We always give the same reply – yes and no. This reply, rather than being evasive is meant to highlight the following:

- At a higher level the theory of marketing is relevant to all exchange relationships. The same principles and concerns apply.
- At the industry sector and operational levels the characteristics of

services may dictate the need to place more emphasis on some marketing element and/or apply other marketing elements in a different way.

With an intangible product and with copyright impossible on many service innovations, marketing staff in the services industries are faced with a special challenge: how can a firm achieve a unique corporate image, product differentiation, and a distinctive reputation in the marketplace? How can one airline seat or one insurance policy be made to appear more attractive than the opposition's broadly similar offering? In such an intensely competitive environment, marketing skills in services will be at a premium.

Some of the traditional business divisions no longer apply and services marketing professionals can learn from people involved in other areas of expertise such as fast moving consumer goods, which has a lot in common with certain services such as package tours. Professionals like architects and solicitors now have to consider how to improve their marketing to both consumers and businesses as a consequence of deregulation. In deregulated businesses in particular, managers have recently seen an urgent need for marketing where none existed previously. Even non-profit making bodies such as charities, hospitals and some government departments – such as the Department of Industry with its Enterprise Initiative – are discovering the need for services marketing.

In this chapter we begin with an overview of the service economy and a consideration of the nature of services. We then examine ways of classifying services to help gain strategic marketing insights and conclude by exploring the role of services in manufacturing.

An overview of the services economy

World War II marked a milestone in the explosive rise of service industries. At the end of the war major social and economic changes transformed Western economies. The restructuring of the shattered European economy brought massive new investment projects, which placed new demands on the financial services sector. Specialization in all areas of production meant that businesses became more reliant upon contracted services. The increased rate of spending on personal consumption services has also been impressive, rising from approximately 30 per cent to over 50 per cent in the last thirty years. Individuals are spending greater proportions of their income on travel, restaurant and leisure services to improve the quality of their lives; on telephone, postal and communication services, reflecting a more dynamic and fast moving environment; and on purchasing better quality health and education services. The growing complexity of banking, insurance, investment, accountancy and legal services has led to greater demands for financial and professional services in each of these areas.over the past forty years the services sector has come to dominate our economy. This trend has been so strong that it has been described as the Second Industrial Revolution.

Table 1.1 provides a breakdown of employment in the UK between 1968 and 1990. On the basis of the government statistics in the table we can see that the proportion of employees in the service sector grew from 50 per cent in 1968 to 70 per cent in 1990. This trend has been evident throughout the world, with the more advanced economies showing the greatest growth in services. Table 1.2 offers an international comparision of civilian employment in twenty-one countries. With the exception of Greece and Portugal all the countries listed have more than 50 per cent employment in the services sector.

Table 1.1 Total UK employees in employment in June 1990 (thousands)

	Service employees	All other	Total in employment
1968	11 242	10 944	22 186
1969	11 243	10 905	22 148
1970	11 294	10 699	21 993
1971	11 358	10 290	21 648
1972	11 667	9983	21 650
1973	12 096	10 086	22 182
1974	12 240	10 057	22 297
1975	12 545	9668	22 213
1976	12 624	9424	22 048
1977	12 698	9428	22 126
1978	12 895	9378	22 273
1979	13 260	9378	22 638
1980	13 384	9074	22 458
1981	13 142	8244	21 386
1982	13 117	7799	20 916
1983	13 169	7403	20 572
1984	13 503	7238	20 741
1985	13 769	7151	20 920
1986	13 954	6932	20 886
1987	14 247	6833	21 080
1988	14 853	6907	21 760
1989	15 319	6908	22 227
1990	15 849	6846	22 695

Source: Monthly *Digest of Statistics* and *Employment Gazette*, February 1991.

Table 1.2 Civilian employment by sector: international comparison, 1988 (%)

	Services	Industry	Agriculture
UK	66.6	29.8	2.3
Australia	67.8	26.4	5.8
Austria	54.5	37.4	8.1
Belgium	68.9	28.3	2.8
Canada	69.9	25.6	4.5
Denmark	67.1	27.2	5.8
Finland	59.6	30.6	9.8
France	62.9	30.3	6.8
FR Germany	56.1	39.8	4.0
Greece	46.2	27.2	26.6
Irish Republic	56.9	27.8	15.4
Italy	57.7	32.4	9.8
Japan	58.0	34.1	7.9
Luxembourg	65.0	31.6	3.4
Netherlands	68.8	26.4	4.8
Norway	67.1	26.4	6.4
Portugal	44.2	35.1	20.7
Spain	53.1	32.5	14.4
Sweden	66.7	29.5	3.8
Switzerland	59.2	35.0	5.7
United States	70.2	26.9	2.9

Source: *Employment Gazette*, February 1991.

There are various reasons for the growth of the services sector. These can be divided into demographic, social, economic and political changes.

Demographic changes

- Life expectancy has risen, producing an expanding retired population. This sector has created new demands for leisure and travel as well as for health care and nursing.

- Structural shifts in communities have affected where and how people live. The development of new towns and regions has increased the need for infrastructure and support services.

Social changes

- The increased number of women in the workforce has led to previously domestic functions being performed outside the home. This has promoted the rapid rise of the fast food industry, child care facilities and other personal services.

- Working women and the resulting two-income households have created a greater demand for consumer services, including retailing, real estate and personal financial service.
- The quality of life has improved. Smaller families with two incomes have more disposable income to spend on entertainment, travel and hospitality services.
- International travel and mobility have produced more sophisticated consumer tastes. Consumers compare services both nationally and internationally and demand variety and improved quality.
- The greater complexity of life has created demand for a wide range of services, particularly legal and financial advice.
- Communication and travel have increased aspiration levels. As a result both children and adults are making new demands on learning establishments, in order to develop the skills needed to compete in our complex and fast changing environment.

Economic changes

- Globalization has increased the demand for communication, travel and information services. This has been fuelled by the rapid changes brought about by new information technology.
- Increased specialization within the economy has led to greater reliance on specialist service providers; for example, advertising and market research have become specialist functions supporting all sectors of the economy.

Political and legal changes

- Government has grown in size, creating a huge infrastructure of service departments. This trend has been augmented by the European Community.
- Internationalism has made increased and new demands on legal and other professional services.

Many of these changes have knock on effects. For example, globalization is producing concentration within many industries – often by acquisition. In one recent example over £15 million was spent on fees to merchant banks, financiers, accountants and legal advisers, over a relatively short period in an unsuccessful attempt to ward off an acquisitor. A large amount was also spent by the acquiring company. As a consequence of the successful acquisition, many staff were made redundant, creating demand for out-placement consultants and external specialists. Management consultants were called in to improve the company's operations and actuaries were used to sort out transference and settlement of pension schemes. Loss adjusters, insurance brokers and insurance companies were involved following a fire, (which was believed to be the result of sabotage). Architects were used to redesign the building, involving the subsequent use of other services.

This example illustrates an important feature of demand for many types of services. The various providers of the services did not have advance warning of the service requirement. They could not plan for the sudden demand on their various specialisms. Each of the services was very much dependent upon people resources, which cannot be stockpiled. The increased demand for services is in part driven by the greater complexity of all business transactions.

A further factor in the current economy is an increasing trend for companies to subcontract out to specialist service providers a wide range of activities which they previously carried out in house. Contract catering, recruitment, advertising, transportation, computer services, training, market research and product design are all examples of such work being delegated to external organizations. Companies are becoming more focused, realizing that increased sophistication in the marketplace and greater competition means that such activities are better performed by external specialists.

The nature of services

The increasing interest in the services sector has been accompanied by considerable disagreement and debate as to what constitutes a service and whether services marketing is a distinctive subject area. Many authors have sought to develop definitive descriptions of a service, yet no adequate agreed definition has emerged.

In a review of over ten different definitions of service one author pointed out that all the definitions he had examined were too limited. Our definition, recognizing that any definition is inherently restrictive, is as follows:

> A service is an activity which has some element of intangibility associated with it, which involves some interaction with customers or with property in their possession, and does not result in a transfer of ownership. A change in condition may occur and production of the service may or may not be closely associated with a physical product.

However, given the diversity of services, examples of services which do not fit any definition can usually be found.

There is often confusion over terminology in this area. We view a **product** as an overall package of objects or processes which provide some value to customers, whilst **goods** and **services** are subcategories which describe two types of product. However, there is no widely used convention and even within the same service industry, terms such as 'product', 'service' or 'service product' may be used interchangeably. Rather than being too concerned with a definition of services, it is more useful to explore what they are and what 'offer' is made to customers.

Phillip Kotler has distinguished four categories of offer, varying from a pure good to a pure service:[1]

- **A pure tangible good** such as soap, toothpaste or salt. No services accompany the product.

- **A tangible good with accompanying services** to enhance its consumer appeal. Computers are an example.

- **A major service with accompanying minor goods and services** such as first class airline travel.

- **A pure service** like baby-sitting and pyschotherapy.

This categorization starts to make it clear why it is difficult either to define or generalize about services. Services vary considerably over a range of factors, including whether they are directed at businesses or individual consumers; whether they require a customer's physical presence; and whether they are equipment intensive or people intensive (e.g. a launderette versus a masseur).

To what extent do services differ from goods? It is frequently argued that services have unique characteristics that differentiate them from goods or manufactured products. The four characteristics most commonly ascribed to services are:

- **Intangibility** – services are to a large extent abstract and intangible.
- **Heterogeneity** – services are non-standard and highly variable.
- **Inseparability** – services are typically produced and consumed at the same time, with customer participation in the process.
- **Perishability** – it is not possible to store services in inventory.

Several authors have pointed out that these characteristics by no means fully describe all services and that some manufactured products have one or more of the four characteristics. Some further comments on these characteristics are appropriate at this point.

Undoubtedly services such as education are highly intangible; however, the customers of a restaurant seek a highly tangible product

– food of high quality. Clearly there is a continuum of tangibility ranging from highly intangible to highly tangible. Both services and goods differ in their degree of tangibility, as is shown in Figure 1.1.

This concept of a continuum is useful when considering each of the four distinguishing characteristics of services. It should also be recognized that at least some characteristics may also apply to goods. The distinction between manufactured products and services therefore becomes less clear. Services can only be described as having a *tendency* towards intangibility, heterogeneity, inseparability and perishability. Any given service will display a different combination of each of the four factors, as illustrated in Figure 1.2. This suggests a continuum for each of the four characteristics. For example, a fast food service is high on tangibility, highly standardized, generally performed near to the customer, and is perishable. Financial services are less tangible, highly varied, can often be performed away from the customer and are generally required immediately.

To define services narrowly as only relating to service industries is clearly incorrect. Services, as will be discussed later in this chapter, are not confined exclusively to traditional service sector businesses. Manufactured products tend to be highly tangible, tightly controlled for variance during production, are often produced away from the customer and can be stockpiled. Today there is an increasing trend to attempt to differentiate products by service elements. Thus one distinguishing characteristic within the highly competitive photocopier industry is the quality of customer service. This has become an inseparable part of the overall product and is a major factor in the buying decision.

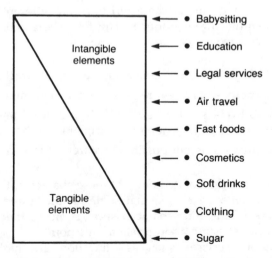

Figure 1.1　The intangibility and tangibility continuum

The emphasis on each of the four service characteristics can vary for a given service, and can also be a source of competitive differentiation. A service which is more easily understood, and whose benefits are more easily assessed, may have a distinct advantage over a less 'tangible' service product.

A food service which is more standardized should have a lower cost base, and may improve its competitive position *vis-à-vis* a less standardized competitor by using its cost position to add value or reduce price. A banking service which places greater emphasis than its competitors on electronic transfer of information and automatic teller machines (ATMs) will have less personal contact with customers outside the bank, but more flexibility of service within the bank. The greater use of technology in banking has made the sector more able to cope with varying demands on personal service delivery.

Understanding the position of a particular service on each continuum, and the position of competitors, is an important steps towards finding possible sources of competitive advantage. In the same way,

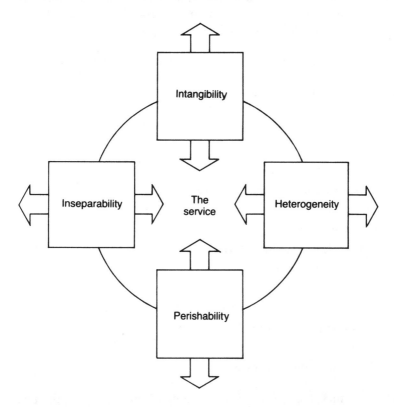

Figure 1.2 A continuum for each of the four service characteristics

manufacturers of products can seek competitive advantage by focusing on 'service' elements. IBM understood this at an early stage in its development, and distinguished itself by excellence in customer service. A customer buying an IBM machine is confident that the support offered by the manufacturer in choosing, installing and maintaining a product will be of the finest quality. Service features are often a major factor in the success of many manufacturing companies.

Classification of services

Researchers have directed much attention to the development of classification systems for services. Such classification schemes help service managers to cross their industry boundaries and gain experience from other service industries which share common problems and have similar characteristics. Solutions to problems and breakthroughs in similar service industries can then be applied by managers to their own service businesses.

At the simplest level we can categorize services by exclusion: services are that part of the economy left over after the exclusion of agriculture, manufacturing and mining. Another means of defining services is to simply list service industries.

A description of services typically includes the following industry sectors:

- Retailing and wholesaling.
- Transportation, distribution and storage.
- Banking and insurance.
- Real estate.
- Communications and information services.
- Public utilities, government and defence.
- Health care.
- Business, professional and personal services.
- Recreational and hospitality services.
- Education.
- Other non-profit organizations.

However, such listings are not very helpful in identifying the features relevant to the marketing of services.

Many other approaches have been used to classify services. Classification schemes use a wide range of factors such as:

- Type of service.
- Type of seller.
- Type of purchaser.
- Demand characteristics.
- Rented versus owned services.
- Degree of intangibility.
- Buying motives.
- Equipment based versus people based.
- Amount of customer contact.
- Service delivery requirements.
- Degree of customization.
- Degree of labour intensity.

More than sixteen studies have discussed classification schemes. (For a review see Bowen[2], and Grönroos[3].) However, whilst some of these classification schemes are useful, many have shortcomings in terms of helping to develop marketing strategies.

There is a need to develop service classification schemes that enable service managers to compare their firm with those in other service industries sharing common characteristics and learn from them. Christopher Lovelock[4] suggests the following key issues with respect to the classification of services:

- Service industries remain dominated by an operations perspective, with managers insisting that their service industry sector is different from other service industry sectors.
- A managerial mind set evident in many service sectors argues, for example, that the marketing of airlines has little in common with the marketing of banking, insurance, motels or hospitals.
- Simple classification schemes of services are not sufficient – they should offer strategic marketing insights if they are to have managerial value.

Researchers have recently sought to classify services in a manner more meaningful to the services marketer. They have been concerned with classification schemes that give insight into the strategic dimensions of services marketing. Lovelock has developed classification schemes which attempt to answer five specific questions. These are each examined in a series of two dimensional matrices and are shown, in summary form, in Figure 1.3. This approach is based on the idea that appropriate *combinations* of classification schemes are more likely to lead to improved strategic marketing insights than classification schemes based on using only one variable at a time. Each of the questions yields strategic marketing insights.

What is the nature of the service act?

Classification 1 in Figure 1.3 considers the intangibility of services and their recipients. It raises a number of interesting questions including whether the customer needs to be physically or mentally present during the service delivery, how the customer benefits, and how the customer is changed by the receipt of the service activity. This helps the service provider address questions of location and schedule convenience where people have to be present to receive the service. It also raises the question of whether service managers can restructure the service activity to standardize it in a way that is more convenient to the customer in terms of service delivery and more convenient for the service provider. For example, offering a pick up and home delivery laundry service may remove the necessity for an expensive high street presence, facilities for customers, and also solve problems of balancing demand for services during the day.

What style of relationship does the service organization have with its customers?

Classification matrix 2 contrasts the nature of service delivery and whether or not there is a formal relationship between buyer and service provider. Membership organizations can benefit from a knowledge of their customers' identities and addresses and can tailor specific offers to the specific customers through targeted direct marketing; market segmentation becomes easier and customer loyalty stronger. This classification system helps yield insights into trade offs between pricing and usage rates. Where no personal relationship exists services can be provided by continuous delivery, where no charge is typically made (e.g. police services), or by discreet transactions, where the user pays for each specific service provided (e.g. the cinema). In the latter case market opportunity is restricted as customers are often anonymous and the service provider does not have much information about them. Where there is no formal relationship the key issue for marketers is whether some form of more enduring relationship can be established through a membership club or subscription series. Airlines such as British Airways and American Airlines and hotel chains such as Hyatt and Sheraton place considerable emphasis on this.

How much room is there for customization and judgement?

Matrix 3 contrasts the degree of customization of service characteristics with the degree of judgement required by customer contact staff. A critical issue for service marketers is to decide to what extent the service offer should be customized. For example, French lessons can be offered via a one-to-one tutor relationship, or by mail through the provision of audio or video tapes and tutorial books. Some service providers seek to limit the number of options: airlines offer first class, business class, economy and standby, or hotels offer suites, double rooms and single rooms. Service marketers need to balance the cost of custom made versus a standard service. Customer contact staff in professional service firms can exercise a high degree of judgement, or may establish a series of routines and procedures – the 'cookie cutter' approach – where contact staff exercise relatively little judgement (e.g. a high street chain preparing individuals' taxation returns).

What is the nature of demand and supply for the service?

The fourth classification matrix contrasts the nature of demand fluctuations over time and the extent to which supply is constrained. Service firms cannot develop an inventory. If the demand exceeds the supply of a particular service the business may be lost to another provider. If one particular restaurant is full and the customer has made up his or her mind to eat out, he or she will go to another. This matrix is useful in contrasting different supply/demand situations – something of concern to nearly all service marketers. This is an important issue and affects profitability in many service firms. It focuses attention on establishing demand patterns over time, understanding why these patterns of demand exist, and considering what strategies could be developed to help change patterns of demand to become more favourable for the service provider, (e.g. by charging premiums for peak periods and discounts for non-peak periods). Methods of generating increased capacity at peak time can also be considered.

How is the service delivered?

The final matrix in Figure 1.3 suggests an examination of the availability of service outlets, ranging from single to multiple site, and the nature of the interaction between the customer and the service provider. This matrix focuses on distribution issues relating to the method of delivery. It helps the service organization review whether it should have a sole outlet or multiple outlets and to consider the interaction opportunities with customers. Customer convenience is a

Classification and dimensions | Classification matrix and examples

1. The nature of the service act
- Nature of service act
- What or who is recipient of service

Nature of service act	Recipient of service	
	People	**Things**
Tangible actions	• Health care • Beauty salon • Restaurants	• Freight transportation • Dry cleaning • Veterinary services
Intangible actions	• Education • Information services • Entertainment	• Banking • Legal services • Insurance

2. Relationship with customer
- Nature of service delivery
- Type of relationship between service organization and its customers

Nature of service delivery	Type of relationship	
	Member relationship	**No formal relationship**
Continuous delivery of service	• Insurance • Banking • AA or RAC	• Police • Radio station • Lighthouse
Discreet transactions	• Commuter ticket • Theatre subscription • Long-distance phone calls	• Car rental • Mail service • Cinema

3. Customization and judgement in service delivery
- Amount of judgement exercised by customer contact staff
- Extent to which service characteristics are customized

Judgement by customer contact staff	Customization of service characteristics	
	High	**Low**
High	• Legal services • Architectural design • Education (tutorials)	• Education (large scale) • Preventative health programmes
Low	• Hotel service • Retail banking transactions • Quality restaurant	• Public transportation • Appliance repair • Cinema

4. Nature of demand and supply for services
- Extent to which supply is constrained
- Extent of demand fluctuations over time

Peak demand often:	Demand fluctuations	
	Wide	Narrow
Met without major delay	• Electricity • Telephone • Fire services	• Insurance • Banking • Legal services
Regularly exceeds capacity	• Hotels • Theatres • Passenger transport	• Services directly above without sufficient capacity

5. Method of service delivery
- Nature of customer/service organization interaction
- Availability of service outlets

Interaction:	Service outlet availability	
	Single site	Multiple
Customer goes to organization	• Theatre • Hairdressing	• Bus service • Fast food chain
Organization comes to customer	• Lawn care • Taxi	• Mail • Emergency repairs
Both transact at arm's length	• Credit card • TV station (local)	• Broadcast network • Telephone company

Figure 1.3 Alternative classification schemes for services

Source: Summarized from C. H. Lovelock, 'Classifying services to gain strategic marketing insights,' *Journal of Marketing* vol. 4, Summer 1983, pp. 9–20.

key consideration here and a review of ways to achieve it has helped some organizations to come up with innovative solutions. For example, First Direct in the UK provides home banking services. By communicating through telephone and mail, First Direct dispenses with the need for multiple sites and avoids the need for customers to visit it. This question also raises the issue of the service provider using various intermediaries as distribution outlets to give wider geographic coverage – for example, hotel reservation organizations, independent financial advisers and airline travel agents. The disadvantage of this is that such agents may represent several competing service providers.

The classification systems outlined above provide a framework for managers of service businesses to consider both the nature of their businesses and to what extent they share common characteristics with other service businesses which may be seemingly unrelated. It will also provide them with an opportunity to look outside their own industries for successful approaches to solving marketing problems that are transferable to their own service businesses. This approach helps those interested in services marketing to consider their businesses in a more appropriate context, avoiding the generalities of broad assertions and at the same time transcending the inherently narrow perspective of considering services on a single industry basis.

Services in manufacturing

We looked earlier at some of the difficulties in attempting to distinguish a good from a service. With the exception of a few commodities, almost all products have a service component. Today many manufacturing companies need to focus on managing their services just as service companies do. As a number of writers have pointed out, it may be more useful to discuss service and manufacturing *activities* rather than service and manufacturing *industries*. The confusion about services is compounded by arbitrary categorization. For example, consider the high-cost activity of large jet engine overhaul. If Pratt and Witney overhaul their own aircraft engines this is part of a manufacturing company's activity and falls within the manufacturing sector. If the engine overhaul is carried out by one of the emerging global companies specializing exclusively in engine overhaul, such as Standard Aero of Canada, it is a service activity and falls within the service sector.

Services have become a vital means of competition in all forms of business – services and manufacturing – and offer the potential to achieve significant competitive advantage. Services that can be added to basic manufactured goods are innumerable and include:

- Delayed payment or leasing systems.
- Training.
- Service contracts.
- Replacement or back up facilities.
- Consultancy services.
- Stockholding of customer parts.

In a wide range of manufacturing industries such as those above, and many more, services are emerging as key areas in which to seek competitive advantage. Reasons for this include the following:

- Flattening out of demand in traditional manufacturing.
- Increased international competition.
- Technological and product features advantages are short lived.
- Services represent an area of significant profit potential.

The preceding discussion has focused mainly on services in the context of service industries and pointed out how these service industries account for 60 per cent or more of Western countries' economies. However, this figure understates the true size of the **service economy**.

Today many companies which would traditionally be classified as manufacturers are heavily involved in services in one form or another:[5]

- General Motors Acceptance Corporation's (GMAC) financial service business represented over 41 percent of GM's US$2.9 billion earnings in 1986.
- IBM derives over 33 per cent of its revenue from services essential to its hardware business, including computer leasing, maintenance and software. Only a small proportion of its total workforce are directly involved in manufacturing.
- Otis Elevators derives over half of its revenues and profits from servicing and marketing and repairing of lifts and elevators.
- Digital Equipment Company generated over one-third of its US$9 billion 1987 revenues from maintenance contracts on its computers.

Thus the real extent of service activities is considerably greater than statistics suggest. In the USA around 76 per cent of all workers are now employed in service industries and, of those working in manufacturing, 65 to 75 per cent perform service tasks such as research, logistics, maintenance, product design, accounting, financial, legal and personnel services. In fact, so prevalent are non-manufacturing services in industries such as publishing, pharmaceuticals and food companies that it is questionable whether they should be classified as manufacturing industries at all.[6]

Services and manufacturing have evolved to a stage where they are highly interrelated and complementary. Quinn and his colleagues have outlined the complex interactions between the service and manufacturing sectors. These are shown in Figure 1.4, which illustrates the economic benefits which flow between the services and manufacturing sector and vice versa.

Many manufacturing firms have the ability to produce goods of a quality equal to those of their competitors. Leading manufacturers are now adding value by the addition of services traditionally outside their existing business domain. Vandermerwe and Rada[7] call this trend the 'servitisation of businesses'; companies are increasingly offering customer-focused bundles of goods, services, support, self-service and knowledge. As a result the dividing line between traditional manufacturers and classic service companies has become less clear.

In a world where competitive imitation is increasing, services are the main instrument for creating differentiation. As Grönroos[8] has pointed out, every firm, irrespective of whether it is a service firm by today's definition, has to learn how to cope with new forms of service competition. Manufacturing businesses are now looking to service businesses in an effort to learn new insights.

Summary

This chapter has provided an introduction to services and the services sector. Services are a large part of the economy and if the 'hidden services sector' is also included, services assume an even greater importance. A number of demographic, social, economic and political changes will continue to fuel the growth of the services sector.

We have suggested that a satisfactory and comprehensive definition of services has yet to emerge. Debate continues on the nature and characteristics of services. Our view is that continued debate on the differences between goods and services as mutually exclusive categories is unproductive. We consider 'the offer' made to the customer a more relevant concept; depending on the context, this may be a good, a service, or more often an appropriate combination of both. In this book, for shorthand familiarity, we use 'the product' or 'the offer' as generic terms covering goods, services and their combination. However, it is rare for the offer not to include some service component. In any given service industry the offer made by two companies can vary. A firm can change the balance in its service/good offer to stress a greater service or good element in an effort to improve its competitive position.

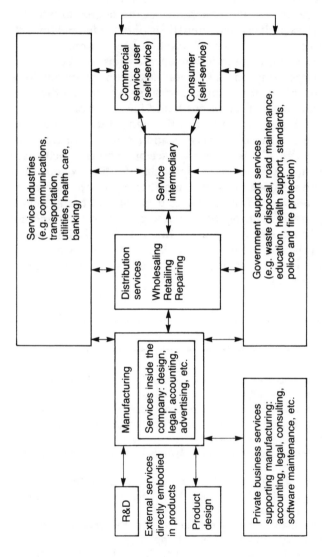

Figure 1.4 Interactions between the service and manufacturing sectors

Source: J. B. Quinn, J. J. Baruch and P. C. Paquette. 'Exploiting the manufacturing–services interface', *Sloan Management Review*, vol. 29, no. 4, Summer 1988.

It is generally agreed that services tend to exhibit four characteristics: intangibility, heterogeneity, inseparability and perishability. However, examples can be found of services that contradict each of these characteristics. It is therefore more appropriate to consider each of these characteristics on a continuum: any specific service combines different degrees of each. An understanding of the degree to which a given service possesses a given characteristic is of considerable import- ance as this will affect the design of a marketing programme.

Until recently marketing in service businesses has lagged behind marketing in manufacturing firms. There has been relatively little cross-fertilization of ideas from one service sector to another. In banking, insurance, education, accounting and law, staff often remain in the same industry, if not the same firm, throughout their careers. As a consequence there is a need for classification schemes of different services to help managers identify other service businesses which share common characteristics. A review is made of classification systems that help to shed light on strategic marketing insights of managerial value.

Services are also relevant to the manufacturing sector. Many manu- facturers are today seeking competitive advantage from service and are learning that services are just as important in goods-based as in service industries. Many of the issues raised in the remainder of this book will be relevant to manufacturers seeking to enhance their competitiveness through addition of services.

Notes

1. P. Kotler, *Marketing Management: Analysis, planning and control*, Prentice Hall, Englewood Cliffs, 7th edn, 1991.
2. J. Bowen, 'Development of a taxonomy of services to gain strategic marketing insights', *Journal of the Academy of Marketing Sciences*, vol. 18, no. 1, 1990, pp. 43–9.
3. C. Grönroos, *Services Management and Marketing*, Lexington Books, Lexing- ton, Mass., 1990.
4. C.H. Lovelock, 'Classifying services to gain strategic marketing insights', *Journal of Marketing*, vol. 47, Summer 1983, pp. 9–20. The following discussion is based on this article.
5. I.D. Canton, 'How manufacturers can move into the service business', *Journal of Business Strategy*, July–August 1988, pp. 40–4.
6. J.B. Quinn, T.L. Doorley and P.C. Paquette, 'Beyond products: services based strategy', *Harvard Business Review*, March–April 1990, pp. 58–67.
7. S. Vandermerwe and J. Rada, 'Servitization of business: adding value by adding service', *European Management Journal*, vol. 6, no. 4, 1988, pp. 314–423.
8. Grönroos, *op. cit.*

2

Services marketing and relationship marketing

The role of marketing

The dynamics of most services markets have changed; low levels of competition have given way to vigorous and intense competition. In this competitive marketplace marketing has become a key differentiator between corporate success and failure. This chapter discusses the role of marketing, introduces an expanded marketing mix for services, describes the evolution of services and relationship marketing and outlines the framework for the remaining six chapters.

Marketing is a process of perceiving, understanding, stimulating and satisfying the needs of specially selected target markets by channelling an organization's resources to meet those needs. Marketing is thus a process of matching an organization's resources to the needs of the market. Marketing is concerned with the dynamic interrelationships between a company's products and services, the consumers' wants and needs, and the activities of competitors.

The marketing function can be considered as consisting of three key components:

- **The marketing mix** – the important internal elements or ingredients that make up an organization's marketing programme.

- **Market forces** – external opportunities or threats which the marketing operations of an organization interact with.

- **A matching process** – the strategic and managerial process of ensuring that the marketing mix and internal policies are appropriate to the market forces.

21

The marketing mix is one of the most universal concepts which has been developed in marketing. Most discussions of marketing focus around four key components of the marketing mix, called the 4Ps. These include:

- **Product** – the product or service being offered.
- **Price** – the price charged and terms associated with its sale.
- **Promotion** – the communications programme associated with marketing the product or service.
- **Place** – the distribution and logistics function involved in making a firm's products and services available.

The concept of the marketing mix has gained wide acceptance in business and covers these four main elements, each of which comprise a collection of subactivities (for example, promotion includes both advertising and personal selling).

Market forces comprise a number of areas which need to be considered, including:

- **The customer** – buying behaviour in terms of motivation to purchase, buying habits, environment, size of market and buying power.
- **The industry's behaviour** – the motivations, structure, practice and attitudes of retailers, intermediaries and other members of the supply chain.
- **Competitors** – the way a company's position and behaviour is influenced by industry structure and the nature of competition.
- **Government and regulatory** – control over marketing which relates to both marketing activities and competitive practices.

The task of the manager in developing a marketing programme is to assemble the elements of a marketing mix to ensure the best match between the internal capabilities of the company and the external market environment. A key issue in the marketing programme is the recognition that the elements of the marketing mix are largely controllable by managers within the organization, and that the market forces in the external environment are, to a large extent, uncontrollable. The success of a marketing programme depends primarily on the degree of match between the external environment and the organization's internal capabilities. The marketing programme can thus be characterised as a matching process, and this is especially important in the services context. This is shown in Figure 2.1.

The external forces in fast moving services markets are not stable.

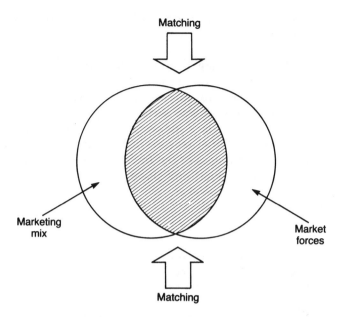

Figure 2.1 Marketing as a matching process

Forces can alter quickly and dramatically, as shown by deregulation in airlines, privatization of services such as water and electricity utilities, increased regulation of financial markets and the emergence of new forms of service competition, to name but a few. Changes in these forces create both marketing opportunities and marketing threats. Thus marketing executives need to monitor the external environment constantly and be prepared to alter their marketing mix to create a better match with market opportunities.

Marketing has come relatively late to services. A study of 400 service and manufacturing firms in the mid-1970s concluded that service firms appear to be[1]:

- Generally less likely to have marketing mix activities carried out in the marketing department.
- Less likely to perform analysis in the offering area.
- More likely to handle their advertising internally rather than go to outside agencies.
- Less likely to have an overall sales plan.
- Less likely to develop sales training programmes.
- Less likely to use marketing research firms and marketing consultants.

- Less likely to spend as much on marketing when expressed as a percentage of gross sales.

Taken as a whole marketing in the services sector today still lags behind the consumer goods and industrial sectors. To some extent the lack of attention directed to marketing of services is surprising considering the size of the service sector. This can be at least partly explained by the relative lack of competition in many services businesses until recently. Other reasons include the complex nature of a service and the restrictiveness of the traditional 4Ps of the marketing mix (product, price, promotion and place) when marketing services. Some service industries, however, are more sophisticated in their approach to marketing.

Services and the marketing mix

The increased attention to the application of marketing in the services sector has brought into question what the key components or elements of a marketing mix for services are, or what they should be. If the elements chosen to develop a marketing mix for a service are not comprehensive, it is likely that a service quality gap will occur between the market requirements and the firm's marketing offer.

It is therefore appropriate to reconsider the traditional marketing mix in the context of services. The 4Ps of the marketing mix are derived from a much longer list developed from the Harvard Business School in the 1960s. The original list consisted of twelve elements, including product plan, pricing, branding, channels of distribution, personal selling, advertising, promotions, packaging, display, servicing, physical handling, fact finding and analysis. Over time, the marketing mix concept gained considerable acceptance and the 4Ps were adopted to capture the key elements.

However, it has been argued that simplifying the original list offers a seductive sense of simplicity which may lead to neglect of some key relevant elements. As a result many authors have added to the basic 4Ps framework. Lists of additional marketing mix elements have been added which extend the 4Ps framework to five, seven and eleven key elements which should be considered in the marketing mix. Several authors have argued that a different marketing mix is needed for services. Some writers have suggested specific marketing mix elements for service industries like banking and airlines, whilst others have suggested different elements for professional services.

Our view of the marketing mix accords closely with that of a colleague, Simon Majaro, who argues that three factors determine whether or not a specific element should be included in a firm's marketing mix. These include the following:[2]

- **The level of expenditure on a given ingredient in the marketing mix**, i.e., how important that element is in the firm's overall expenditure.

- **The perceived level of elasticity in customer responsiveness**; for example, in the case of a monopoly or government body, prices may be set externally and thus need not be included in the marketing mix.

- **Allocation of responsibilities** is based on the belief that a well defined and well structured marketing mix needs a clear cut allocation of responsibilities.

We consider the 4Ps model unnecessarily restrictive; an expanded marketing mix is more appropriate. At the same time we should recognize the diversity of the services economy, described in Chapter 1, which includes both services firms as well as manufacturing firms to whom services are important. We advocate the expanded marketing mix shown in Figure 2.2. This reflects the traditional elements of the marketing mix – product, price, promotion and place, plus three additional elements – people, processes and the provision of customer

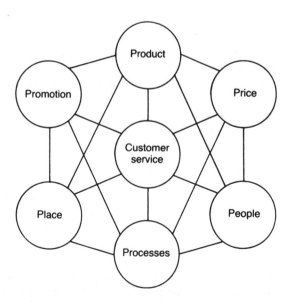

Figure 2.2 Expanded marketing mix for services

service. We regard this as a framework particularly appropriate for services, but also relevant for non-service industries, given the importance of the service dimension in most manufacturing companies.

We shall return to a more detailed discussion of developing a marketing mix programme for services in Chapter 6. However, at this point it is appropriate to briefly comment on why these three additional elements are important:

- **Customer service.** There are several reasons for including customer service as an element in a services marketing mix. These include more demanding consumers requiring higher levels of service, the increased importance of customer service (in part due to competitors seeing service as a competitive weapon to differentiate themselves); and the need to build closer and more enduring relationships with customers.

- **People.** In the last chapter we described the inseparability characteristic of services. People are an essential element in both the production and delivery of most services. People are increasingly becoming part of the differentiation by which service companies seek to create added value and gain competitive advantage.

- **Processes.** Processes are all the procedures, mechanisms and routines by which a service is created and delivered to a customer, including policy decisions about some of the customer involvement and employee discretion issues shown in Figure 1.3. Process management is a key aspect of service quality improvement.

Given the diversity of the services sector and the different emphasis that is needed in its various kinds of marketing activity, it may be necessary to vary this list. Nevertheless, it is sufficiently robust to cover most services marketing situations. It is equally clear that the 4Ps model does not capture the full complexity of services marketing in practice and does not recognize the essential interrelationships between key aspects of marketing in service businesses.

The evolution of services marketing

Over the past few decades we have seen the focus of the formal study of marketing directed at an increasing number of specific sectors. In the 1950s consumer goods companies were recognized as the most sophisticated marketeers. They were often the first companies to develop formal marketing plans and much academic effort was directed at analyzing and researching consumer markets. In the 1960s considerable attention was paid to industrial markets and marketing texts and journals dealing specially with industrial markets started to appear. In the 1970s marketing in non-profit organizations and the associated areas of public sector and societal marketing received attention. It was only in the 1980s that services marketing started to attract attention, which is surprising considering the size and rapid growth of the services sector.

Despite the recent emphasis on services marketing, there is still a considerable misunderstanding within much of the service sector as to what constitutes effective marketing. To some it is still primarily equated with selling and the pursuit of sales, rather than customer satisfaction. To others, for example those offering professional services, it is viewed as the production of brochures, advertising and low-level marketing communications. Even amongst those service firms which have developed more sophisticated marketing approaches, few have capitalized on the full potential of marketing, and recognized that everyone within an organization has the ability to contribute to external or internal marketing initiatives. Many organzations are still reluctant to make the changes necessary to focus on the marketplace, even when the need for more active marketing is generally agreed.

Service organizations have tended to move through a series of stages in seeking to adopt marketing. This is illustrated in Table 2.1, which shows some of the main stages through which service firms typically evolve, including the following:

- Selling.
- Advertising and communications.
- Product and service development.
- Differentiation and competitor analysis.
- Customer service.
- Service quality.
- Integration and relationship marketing.

These stages are illustrative and clearly not all service companies will go through all these stages of evolution, nor will they necessarily pass through them in the order shown in Table 2.1.

Banks are a good illustration of some of these stages of development, although there is overlap between the stages. Up to the 1960s banks did not worry much about marketing. However, as competition intensified in the 1970s they expended considerable efforts on selling, sales promotion and advertising both to attract funds and promote bank products and services. The emphasis here was on sales rather than customer satisfaction. This was followed by emphasis on new

Table 2.1 Adoption of marketing by service organizations

	Stage 1 Selling	Stage 2 Advertising and communication	Stage 3 Product development	Stage 4 Differentiation and competitor analysis	Stage 5 Customer service	Stage 6 Service quality	Stage 7 Integration and relationship marketing
Some key components	• Competition emerging • Sales programmes • Selling skills courses and training • Recruit more new customers	• Increased advertising • Appointment of multiple agencies (advertising, public relations, etc.) • Promotional enticements • Brochures and point-of-sale materials	• Recognition of new customer needs • Introduction of many new products and services • Emphasis on new product development process	• Strategic analysis • Positioning maps • Seeking differentiation • Restricted planning • Marketing training • Market research	• Customer service training • Smile campaigns • External promotion of improved service • Improved front office layout and facilities	• Service quality gap identification • Service blueprinting • Customer contribution analysis • Customer research	• Regular research on customers and competitors • Focus on all key markets • Rigorous analysis and integration of marketing plans • Data-based marketing
Some typical outcomes	• Focus on sales not profits • Lack of emphasis on customer satisfaction • Improved sales capability	• High customer expectations • Outputs often not easily measurable • Competitive imitation • Expectations often not met	• Product and services proliferation • Confusion at branch level • Competitive imitation • Some market segmentation • Establishment of stronger branding	• Clarification of strategy • Improved branding • More sophisticated segmentation • Implementation problems • Failure to deliver on positioning	• Low impact on profitability • Not sustained • Not supported by processes and systems • Payoff not measured • Lack of competitive differentiation	• Some focus diverted from: – marketing planning – other relevant markets • Customer retention not emphasized	• Balanced marketing activity • Improved processes and systems • Challenging but realizable goals • Improved customer retention

product and new service development, in the 1980s. However, there is little patent protection and few secrets in services. As a consequence innovations can be quickly copied. Services are especially prone to competitive imitation and advantages from product development tend to be short lived. This resulted in a 'sameness' in bank products and, to the branch banker, a large and potentially confusing array of products to try and sell.

During the early 1980s banks undertook more rigorous competitive analysis and developed more sophisticated marketing and strategic plans. They also started to understand positioning and became more adept at market segmentation, as well as identifying strategic means of differentiation.

In the mid-1980s banks also discovered (or rediscovered) the customer and developed 'putting the customer first' programmes. These often tended to be 'smile campaigns', aimed at making the service provider more friendly, and were accompanied by changes in the physical environment of the bank to make it warmer and more attractive. This may have given an initial advantage to early adopters of this approach but other banks quickly followed suit. Today virtually all the major financial services players in the UK have launched some form of customer care programme.

With the arrival of the 1990s some banks have started to reassess their customer service programmes and have begun a more rigorous pursuit of service quality based on identification of service quality issues and service quality gaps using a variety of techniques, including service blueprinting. This has been accompanied by a more disciplined approach to customer and market research.

The last stage in Table 2.1, integration and relationship marketing, involves the integration of past effort within a relationship marketing context. This challenges both bankers and other service marketeers to do as follows:

- Integrate various marketing initiatives.
- Capitalize on the use of data-based marketing techniques.
- Develop a more disciplined, realistic and focused approach to marketing planning.
- Focus on the development of a marketing oriented culture.
- Recognize the potential of external and internal marketing and its use in a number of relationship markets not usually considered in the domain of marketing activity.
- Increase profitability through improved customer retention.

In the 1990s a new emphasis on marketing is likely to emerge – relationship marketing. Relationship marketing has the potential to draw together the streams of marketing focus into an integrated whole, as shown in Figure 2.3. Relationship marketing draws heavily on services marketing thinking but also has applications to other sectors.

Relationship marketing

The term 'relationship marketing' was introduced during the 1980s and is a relatively new and evolving concept. An early definition is provided by Leonard Berry: 'Relationship marketing is the attraction, maintaining and . . . in multi-service organisation . . . enhancing customer relationships. The marketing mind set is that the attraction of new customers is merely **the first step** in the marketing process.'[3]

Our view of relationship marketing extends this definition. This broadened view has three complementary perspectives:[4]

- The nature of the way the companies view their relationships with customers is changing. Emphasis is moving from a transaction focus to a relationship focus with the aim of long-term customer retention.
- A broader view is emerging of the markets with which the company interacts. In addition to customer markets the organization also becomes concerned with the development and enhance-

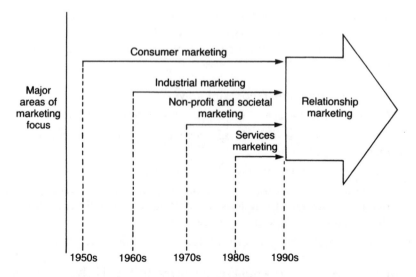

Figure 2.3 The changing emphasis on marketing

ment of more enduring relationships with other external markets including suppliers, recruitment, referral and influence, as well as internal markets.

- A recognition that quality, customer service and marketing activities need to be brought together. A relationship marketing orientation focuses on bringing the three elements into closer alignment and ensuring their combined synergistic potential is released.

The first two of these perspectives deal with the different market domains that can be considered; we will discuss them at this point and return to the third perspective later in Chapter 8.

Figure 2.4 illustrates 'The six-markets model' – a broadened view of where marketing can be applied. It suggests that companies have six key market areas where they should consider directing marketing activity and where the development of detailed marketing plans may be appropriate. In addition to existing and potential customers, those markets are referral markets, supplier markets, recruitment markets, influence markets, and internal markets.

Customer Markets

Customers must, of course, remain the prime focus area for marketing activity. But the focus needs to be less on 'transactional marketing' – an emphasis on the one-off sale or hooking a new customer – and more

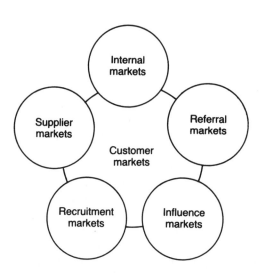

Figure 2.4 The six-markets model: a broadened view of marketing

on the building of long-term client relationship. These two approaches can be contrasted as follows:

Transaction marketing	Relationship marketing
• Focus on single sale.	• Focus on customer retention.
• Orientation on product features.	• Orientation on product benefits.
• Short timescale.	• Long timescale.
• Little emphasis on customer service.	• High customer service emphasis.
• Limited customer commitment.	• High customer commitment.
• Moderate customer contact.	• High customer contact.
• Quality is primarily a concern of production.	• Quality is the concern of all.

Whilst a relationship focus has been fully adopted by some service businesses it is noticeably absent in others. Unfortunately, many companies take the transactional route. The investment made in winning a new customer, once successful, is immediately transferred to the next prospect. Little effort goes into keeping that customer. We will explore the economic benefits of customer retention in Chapter 8.

Firms today are now starting to recognize that existing customers are easier to sell to and are frequently more profitable. However, whilst managers intellectually concur with this view, much greater emphasis and resources are often devoted to attracting new customers, and existing customers are taken for granted. It is only when some breakdown in service quality occurs, and the customer leaves or is on the point of defection, that the existing customer becomes important.

An example from a large, City law firm provides a good illustration of this. In this law firm two events occurred within a short time. The first involved the gaining of a contentious piece of litigation work from a new client. This work, worth around £100 000 was likely to be a one-off piece of business as the client's existing law firm did not wish to handle it. The law firm's partners were jubilant and everyone was excited about 'Johnson's brilliant coup in bringing in this new client'. Six weeks later another partner persuaded a large corporate client, who dealt with several law firms, to give his firm all the company's conveyancing work. Prior to this, the firm had only worked in one area of the law for this client. This represented additional work of about £150 000 in the first year and would be a continuing and growing source of future fees. There was little reaction to this news in the partnership except for the comment 'Roberts has finally got off his backside and done what he should have been doing all along'.The conveyancing work was on-going. As such it represented, in net present value terms, perhaps five times as much profit as the litigation; yet other members of the firm paid little attention to it.

This is not to say that new customers or clients are not important – indeed they are vital to the future most service businesses. Rather, a balance is needed between the effort directed toward existing and new customers. Figure 2.5 shows the relationship marketing ladder of customer loyalty which emphasizes this point. It is apparent that many organizations put their main emphasis on the lower rungs of identifying prospects and attempting to turn them into customers rather than on the higher 'relationship' – and ultimately more rewarding – rungs of turning customers into regular clients and subsequently into strong supporters and eventually active advocates for the company and its products. But moving customers up the loyalty ladder is not simple. Organizations need to know explicitly and in depth exactly what each customer is buying – and every customer is different – and how it can continue to offer additional satisfactions that will differentiate its offering. Essentially, the only way to change someone from customer to advocate is to replace customer satisfaction with customer delight – by offering service quality that exceeds expectations.

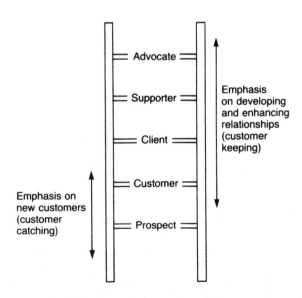

Figure 2.5 The relationship marketing ladder of customer loyalty

Referral markets

The best marketing is that which is carried out by your own customers; this is why the customer loyalty ladder and the creation of advocates is so important. But existing customers are not the only sources of referral. Referral markets go under many names – intermediaries, connectors, multipliers, agencies and so on.

An example from a bank will serve as an illustration here. Referral sources for the bank included insurance companies, real estate brokers, accountancy and law firms as well as existing customers and internal referrals. For this bank, an internal study of the amount of business (both historic and projected) which originated from referral sources showed how important these sources were, although the bank had traditionally done little to promote itself in this area.

A strategy retreat was subsequently organized which included sessions on referral sources, including presentations from several important intermediaries. The bank was surprised at the criticism it received during these presentations. Aware through its research of the importance of this business, the bank established a task force to develop better relations with referral sources and establish a marketing plan to deal with the referral markets. The result was noticeable and continued improvements in business generated by referral sources.

Most organizations will need to take similar action. The current and potential importance of referral sources should be established and a plan developed for allocating marketing resources to them. Efforts should also be made to monitor results and cost benefits. However, it is worth emphasizing that developing these relationships takes time and that the benefits of increased marketing activity in this area may not come to fruition immediately.

Supplier markets

The relationship between an organization and its suppliers is undergoing some fundamental changes – mainly under the influence of the Japanese. The old adversarial relationship where a company tried to squeeze its suppliers to its own advantage, is giving way to a relationship based much more on partnership and collaboration. There is good commercial sense in this. Manufacturers in the United States typically spend over 60 per cent of total revenue on goods and service from outside suppliers.

The new relationship can go under a number of different names. At AT&T it is 'vendorship partnership'; at electronics group Philips in Europe it is called 'co-makership'. In the USA it is being referred to as 'reverse marketing'. Whatever the term, however, the aim is close cooperation between customer and supplier from a very early stage, mutual concentration on quality, commitment to flexibility, lowest costs and long-term relationships.

From the marketing point of view, the concern is to 'sell' the new attitudes implicit in such a collaborative arrangement both to suppliers and, equally importantly, inside the company, since in the past internal reward systems may have operated in a traditional antagonistic relationship.

Recruitment markets

The key scarce resource for business (and other) organizations is no longer capital or raw materials – it is skilled people, a vital, perhaps *the* most vital, element in customer service delivery. And the situation is not getting any easier, even if unemployment climbs to historic levels. The reason is demographic trends.

In the United States the percentage of people in the age range 16–24 is expected to fall from around 20 per cent in 1985 to 16 per cent in 2000 and in the 25–34 age group from 23 per cent to 19 per cent over the same period. The same is true in most Western countries. Obviously new skilled workers entering the labour market originate from these key groups. If, as seems possible, demand outstrips supply, then effectively marketing an organization to potential employees will become a vital success factor. A brief case study shows the kind of effort that may have to be made.

Several years ago a large and well known accountancy practice was having problems attracting new young recruits. The reasons were not hard to discover. Its recruitment literature was old fashioned and lacked visual impact. On visits to university campuses – a traditional recruitment source – the company was represented by an old and uninspiring partner and bored administrative staff. A marketing plan to try to improve the situation involved redesigning recruitment literature (with the help of recent graduates), sending the brightest partners on university visits with managers with interesting experiences to recount, and sponsoring awards and prizes at target universities. As a result of this marketing plan, the firm's offers to acceptances ratio increased by nearly 200 per cent within two years.

Influence markets

Influence markets tend to vary according to the type of industry or industry sector that an organization occupies. Companies involved in selling infrastructure items, such as communications or utilities, will place government departments and regulatory bodies high on the list of markets they must address. Most companies also place the financial community in its various forms – brokers, analysts, financial journalists and so on – in the influence category. Other examples include standards bodies, political groups, consumer associations, trade associations, activist groups, environmental control authorities, etc.

A good example of influence markets that needs to be addressed is provided by MCI Communications Corporation in the USA. William G. McGowan, Chairman and Chief Executive of MCI Communications faced some key marketing tasks with respect to influence markets in the early days of MCI. These influence markets included the following:

- **The venture capital business** – McGowan had a capital starved communications company. He had to raise sufficient finance from venture capitalists.

- **The regulators**, who needed to be convinced that McGowan could construct and satisfactorily operate a long-distance telecommunications network.

- **Lobbyists** – communications is an industry highly subject to regulation by the Federal Communications Commission and one which is dominated by AT&T. MCI had to become a skilled lobbier. It was for this reason that it established its headquarters in Washington DC.

- **Litigators** – in challenging AT&T's domination of long-distance telephone lines through a private anti-trust case, MCI became involved in complex litigation. (MCI were at one time described as a 'law firm with an antenna on top'.) Relationships with law firms and lawyers became critical.

MCI had to focus on its important influence markets as well as its original core mission. This suggests that involvement in other activities may be essential to protect the core business. These key activities were the principal focus of McGowan's efforts in the early stages.

Whilst such activity is often carried out under the banner of public relations or public affairs, it is important that it is recognized as an essential element in the overall marketing activity, and that appropriate resources are devoted to it.

Internal markets

Internal marketing involves two main concepts. The first is that every employee and every department in an organization is both an internal customer and an internal supplier. The optimal operation of the organization is ensured when every individual and department both provides and receives excellent service.

The second concept is making sure that all staff work together in a way that is aligned with the organization's stated mission, strategy and goals. The importance of this has become particularly transparent in service firms, where there is a close interface with the customer. Internal marketing aims at ensuring that all staff provide the best representation of the organization through successfully handling telephone, mail, electronic and personal contacts with customers (including customers from the other markets outlined above).

Internal marketing is recognized as an important activity in developing a customer-focused organization. In practice, internal marketing is concerned with communications and, with developing responsiveness, responsibility and unity of purpose. The fundamental aims of internal marketing are to develop internal and external customer awareness and remove functional barriers to organizational effectiveness.

While little has been codified about internal marketing practice it is clear that a consideration of internal markets is essential. Where internal marketing is concerned with the development of customer orientation, the alignment of internal and external marketing ensures coherent relationship marketing. It also plays an important role in employee motivation and retention. This area is one which should receive considerable attention over the next five years and research is needed to identify success factors and barriers, particularly in the areas of structures, systems and people.

Determining market emphasis in relationship marketing

These six markets – customer, referral, supplier, recruitment, influence and internal – do not necessarily need their own formal written marketing plan, although some organizations will find it helps them. But companies do need to develop some form of marketing strategy for each. The adoption of the relationship philosophy as a key strategic issue is more important than a written plan. For example, a formal marketing plan for an internal market is of little value if customer contact staff are not motivated and empowered to deliver the level of service quality required. The needs of members of all these markets need to be addressed in exactly the same way as customer markets – and high levels of service quality are essential in establishing and maintaining relationships with them.

However, not all markets require equal levels of attention and resources. A decision on the appropriate level of attention can be arrived at through the following steps:

- Identify key participants in each of the markets.

- Research to identify expectations and requirements of key participants.
- Review current and proposed level of emphasis in each market.
- Formulate the desired relationship strategy and determine if a formal market plan is necessary.

The relationship marketing spidergram shown in Figure 2.6 can be used to help identify the present level of effort and desired level of emphasis on each market. The spidergram has seven axes– two for customers (existing and new) and one each for the other five relationship markets. Each axis represents the degree of emphasis placed on each market. The division of customers into new and existing reflects the two tasks of customer attraction and customer retention.

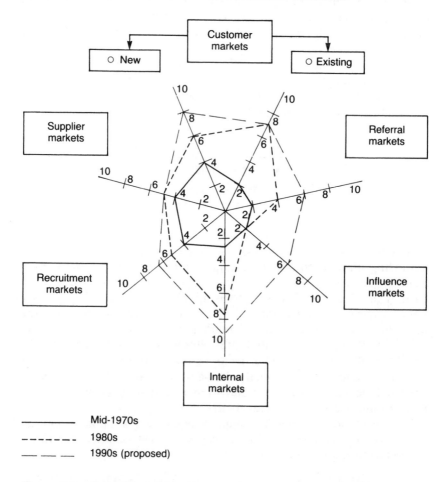

Figure 2.6   Illustrative relationship marketing spidergram for British Airways

As noted earlier, many service companies place too much emphasis on attracting new customers and too little on retaining existing ones. We have met many managers during our consultancy work and on courses at Cranfield who agree that their companies are guilty of this. An objective approach to determining the level of emphasis is to examine in detail the resources, in terms of both money and executive time, expended on each of these two tasks. In many cases where a quantitative assessment has been undertaken it has been apparent that the majority of the marketing mix, marketing expenditure and managerial time is directed at attracting new customers. We shall return to the justification for spending more on customer retention in Chapter 8.

The spidergram approach in Figure 2.6 can be illustrated by reference to British Airways (BA). This is based on the views of a group including two former senior executives in British Airways, and represents an external view of developments in BA. In the 1970s British Airways was in poor shape. Its financial position was terrible and it lacked market focus. Following the appointment of Lord King and Colin Marshall in the 1980s a revolution took place in BA. Considerable emphasis was placed on the internal market, and a series of customer care programmes were promoted, including 'Putting the Customer First' and 'A Day in the Life'. Towards the end of the 1980s BA recognized the importance of customer retention and this led to a number of initiatives aimed at retention including the Airmiles and Latitudes programmes. Marketing to new and existing customers, travel agents and other referral markets greatly improved. Saatchi and Saatchi developed a series of outstanding global television commercials aimed at most of the relationship markets.

In the early 1990s BA might consider a number of issues in the relationship market spidergram, as shown in '1990s proposed' in Figure 2.6. These involve the following:

- Greater attention to gaining new customers. (BA has placed much emphasis on customer retention. Should more attention now be directed at new customers?)

- A reinforcement of customer care and service quality issues with internal staff.

- Greater attention to influence markets – especially government. (The recent granting of rights to use Heathrow to several US carriers, following the departure of Mrs Thatcher as Prime Minister, raises an important issue. Should more widely-based relationships have been forged by BA both within the government and the opposition parties?)

The six-markets model illustrates how service organizations have a network of relationships with different markets. Each of these interactions needs to be managed, where appropriate with a formal strategy and marketing plan.

The six-markets model has been used in a diverse range of service businesses to develop marketing plans for each of the six markets and to illustrate the relationship marketing concept, including:

- An insurance broker.
- A hotel.
- A division of a major railway.
- A subsidiary of a Dutch consulting engineering firm.
- An international airport.
- A university.
- A hospice.

This model has proved a robust means of considering the network of relationships that services organizations need to address. In each of the seven cases studied above, important areas that had not previously received attention were highlighted, as a result of using this approach. While most of the rest of this book is concerned with applying marketing to customer markets, the relevance of marketing techniques to these other market areas should also be considered by service marketers.

The essence of services marketing

It is possible to address the process of services marketing in a number of ways. The approach adopted in this book is to explore key aspects that are important from a managerial perspective. The remaining six chapters of the book explore the following key managerial dimensions of services marketing:

- **Developing an effective service mission** (Chapter 3). The development of effective service mission involves asking two interrelated questions: 'What business should we be in?', and 'What business are we in?' Chapter 3 examines the nature of service missions and explores why they are important.
- **Services market segmentation** (Chapter 4). This chapter, and the following one, examine how to focus the firm's activities on specific markets. The process of segmentation is outlined and examples are presented.
- **Positioning and differentiation of services** (Chapter 5). Positioning

involves decisions about how an organization should differentiate itself in the marketplace. Given the intangible nature of services, positioning is a major opportunity to create differentiation from the competition.

- **The services marketing mix** (Chapter 6). This chapter examines the elements of the expanded marketing mix outlined earlier in this chapter, and their interaction.

- **Marketing plans for services** (Chapter 7). The preparation of practical marketing plans is essential to manage the services marketing function. The ten key steps involved in doing this are outlined.

- **The customer-focused service organization** (Chapter 8). This final chapter explores an approach to create a customer-focused and marketing-oriented corporate culture, involving a focus on service quality.

Notes

1. W.R. George and H.C. Barkdale, 'Marketing activities in service businesses', *Journal of Marketing*, October 1974, p. 65.
2. S. Majaro, *Marketing in Perspective*, George Allen and Unwin, London, 1982.
3. L. Berry, 'Relationship marketing', in L. Berry, G.L. Shostack and G.D. Upah, *Emerging Perspectives on Services Marketing*, American Marketing Association, Chicago, 1983, pp. 25–8.
4. M. Christopher, A.F.T. Payne and D. Ballantyne, *Relationship Marketing: Bringing quality, customer service and marketing together*, Butterworth-Heinemann, Oxford, 1991.

3

Developing an effective service mission

A mission for services

The development of an effective mission statement is especially important in services because of the need for focus and differentiation in service sector businesses. Given the intangibility of services and the significance of people in service operations, organizations need to develop a clear statement of purpose or 'mission' to ensure that the appropriate attention is directed at the key elements of their strategy. In this chapter we discuss mission statements and consider what is required to develop an effective mission statement for a service business. Mission statements of a written form are the subject of attention here, although it is recognized that some organizations may have unwritten missions which are nevertheless strongly embedded within their corporate culture.

Mission statements or 'missions' go under various guises including: business definitions, statements of business philosophy, belief statements, credos, vision statements, statements of purpose and so on. We will use the term generally here to include these different forms, whilst recognizing that some companies, and writers, distinguish between them. We define a mission as follows:

A mission is an enduring statement of purpose that provides a clear vision of the organization's current and future business activities, in product, service and market terms, its values and beliefs, and its points of differentiation from competitors. A mission helps determine the relationships in each of the key markets with which the organization interacts, and provides a sense of direction and purpose which leads to better independent decision-making at all levels of the organization.

Such a mission statement should explicitly reflect the underlying beliefs, values and aspirations, and strategies of the organization. However, many companies' mission statements display bland similarity and consist of generalizations rather than unique commitments to a specific set of values and corporate direction.

Companies' purposes in writing a mission can vary. Whilst some do it for public relations purposes, we view a mission statement as a means of strategically focusing an organization's business activities. Essentially a mission statement should represent a long-term view of the company in terms of what it wants to be and where it wants to go.

During the last decade many services organizations have started to develop mission statements. Over this period there has been increasing recognition of the potential value of mission statements and some companies have spent enormous amounts of time and effort in developing them. However, whilst much effort has gone into the development of missions in service organizations they have often not resulted in satisfactory end products. In discussing mission statements with hundreds of managers from diverse service businesses ranging from banks and hospitals to actuarial firms and airlines, several problems become apparent:

- Intense frustration is common in groups of managers trying to develop a useful mission.
- The missions of many service firms are not considered satisfactory or useful by their senior managers.
- Employees often see their mission statement as bland and meaningless, and in some cases treat it with scepticism and derision.

We will now consider the key issues in developing a good mission statement for a services business and how to try and avoid the problems listed above.

The nature of corporate missions

A consideration of the literature on mission statements suggests a number of key issues are important:

- It is dangerous to define an organization's mission too narrowly or too broadly.
- The audience for a mission should be carefully considered.
- It is crucial to understand what business you are in.

- A mission statement should be unique.
- It is essential to have a mission statement which is market rather than product oriented.

Each of these issues can be expressed as questions.

What is the balance between narrowness and breadth?

A frequently quoted services sector which defined its business too narrowly is the railway industry in the USA. Theodore Levitt argues that by defining itself as being in the locomotive business, rather than as helping people solve their transport needs, the railway industry as a whole failed to capitalize on opportunities and placed itself under severe threat.[1] One example of a railway that did redefine its corporate mission more broadly as 'transportation services' is the Southern Railways Company, which has one of the highest earnings per share of any company in the railroad industry in the USA. Southern Railways Company achieved this position through a carefully integrated programme of acquiring other railroads and by developing and maintaining a mission of providing useful and relevant transport services to its customers.

However, just as there are dangers in defining a business too narrowly, so there are also dangers in defining a business too broadly. In the past, American Express has defined its business quite broadly in terms of being in the information and leisure businesses. This definition led to unsuccessful attempts to acquire McGraw Hill and Disney. Fortunately for American Express these attempts failed. Had they succeeded the acquisitions would have involved them in a series of businesses with little direct relationship to their existing core business and of which they had little understanding. More recently American Express have developed a much more focused and coherent view of their mission which is focused around financial and travel-related services to affluent clients. This has fuelled their subsequent strategic moves into investment banking and brokerage, and towards becoming a diversified financial services company.

In developing a mission statement the key is to achieve a balance between not being so narrow as to restrict growth opportunities and not being so broad as to lose focus. The value of this balance in developing a mission statement to guide the firm's strategic moves becomes apparent when the recent activities of a number of UK banks and retailers are considered. Some banks which diversified away from their core business into stockbroking and investment banking, with disastrous results, are now reconsidering their strategy. Similarly, a number of retailers that have diversified away from their core businesses, have been unprofitable in these new areas, and are now leaving them and consolidating back into their core retailing business. If effective mission statements had been formulated, with the requisite strategic focus that this implies, it is questionable whether some of these firms would have diversified into the loss-making, non-core and unrelated business areas that they entered in recent years.

Who are the target audiences for the mission and what are their expectations?

Before formulating a mission statement the target audiences for the mission and their relative importance should be considered. Many mission statements are primarily directed at shareholders and senior management and fail to understand the critical role of non-managerial front-line service providers within a service company. Without such a statement of organizational values employees have to derive these from their own interpretation of where the organization is headed and what its values are, and such interpretations may vary considerably. Without the energy, enthusiasm and commitment of staff it is unlikely that the strategy of the service provider will be realized. The sophistication of the mission needs to be reviewed taking into account the audience to whom it is addressed. Figure 3.1 outlines some of the key potential audiences for a mission and some of their expectations, based on a consideration of stakeholders in the six relationship markets described in the last chapter. A mission statement aims to capture the values and beliefs of the organization and provide guidelines for the way it should interact with its identified markets – customers, internal employees, influence markets (including shareholders), suppliers, referral markets, as well as the recruitment markets for employees.

These are the major areas for consideration, but there may be others. For example, there may be other influence markets. In construction engineering services for the oil industry environmentalists could be a important influencer market. It might also be appropriate to further subdivide some of the markets shown in Figure 3.1. For example, internal staff could be divided into senior management, junior management and salaried employees; each group might have differing expectations.

Figure 3.1 provides a framework for considering the relative importance of each of these groups. It should be clear that a mission which attempts to address every one of these groups equally could become extremely long and consist of general 'motherhood' statements. There are also potential conflicts of interest between the different market areas. In considering the various markets outlined above the company needs to consider how the company intends to serve each of them and to what extent it wants to incorporate a recognition of them within the mission.

Customers
- Good service quality
- Trustworthiness
- Fair prices

Suppliers
- Clear requirements
- Partnership
- Large orders
- Reliable settlement

Internal staff
- Recognition
- Rewards
- Security
- Opportunity for advancement

Bank

Employees (potential)
- Job supply
- Image of 'first choice' employer
- Courteous treatment

Referral sources
- Reliability
- Performance
- Recognition
- Reciprocation

Influencers

1. Shareholders
   - Returns
   - Growth
   - Compliance
   - Good corporate citizen

2. Government and regulators
   - Credit rating
   - Compliance
   - Reliability
   - No surprises

Figure 3.1 Expectations of relationship market/stakeholders

The decision on target audiences for the mission should be based on the context of the particular service firm and its current position within the industry sector. Most senior managers in service firms consider that the key messages in the mission statement should be concerned primarily with providing a strategic direction for the organization and motivating and focusing its internal staff. In a number of cases we examined a mission statement was developed and aimed specially at this internal audience, with a modified version being used for external purposes and reflecting consideration of other stakeholders.

What business are we in?

Consideration of the mission for a service organisation involves asking two interrelated questions: What business are we in and what business should we be in? The mission should provide the target audience determined above, including employees and other relevant stakeholders, with an understanding of the strategic direction and scope of the organization.

The mission is a key vehicle for developing and reviewing the strategic market and service options. In considering the basic purpose of the business it is essential that these strategic growth options are considered, otherwise the mission may simply be a series of elegant words used to reinforce the existing status quo. To do this we need to consider the service and market areas in which the organization may wish to develop. Figure 3.2 outlines the product/market options which the organization needs to consider. These include the following:

- Market penetration.
- Market development.
- Product or service development.
- Diversification.

Each section of the matrix in Figure 3.2 represents a core marketing strategy based on combinations of focus on existing markets, new markets, existing services and products or new services and products. We shall review the matrix briefly here but will return to discuss it in more detail in Chapter 6 in the context of product decisions.

Four possible approaches are available to the services firm. In expanding its market position (market penetration) it can attempt to penetrate the existing market for its services by attracting customers away from competitors, by increasing usage rates amongst existing competitors or by improving customer retention. A second option (service development) involves introducing new services to the existing marketplace. Many of the banks are following this strategy by introducing a continuous array of new products including investment and insurance services. A third option (market development) is to

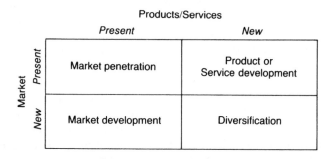

Figure 3.2 The product–market matrix

develop new markets for the existing services. This could involve identification and attack of new market segments or may involve regional or global geographic expansion. The fourth option (diversification) involves offering new services or products to new markets.

Developing a mission involves consideration of what services and markets the company wants to be in, not just those in which it is involved at present. A mission can help identify a policy defining future business growth and probability, based on these four growth options.

How unique is the mission statement?

A mission statement needs to be unique to the organization under consideration: a key method of obtaining competitive advantage is to be different in a preferred way to a selected customer base. The mission statement should articulate the point of differentiation and at the same time act as a framework for helping evaluate current and future activities. The acid test of a good mission statement is the substitutability test. If another company's name can be substituted into your mission and it still makes sense, it is a clear indication that your mission is too general and not sufficiently focused. A mission statement should differentiate the company from other companies operating in the same sector and help to establish an organization's individuality and uniqueness.

Is the mission market oriented?

It is particularly important to avoid mission statements that are product oriented, i.e. the mission should be defined in a way that reflects customer needs rather than product features and attributes. The dangers of product-oriented mission statements become obvious when we consider manufacturers of products such as candlesticks and slide rules, which have seen their markets largely disappear. In the long run, companies which appreciate that they are in the business of satisfying underlying market needs such as illumination or computational aids, rather than producing specific products, are likely to be much more successful than companies which are product oriented.

The value of a mission statement in the context of a physical product is easy to comprehend. In the services sector definition of business scope can be more subtle. The replacement of 'greasy spoon' sit down hamburger restaurants by restaurant chains such as McDonalds suggests that customer needs include speed, uniformity of service and product, cleanliness and the McDonalds' experience. This issue of underlying service needs is of concern to a diverse range of service firms which need to make a decision about the nature of what they offer. Organizations such as airlines, hotels and banks need to consider customer needs carefully and use this knowledge to make an input into the design of the services that are offered.

Unfortunately, many companies' mission statements do not satisfactorily answer the five questions posed above. Common problems with mission statements are that they are merely 'motherhood' statements, fail to support a relationship focus, are either unnecessarily broad or restrictingly narrow, and may prevent management taking advantage of new opportunities. A mission statement should articulate the right balance in terms of the desired long-term direction of the organization, determine to whom the mission is addressed, indicate the services to be offered and markets to be served, be unique and focus more on customers' needs rather than on the characteristics of the products and services offered.

Service mission statements

Relatively little research has been undertaken on the nature of mission statements and their content, and clear agreement as to how they should be developed, and what they should include, has not emerged. However, the studies that have been undertaken provide some useful guidelines.

David[2] has identified nine components of mission statements. These include the following:

1. **Customers** – who are they?
2. **Products or services** – what are the firm's major products or services?
3. **Location** – where does the firm compete?
4. **Technology** – what is the firm's basic technology?
5. **Concern for survival** – what are the firm's economic objectives?
6. **Philosophy** – what are the basic beliefs, values, aspirations and philosophical priorities of the firm?
7. **Self-concept** – what are the firm's major strengths and competitive advantages?
8. **Concern for public image** – what are the firm's public responsibilities and what image is desired?
9. **Concern for employees** – what is the firm's attitude towards its employees?

In a study of mission statements from forty-five service firms and thirty manufacturing firms David found that service firms stressed different competitive advantages in the marketplace from manufacturers. He concluded that service firms generally have less comprehensive mission statements than manufacturing firms. For example, less than 14 per cent of the mission statements of service firms addressed issues such as the technology, philosophy, location and self-concept. Service firm missions did, however, include a focus on customers' orientation and public image issues, with 76 per cent of service firms including the 'concern for customers' component, and 67 per cent of service firms including the 'concern for public image' component.

In this study, derived from 181 responses sent to the *Business Week*, 1000 top corporations in the USA, 59 per cent of responding chief executives indicated that their firm had not developed a formal mission. Thus development and communication of a clear mission appears to be a commonly neglected task in the formulation of business and marketing strategy amongst these companies.

Our observation is that relatively few service organizations have developed effective missions. There is considerable evidence of the poor quality of mission statements. A study by Byars and Neil[3] examined 157 mission statements from 208 respondents who are members of the Planning Forum, the world's largest membership organization on planning and strategic management. The study concluded that most mission statements were so broadly written that they had little meaning.

Those service companies that have taken the development of a mission seriously and have understood what is needed to develop one have, however, benefited. Dr Thomas Frist Jr. who is president and chief executive officer of the Hospital Corporation of America (HCA), has pointed out the value of an effective mission:

> I cannot stress enough how important the development of our written mission and philosophy has been to this company . . . far more important than any value received from the external public knowing our mission and philosophy has been the internal discipline and direction it has provided our employees throughout all levels of the organisation[4].

Examples of service organization mission statements

In examining actual mission statements for service companies, it is clear that there are vast differences in their length and content. Some are more general statements of philosophy whilst others are much more specific. In this section we will review some examples of different approaches to the development of service organization missions and illustrate the wide range of approaches that are adopted.

Although attention to missions is relatively recent in the management literature some service organizations have had mission statements for a long time. The 'mission statement' developed in 1888 for the Northwestern Mutual Life Insurance Company is shown in Figure 3.3. This mission developed by their executive committee in 1888 helped the company exist and flourish for over a hundred years in the highly competitive insurance industry.

Thomas Watson, IBM's founder, articulated his company's philosophy in the phrase 'IBM means service'. IBM defines itself as a service company and the corporate philosophy articulated by Watson was not just to be a good service company, but be the best service company – in any industry in the world. The IBM mission espoused by Watson in the 1960s is shown in Figure 3.4.

Watson argued that the basic philosophy of the organization was more connected with its performance than its technical or economic resources, organizational structure, innovation or timing. Some twenty years later the then IBM chairman stated: 'We've changed our technology, changed our organisation, changed our marketing and manufacturing techniques many times, and we expect to go on changing. But through all this change, his three basic beliefs remain. We steer our course by those stars.'

The Northwestern Mutual Way

The ambition of The Northwestern has been less to be large than to be safe; its aim is to rank first in benefits to policy owners rather than first in size. Valuing quality above quantity, it has preferred to secure its business under certain salutary restrictions and limitations rather than to write a much larger business at the possible sacrifice of those valuable points which have made The Northwestern pre-eminently the policy owners' Company.

Figure 3.3   The Northwest Mutual Life Insurance Company mission statement

---

IBM

■ Respect for the individual.
■ Provide the best customer service of any company in the world.
■ Pursue all tasks with the idea that they can be accomplished in a superior fashion.

Figure 3.4   Organization statement of philosophy for IBM

Such missions, which are statements of business philosophy, give overall guidance in terms of values but do not focus on service and product areas or markets. Today many service organizations are seeking to spell out their mission in more detail. The British Airways mission outlined in Figure 3.5 focuses on a number of key themes which include corporate charisma, creativity, business capability, competitive stance and training philosophy. Ultimately the company's

THE BRITISH AIRWAYS MISSION

To be the best and most successful company in the airline industry

OUR GOALS

■ Safe and Secure
To be a safe and secure airline

■ Financially Strong
To deliver a strong and consistent financial performance

■ Global Leader
To secure a leading share of air travel business worldwide with a significant presence in all major geographical markets

■ Service and Value
To provide overall superior service and good value for money in every market segment in which we compete

■ Customer Driven
To excel in anticipating and quickly responding to customer needs and competitor activity

■ Good Employer
To sustain a working environment that attracts, retains and develops committed employees who share in the success of the company

■ Good Neighbour
To be a good neighbour, concerned for the community and the environment

To achieve these goals, we must:

Deliver friendly, professional service consistently through well-trained and motivated employees.

Search continuously for improvement through innovation and the use of technology.

Employ planning and decision-making processes that provide clear direction and sense of purpose.

Foster a leadership style throughout the organisation which encourages respect for individuals, teamwork and close identification with customers.

Strive constantly to achieve agreed standards of quality at competitive cost levels.

BRITISH AIRWAYS   BRITISH AIRWAYS

Figure 3.5   British Airways' mission statement

mission needs to reflect the shared values which are held within the organization as part of its strategic focus. Within the industry sector in which it competes, British Airways aims to be 'the worldwide symbol of creativity, value, service and quality'. This mission statement is one of a series of missions which have been developed over a period of time to progressively refine BA's view of its business.

The mission for DHL in Figure 3.6 focuses on many of the key issues we consider should be addressed in a mission statement for such a firm. It also illustrates the need to develop corporate objectives (discussed in Chapter 7) which are highly integrated with the mission statement. Without a strong linkage which provides a means of measuring whether the mission can be achieved, much of the potential value of a mission can be dissipated. The relationship between

WORLDWIDE MISSION STATEMENT

DHL will become the acknowledged global leader in the express delivery of documents and packages. Leadership will be achieved by establishing the industry standards of excellence for quality of service and by maintaining the lowest cost position relative to our service commitment in all markets of the world.

Achievement of the mission requires:

☐ Absolute dedication to understanding and fulfilling our customers' needs with the appropriate mix of service, reliability, products and price for each customer.

☐ An environment that rewards achievement, enthusiasm, and team spirit and which offers each person in DHL superior opportunities for personal development and growth.

☐ A state of the art worldwide information network for customer billing, tracking, tracing and management information/communications.

☐ Allocation of resources consistent with the recognition that we are one worldwide business.

☐ A professional organisation able to maintain local initiative and local decision making while working together within a centrally managed network.

The evolution of our business into new services, markets, or products will be completely driven by our single-minded commitment to anticipating and meeting the changing needs of our customers.

Figure 3.6   DHL mission statement

corporate objectives and mission has been well summed up by the
Chairman and CEO of General Mills:

> We would agree that unless our mission statement is backed up with
> specific objectives and strategies, the words become meaningless,
> but I also believe that our objectives and strategies are far more likely
> to be acted upon where there exists prior statement of belief [i.e. a
> mission] from which specific plans and actions flow.

Shared corporate values and awareness of customer needs signal a
likely commitment by staff. Figure 3.7 shows the mission statement for
the Royal Trust Bank, a Canadian bank based in London. The strategic
process of development of a mission statement involved detailed

ROYAL TRUST BANK

MISSION STATEMENT

We aim to strengthen and focus our role in the United Kingdom as
a leading relationship bank offering our clients selected lending and
investment products together with fiduciary and advisory services
designed for developing companies, wealth-producing
entrepreneurs and professional individuals.

We will create wealth for our clients, employees and shareholders.

Our aim will be achieved by:
Earning the loyalty of our clients and their recommendation of our
people through:
● quality products and good advice
● dependable delivery
● efficient administration

Giving our employees purpose and pride through:
● training
● authority commensurate with responsibility
● recognition for performance

Maintaining the confidence and support of our shareholders through:
● prudence
● foresight
● progress

Figure 3.7 Royal Trust Bank mission statement

consideration and input from the board and senior management team. For the Royal Trust Bank this led to a reappraisal of its key business areas. In particular the bank recognized the importance of customer service at the strategic level and its role 'as a leading relationship bank'.

Mission statements can be an empty statement on a piece of paper or can reflect and underpin the fundamental values of an organization. In Royal Trust Bank's case the importance of a relationship strategy was emphasized as the primary means by which its basic business objectives were to be achieved.

Degree of sophistication

It is important that the degree of sophistication in the wording used in a mission is appropriate to the organization concerned. The use of technical academic terms appropriate for a strategy consulting firm's mission would be totally inappropriate to a small company operating in road transportation. An example of a less sophisticated services mission from Red Star Parcels, part of British Rail, appears in Figure 3.8.

Red Star Parcel's mission has specific objectives relating to:

- Quality.
- Access.
- Product development.
- Product/market segments.
- Costs.
- People.

Red Star Parcels developed a mission that could be understood by front-line blue collar workers, including some who may have worked for thirty years or more at British Rail. The notion of helping customers save time, helping them make more money, and tailoring delivery requirements to the customers' specification represented a considerable shift from previous thinking in front-line service staff.

RED STAR PARCELS MISSION STATEMENT

Helping our customers to save time and make more money by tailoring fast, precise and consistent delivery of packages to, from and within Great Britain.

Figure 3.8 Red Star Parcels mission statement

ANZ BANK BRANCH BANKING UNIT MISSION STATEMENT

- To not only be known for quality customer service but to be renowned for it
- To know our customers
- Give them the service and products they want
- And do it better than anybody

Figure 3.9   ANZ Bank Branch Banking Unit mission

The ANZ Bank in Australia adopted the mission shown in Figure 3.9 for its branch banking unit. Whilst a more sophisticated approach may be appropriate for the bank as a whole, this is aimed at retail branch bankers at the front line.

Mission statements such as those for Red Star Parcels and ANZ Bank may not include the strategic element of the previous missions, but are nevertheless important devices for getting basic messages across to front-line service staff. More detailed, or more sophisticated, missions, aimed at more senior levels of management, can be developed if appropriate.

Levels of mission statement

Just as companies have different levels of objectives, ranging from strategic objectives through to tactical objectives and action plans, a service organization should consider to what extent it should develop mission or purpose statements at lower levels. For example, a bank with diverse financial services operations could have a mission statement for the bank as a whole as well as individual missions for each business unit. Thus it might develop missions for retail banking, corporate banking, international banking, investment banking, and its insurance and stockbroking activities. Many multi-business service organizations are in a similar position of needing to develop missions for their constituent parts.

It may also be appropriate to have missions at individual functional levels. For example, missions could be developed for internal service functions. An example of a mission for a human resource department is shown in Figure 3.10. Some organizations develop a range of missions for internal service activities and departments. A customer service mission statement, for example, expresses the company's philosophy and commitment to customer service, recognizing that service quality is an important means of gaining competitive advantage. In some cases customer service and quality missions are stated separately, in others they may be combined as part of the statement of a firm's overall mission.

To develop and promote the highest quality human resource practices and initiatives in an ethical, cost effective and timely manner to support the current and future business objectives of the organization and to enable line managers to maximize the calibre, effectiveness and development of their human resources.

This will be achieved through working with managers and staff to:

■ Develop an integrated human resource policy and implement its consistent use throughout the organization

■ Enhance managers' efficient use of human resources through the provision of responsive and adaptable services

■ Be the preferred source of core strategic HR services

■ Provide high quality tailored HR consultancy

■ Introduce methods to plan for the provision of required calibre and quantity of staff

■ Ensure consistent line accountability throughout all areas within the organization

■ Assist the organization in becoming more customer aware and responsive to changing needs.

■ Define and encourage implementation of an improved communications culture throughout the organization

■ Maintain an innovative and affordable profile for HRM

Figure 3.10 Human resource mission statement

In each case the 'mission' should focus on the company, business unit or functional service activity. Where missions are formulated, for example, at the departmental level, they should be consistent with higher level missions within the organization.

Developing a service mission

We have now illustrated a range of service missions, discussed how the levels of sophistication required vary according to the target audience to which they are addressed, and outlined how missions can be developed for different units or levels within the organization. We will now examine alternative approaches to developing a mission, and consider its communication and realization.

The first point in developing a mission statement is to consider if the organization is ready to proceed with the task. Two US authors, Frohman and Pascarella, have suggested if a company cannot answer 'yes' to the following questions, it should weigh up carefully whether to proceed with developing a mission statement. These questions include the following:[5]

● Are we confident that the benefits of a mission statement justify the time and effort required?

- Do we really believe we have something to say about the mission of our business in the future that will make a difference now?

- Do we really believe we have something to say about our management practices and values that is important to our success over the long term?

- Can we afford to invest the time now to do the work necessary to prepare an effective mission statement?

- Are we willing to be objective in the examination of our management practices and relationships?

- Are we willing to solicit and use feedback from our customers, competitors and others to help us understand the needs we satisfy and how our performance is perceived?

- As a top management group, are we willing to take a stand about our business and values and commit ourselves to setting the example?

- Do we think we can come up with a mission that is general enough to guide the entire organization but specific enough to be meaningful for planning and decision making?

- Is there a champion for the development of a mission statement who is in a position to drive it?

If the company agrees, after considering these questions, that it is worthwhile to develop a mission, it then needs to consider how to do this.

Whilst a mission statement can be developed in isolation by a chief executive or management consultant, such an approach misses out on a vital part of the strategic process – that of gaining organizational acceptance. The involvement and participation in the development of the mission of managers and other staff within the organization will greatly enhance the prospects of achieving it. A number of different approaches can be used for the development of a mission.

A workshop approach
This typically takes place in the context of a strategy or marketing planning workshop with senior executives from the organization. A period is spent explaining the purpose and role of a mission statement and the different types of mission that can exist at different levels. This incorporates a review of many examples of both good and bad mission statements and a critique by participants. This is followed by syndicate exercises, where groups of about five people spend a sufficiently long period to produce a first draft mission. The missions from a number of different syndicates are then presented and the strengths and weaknesses of each are discussed in detail. A task force can then be used to

repeat the process at different levels of management and in different business units within the organization, leading to the eventual development of a mission statement.

A top team approach
Another approach is one we have used with several boards of directors, with groups of up to eight people. The session starts with the senior management, or board, being asked the purpose of their business. Each member is asked to write his or her view of the mission on a card. Significant variations are often found. After an appropriate period the missions on the cards are collected and shuffled, and during a coffee break they are written up on large sheets of paper and pinned to the walls. The mission statements do not identify their authors. The team is then invited to write a second version of the mission on a card and again these are collected and written on large sheets of paper which replace the ones on the wall. At this point a more detailed discussion follows. After two or three iterations a good draft mission may start to evolve, although in some cases more fundamental analysis may be needed.

The time devoted to the development of a satisfactory mission can be considerable. In one organization a group met for one afternoon each fortnight for nearly a year before a satisfactory mission statement was developed. However, group procedures like those above can speed up this process.

The development of a mission statement can be assisted by the use of an external catalyst such as a consultant or business school academic who challenges existing internal points of view and biases, and plays a facilitative role. Such a person may also be able to help drafting the mission statement and improving its potential as a communication tool.

Once completed, mission statements change only infrequently. The emergence of a new opportunity, a decline in the company's existing markets or a new technology offering a breakthrough in service delivery can create the need for change. A mission should be sufficiently robust to last for some time but should be reviewed on an annual basis, and be subject to revision if this is warranted by changes in the external environment. Whilst the development of a mission is highly contingent on the circumstances of the organization in question, a number of key factors need to be considered during its development. A good mission should do the following:

- Define the purpose of the organization.
- Identify relevant services and markets.
- Assist in reviewing current and future strategic options.

- Create a balance between narrowness and breadth.
- Differentiate the organization from others in its sector.
- Be specific enough to have an impact on the behaviour of the organization.
- Be realistic, attainable and flexible.
- Focus more on customer needs and their satisfaction than on the characteristics of the services themselves.
- Reflect the core competences of the organization.
- Permit close integration with corporate objectives, so that success in achieving the mission can be measured.
- Be clearly understood and widely communicated through the organization.

The nine components of a mission outlined earlier in this chapter, together with the list above, can act as a check-list when developing a mission.

Whilst there is a some agreement on the aspects that a mission statement should attempt to address, there is considerable diversity of opinion as to its appropriate length and structure. For some firms a short paragraph is considered sufficient, while others have documents that run to several pages. Our view is that it should be no longer than one page in large typeface. If necessary, a briefing document can be attached which discusses specific issues in the mission statement in greater detail; this can help managers in explaining the statement to staff. In terms of structure, we advocate a general statement which outlines the overall scope of the business together with a statement such as 'this will be achieved by', followed by a series of bullet point items which spell out in some detail how the mission statement is to be achieved. Whilst some writers argue that there should be some quantification within a mission statement we contend such quantification should be reserved for corporate objectives.

Communicating the mission statement

Once a satisfactory mission statement has been developed, consideration needs to be given to communicating it within and, where appropriate, outside the organization, and to deciding to what extent subsidiary missions should be formulated at lower levels. Organizations approach the communication of their mission statements in different ways. Some draw attention to it by reproducing it on posters and placing it on walls throughout the company. Others produce the mission on a plastic card that can be conveniently carried or placed on a desk. A leading strategy consulting firm has it printed on a card that becomes the front page of a loose leaf personal organizer used within the firm.

One approach that we used in a bank will serve as an illustration of how a mission can be successfully introduced. In this case the mission statement together with a letter from the chief executive explaining how the mission statement had been developed, why it was important, and how it was planned to use it, was circulated to all staff. The letter outlined how the thinking and philosophy behind it would be explained in a series of forthcoming workshops for the staff. This was followed up by small group workshops for the staff. The workshops involved all staff ranging from receptionists and secretaries up to board level.

In the workshops the mission statement was discussed, the bank's strategy was explained and key customer service strategies were identified. The workshop involved two syndicate exercises which focused around key improvement areas identified in the mission. Each workshop concluded with every syndicate making presentations to the chief executive and members of the board of directors. The chief executive then addressed each issue raised and in many cases immediately implemented suggestions made by the syndicates. In some cases it was explained why some things could not be done. In other cases a task force was set up to report to a member of the executive committee via a project team manager. This resulted in a high level of enthusiasm, raised morale, a clear understanding of what the mission stood for, and an on-going work programme which supported the task of achieving the mission.

The mission can also be communicated from senior management down to front-line service providers by a cascade process in which each level of management provides a briefing to the level below, or by a series of workshops run by facilitators based around key issues in the mission. Whatever approach is used the cascade process should be supported by an appropriate internal communication programme. Such an approach can:

- Help acceptance of the core values in the mission statement.
- Involve workers and give them a wider perspective on their company.
- Create a positive impact on organizational behaviour.
- Improve commitment.
- Focus attention on the key objectives of the company.
- Assist the internal marketing effort.

If a service providing firm is serious about the mission and the core values contained in it, it can test – by internal market research – to what extent employees are familiar with the mission statement and supportive of the core values it represents. The mission statement can thus be used to identify to what extent the core values are accepted as relevant and appropriate to the organization.

The value of a mission statement does not end when the mission statement is finally written down. It should be something that is constantly rearticulated and reinforced by top managers throughout the organization on an on-going basis. It should also be introduced to new employees on their first day of their induction programme so that they are familiar with the mission and what it represents.

The realizable mission

An effective mission is a fundamental element of a service firm's marketing strategy. A mission statement, whilst seemingly simple in its completed form, may be the result of intensive and critical self-review for the company. The mission should position the services firm clearly in the markets in which it seeks to serve its customers and should provide an animated vision with which employees can identify.

Describing a mission statement as an 'animated vision' suggests that it should be forward thinking, inspirational and dramatized. When the mission is communicated it should have the capacity to motivate the workforce towards organizational goals.

Figure 3.11 illustrates that it is necessary to develop a strong overlap between intellectual agreement (the statement of mission) and emotional commitment (the shared values of employees). It is this linkage between mission and values, made by management and other employees, that determines the extent to which the mission is realizable. This was well summed up by Jack Crocker, President of Super Value Stores Inc., who said. 'If a corporation is to succeed and experience continuing, long-term growth, there must exist a meaningful company philosophy [a mission] that justifies the personal commitment and dedication of its people' Several writers have compared missions to New Year's resolutions. People must be motivated to want to carry them out. The true value of a mission is evident when the statements in it are translated into actions. If the mission has value, people in the organization should believe in and follow the principles it espouses. Thus it is essential for the staff's shared values to be congruent with the mission.

Research has not been undertaken on the links between a realizable mission – where the intellectual content of the mission statement and emotional commitment to it are highly integrated – and business

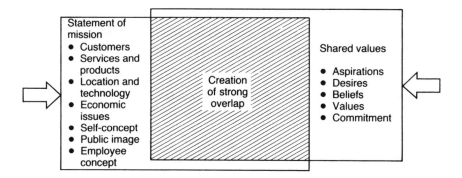

Figure 3.11 The 'realizable' mission: combining intellectual agreement and emotional commitment

profitability. However, research carried out by Johnson and Johnson in connection with the Business Roundtable Task Force on Corporate Responsibility and the Ethics Research Centre in Washington provides some evidence of such a linkage.[6] The researchers set out to identify companies which had a written codified set of principles outlining their philosophy (i.e. a mission). They then looked for solid evidence that the mission had been promulgated and practised by the organization for at least a generation, and examined the performance of the companies in terms of profits and rewards to the shareholder over a thirty-year period.

From an original sample of twenty-six companies, eleven had to be excluded because of the lack of comparable data. The fifteen remaining companies, on average, showed annual compound growth of 11 per cent over the thirty-year period. This represented more than three times the growth of the gross national product over that period. From a shareholder's perspective if US$30 000 had been allocated in the Dow Jones Index over a thirty-year period this would have compounded to US$134 000. If the same US$30 000 had been divided equally amongst the fifteen companies this would be worth more than US$1 million. Whilst the methodology can be criticized, this study presents some evidence that companies with high profit performance have achieved a realizable mission by integrating a statement of mission with the shared values of employees.

The most comprehensive and useful research on the value of mission statements has been undertaken by Andrew Campbell and his colleagues at Ashridge. They identify the following four elements as important in a mission:[7]

- **Purpose** – why the company exists.
- **Strategy** – the competitive position and distinctive competence.

- **Values** – what the company believes in.

- **Standards and behaviour** – the policies and behaviour patterns that underpin the distinctive competence and the value system.

They argue that a strong mission exists when these four elements link together tightly and describe some key guiding principles or how to create a long term 'sense of mission'. These include the following:[8]

- **It takes years not months.** Creating a sense of mission is a long-term project. One company has been actively working at it for ten years and has still not fully succeeded. On the other hand, if the sense of mission is imposed from above, and is combined with sweeping management changes, a shorter period, say less than three years, seems to be reasonable.

- **True consensus is necessary within the top team.** Normally a few people within a company, sometimes as few as two, form the power group at the centre. It is necessary for this group to have a sense of mission if the organization is to have one.

- **Action is a better communicator than words.** The reason why the top team must have a true belief in the values is because it is their actions that will send out the message. Values are not easily communicated by speeches. They only live in an organization when managers act them out.

- **Top team visibility is essential.** The values of the organization are its ethos and personality. It is much easier for employees to identify with the ethos if they can associate it with a leader or leadership group. It is hard to believe in an organization if you feel out of touch with the leadership.

- **Top team continuity.** Continuity of leadership is one of the biggest contributors to creating a sense of mission. Not only does it give the leaders time to think through the connections between values and strategies and to identify pivotal behaviour, it helps to make the leaders more visible, makes consensus more likely and promotes consistency, one of the most important aspects of communicating a message.

- **Statements of mission should have personality.** The most highly regarded published statements were those that reflected the organization's personality and leadership. Frequently they were straight talking, using blunt terms rather than advertising copy.

- **Strategy and values should be formulated together.** An essential part of creating a mission is the resonance between strategy and values.

- **Management should focus on the link between behaviour and**

values. Employees feel a sense of mission when they believe in what they are doing.

As noted earlier, this discussion has been concerned with a formal written mission. A mission does not have to be written down. In smaller organizations the mission is often unwritten but is made explicit by the owner's personal behaviour. However, in large organizations written missions are much more common. In the Byars and Neil's study only 16 per cent of organizations surveyed had informal word of mouth missions.

Most significant service companies believe it is important to have a formal written codification of their principles and ambition to help guide staff. Many missions make the mistake of focusing on shareholders, customers and managers and do not attempt to motivate the non-managerial workforce. Companies should make employee focus a high priority in their mission statements, as in a service organization it is often the collective behaviour of employees which brings success or failure.

Notes

1. T. Levitt, 'Marketing myopia', *Harvard Business Review*, July-August 1960, pp. 45–56.
2. F.R. David, 'How companies define their mission', *Long Range Planning*, vol. 22, no. 1, 1989, pp. 90–7.
3. L.L. Byars and T.C. Neil, 'Organisational philosophy and mission statements, *Planning Review*, July-August 1987, pp. 32–5.
4. J.K. Brown, 'Corporate soul searching: the power of mission statements', *Across the Board*, March 1984, pp. 44–52.
5. M. Frohman and P. Pascarella, 'How to write a purpose statement', *Industry Week*, 23 March 1987.
6. T.A. Falsey, *Corporate Philosophies and Mission Statements*, Quorum Books, Westpoint, Connecticut, 1989, pp. 55.
7. A. Campbell, M. Devine and D. Young, *Sense of Mission*, Economist Books/Hutchinson, London, 1990.
8. A. Campbell and S. Yeung, *Do You Need a Mission Statement?*, Economist Publications Management Guides, London, 1990.

4

Services market segmentation

The process of market segmentation

Market segmentation has long been considered as one of the most essential marketing concepts available to managers concerned with marketing products. However, within the services sector marketing the concept is, in general, underutilized, with many organizations adopting an unsophisticated approach to segmentation or merely paying lip service to it. The approach taken is often to wait and see which clients or customers come forward to buy a service, or to offer a range of services without focusing on the specific needs of identified segments. This chapter identifies the particular importance of market segmentation for service industries, outlines a framework for the segmentation process, describes appropriate bases for segmenting markets, and provides examples of successful approaches to segmentation.

Broadly, a service company has the following three alternatives to target market selection:

- An **undifferentiated marketing approach**, where there is no recognition of distinct segments in the market. This is sometimes termed market aggregation.

- A **differentiated marketing approach** where a company identifies, for example, five segments in the market, and develops separate marketing mix programmes aimed at each segment.

- A **concentrated marketing approach** where, although there is a recognition that there are a number of discreet segments, the company focuses its marketing mix primarily at one specific segment.

These segment choices are illustrated in Figure 4.1.

Not many service companies can rely on an undifferentiated marketing approach to maximize their financial returns. Service organizations with monopolies have attempted to do this in the past. Now, with deregulation and privatization, former monopolies are increasingly aware of the need to consider market segments rather than adopting a market aggregation approach. The entry of the Mercury service into the UK telecommunications market, once the sole territory of British Telecom, is a good example of this. However, many service organizations still undertake their marketing activities as if **every** person in the market (or company, in the case of a corporate market) will want their

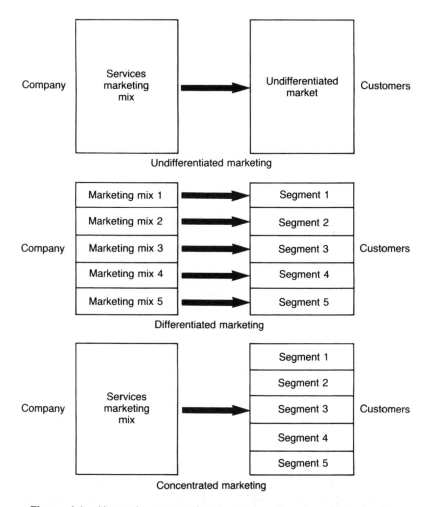

Figure 4.1 Alternative approaches to services target market selection

services. More sophisticated service providers achieve improved performance by targeting those segments most likely to buy their services, and differentiating their offer to them.

The segmentation process divides a heterogeneous market into specific homogeneous segments. This allows identified segments to be targeted with specific services and a distinctive marketing mix. It therefore aims at satisfying customer needs more effectively, ensuring customer retention and loyalty. Market research, which is often required in order to successfully divide the market into segments, ensures that targeted customers are supplied with the service offering which they need and require, thus avoiding the pitfalls of trial and error marketing. On-going analysis of specific market segments is the basis for long-term planning of marketing activity. It also has the advantage that it can help with the development of specific new services and products aimed at satisfying the needs of a particular market segment. Products and services can be planned in the light of knowledge of the requirements of distinct segments.

Market segmentation is especially important for services in the current competitive marketplace. Service industries are suffering from increasing competition both in the numbers of competitors and in the proliferation of service offerings. Market segmentation helps prevent the waste of valuable resources by directing effort into those areas that will help achieve success.

Service products are frequently not clearly differentiated. Market segmentation offers the opportunity of gaining competitive advantage, in a highly contested market, through differentiation. The market segmentation approach involves identification of the benefits which different homogeneous groups seek, allowing relevant features and requirements to be determined and used as a source of service differentiation.

An example from the airline industry provides an illustration of successful market segmentation strategy. SAS is a small airline with a home base in Scandinavia where there is only a small population to serve as a customer base. The airline has been extremely successful in competing with large airlines in centres of high population. The airline successfully identified a distinct segment of the market – the business traveller – which had previously largely been neglected. By offering this segment a highly tailored service, SAS has reaped rich rewards.

Research was used to identify the specific needs of business executives. This group requires timetabling to fit busy work schedules, punctuality of service, appropriate cabin service, features conducive to working on board the aircraft, and back up ground services such as late check-in facilities. SAS developed a service which met these requirements and reaped the rewards from a much less price sensitive market than that for undifferentiated mass travel.

The whole of SAS was redesigned around the needs of the business traveller. Reservations, ticketing, check-in facilities, choice of aircraft, cabin service, schedules,routes and pricing were all designed to meet the service requirements of this distinct market segment. Competitors who wished to compete for the business traveller segment had to change their services to match those of SAS, but they were often not as successful as they still tried to serve several market segments at the same time. For example, some competitors were not able to provide the ground support for a late check-in service.

Different customers have different needs. A hotel which aims to satisfy the prestige executive market needs to consider the specific requirements of this segment. These might include full secretarial and office facilities, conference amenities, twenty-four hour catering, a fitness facility and late check-out options. Successful marketing identifies specific needs and preferences for services, and then develops strategies to satisfy these preferences.

A single service or product cannot meet the needs of all customers, but it can meet the needs of a specific group of customers. A service business should be positioned to serve particular segments of the market. A service company therefore needs to identify the most attractive parts of the market so that it can serve them effectively and produce the greatest profit. For example, within the financial services industry, the credit card serves a variety of credit, convenience and prestige requirements. American Express focuses on the prestige travel and entertainment market, offering a higher-priced card targeted at the business and high status market segments. The actual service product is very similar to that of Visa and Mastercard, but American Express has concentrated on more distinct prestige market segments and positioned itself accordingly. It has attracted up-market users who are not concerned about the fees charged for the service.

The segmentation process, shown in Figure 4.2, is concerned to divide a heterogeneous market into specific homogeneous segments. The segmentation process follows four broad steps:

- The definition of the market to be addressed.
- The identification of alternative bases for segmentation.
- An examination of these bases and the choice of the best base or bases for segmentation.
- The identification of individual market segments, an assessment of their attractiveness and the selection of specific target segments.

Once the market segment has been selected, the process of target marketing involves developing a positioning for the target segments selected and then developing a marketing mix for each target market.

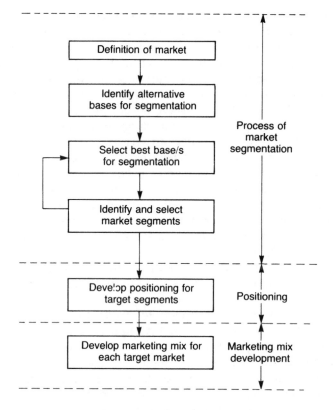

Figure 4.2 Services market segmentation

Definition of the relevant market

The definition of the relevant market to be addressed involves specifying the customer group to which the company is seeking to market its services. This can be a broad group such as retail customers for a supermarket in a given geographic region, or a much more specific group which can be further segmented. For example, an investment bank may focus on very high net worth individuals with personal assets exceeding one million pounds. A hotel chain may focus on the business traveller market. A restaurant may focus on family customers.

The definition of a relevant market will have already been addressed in the development of the mission statement, discussed in Chapter 3. In defining its market the firm needs to conduct an internal audit of its strengths and weaknesses and a review of the resources which are available to it. It also needs to consider carefully the overall strategic objectives of the firm (this is discussed further in Chapter 7). The choice of the market to be addressed or served will be based on decisions relating to the following:

- The breadth of the service line.
- The types of customers.
- Geographic scope.
- Areas of the value-added chain in which the service firm decides to participate.

Successful market segmentation means satisfying the needs of existing and potential customers in a clearly defined market. This involves understanding customer attitudes, and customer preferences, as well as the benefits which are sought. Definition of the target market and its requirements is the first essential step in the segmentation process.

Identifying alternative bases for segmentation

Once the market to be addressed has been identified the next step is to consider alternative means of segmenting the market. Figure 4.3 provides an overview of some of the key approaches, known as 'segmentation bases', which can be used in segmenting a market. We will now review each of these briefly.

Demographics and socio-economics

Demographic segmentation includes a number of factors including sex, age, family size etc. Socio-economic variables may also be considered here, including income, education, social class and ethnic origins. Many retail stores target different customer groups, e.g. Harrods, Marks and Spencer and Littlewoods are targeted at specific socio-economic groups. By profiling demographic segments an organization can identify strengths and weaknesses in its current offerings.

An interesting example of market segmentation is seen in the banking patterns of consumers based on the lifecycle of the household. Whilst other factors such as socio-economic level are also important, the age and family composition of the lifecycle concept are particularly valuable predictors of a household's propensity to either save or

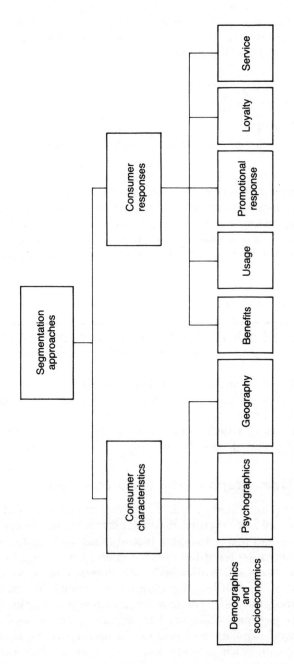

Figure 4.3 Major approaches to services market segmentation

borrow. One study of retail banking in the USA identified the following six lifecycle stages:

- **Bachelor** – a household in which the household head is under 40 years of age, living alone in 'empty nest' status.
- **Young married** – a household in which the household head is married and under 40 with no dependent children in the household.
- **Young full nest** – a household in which the household head is under 40 years of age with at least one dependent child.
- **Older full nest** – a household in which the household head is 40 years of age or older with at least one dependent child.
- **Older empty nest employed** – a household in which the household head is 40 years of age or older, employed full time, with no dependent children.
- **Older empty nest retired** – a household in which the household head is 40 years of age or older, retired, with no dependent children.

An analysis of the stages within the customer lifecycle determines what kinds of banking relationships are needed to meet the demands of the household. These needs change significantly from a bachelor who wants easy credit facilities and convenient transactions, young marrieds requiring higher levels of credit facilities, through to older families at the peak of their earning and spending potential, and then older people without children at home who have a higher propensity to save. A financial institution can therefore direct various service offerings to individuals based on their stage within the lifecycle model. Figure 4.4 shows a variation of the family lifecycle model used by American Express to determine demand patterns for selected financial services.

Psychographic segmentation

This form of segmentation cannot be explained in clearly defined quantitative measures: it is concerned with people's behaviour and ways of living. Psychographics can be especially helpful if other more traditional means of segmentation, such as socio-economics or demographics, do not produce clear or useful segments. Rather than being concerned directly with such factors as age, education, income, occupation and marital status, psychographic segmentation is concerned with analyzing lifestyle characteristics, attitudes and personality. This includes investigation into lifestyle dimensions such as those shown in Table 4.1. Often these elements are examined in conjunction

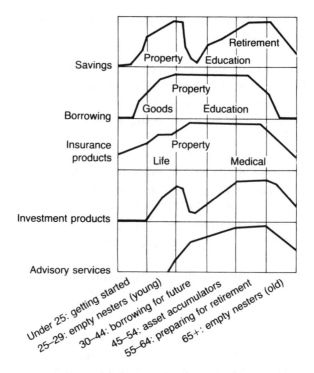

Source: American Express Company, *Annual Report 1982*.

Figure 4.4 American Express life-cycle model

with demographic variables. Service companies are increasingly starting to look at psychographic segmentation, although some attempts at
this have been unsuccessful.

Midland Bank was one of the first British banks to develop specific
brands aimed at different lifestyle segments. Its Vector brand, introduced in 1987 aimed at young, less financially committed consumers
who were high spenders. This was followed by products aimed at two
further target markets, Orchard for home owning, family-oriented and
budget-conscious consumers and Meridian for high income empty
nesters. However, despite gaining 330 000 Vector customers Midland
has decided to stop selling its Vector brand, in part because of shifting
patterns in demographics. Emphasis on the other lifestyle segments
has also been abandoned.

Such segments are usually identified by asking a series of questions
about topics like those shown in Table 4.1, as well as product usage
questions. An illustration of a lifestyle segmentation for a US bank is
shown in Table 4.2. This illustrates how psychographics offers service
providers rich insights into the nature of their customers.

Table 4.1 Illustrative lifestyle dimensions

Activities	Interests	Opinions
Work	Family	Selves
Hobbies	Home	Social issues
Social events	Job	Politics
Vacation	Community	Business
Entertainments	Recreation	Economics
Club membership	Fashion	Education
Community	Food	Products
Shopping	Media	Future
Sports	Achievements	Culture

Geography

Geographic segmentation divides customers according to where they live or work and correlates this with other variables. This is appropriate where customer needs vary in different areas, or where local and regional trends favour particular types of service offerings. For example, a client may use a local or regional law firm for routine legal work, but city law firms for complex litigation or corporate legal matters. Regional law firms therefore often focus on standard work and may not try to compete with the service offered by large, city law firms who have greater professional resources.

As geographic analysis is a relatively simple means of segmenting a market, it is frequently one of the first segmentation variables to be considered by a service firm. Geographic segmentation dimensions are typically grouped into market scope factors and geographic market measures.

- **Market scope factors** include a consideration of where the markets to be served are located: this may be local, national, regional or global. To be a major player in some service businesses requires a regional or global presence: airlines wishing to be significant players are recognizing this. Many airlines are seeking increased scale of operations through mergers and strategic alliances. Both SAS and British Airways have been active in this area. BET, a diversified specialist support services company operating in the business services, plant services and distribution services sectors, operates in local as well as national markets in the UK, Europe and the USA depending on the underlying characteristics of the market served and the services being offered. In some cases geographic segmentation can be an inexpensive yet effective segmentation approach. *College Football*, a yearbook produced in the USA uses

Table 4.2 Lifestyle segmentation for a US bank

Cluster I profile (10%) Upper level, white collar	Cluster II profile (18%) New retiree	Cluster III profile (9%) New, blue collar	Cluster IV profile (15%) Price conscious	Cluster V profile (13%) Savings conscious, debt avoidance	Cluster VI profile (24%) Older, lower income, blue collar
Most important factors Integrity Ego enhancement Expertise	*Most important factors* Time convenience Bank philosophy Pricing	*Most important factors* Location convenience Time convenience	*Most important factors* Time convenience Location convenience Pricing	*Most important factors* Location convenience Bank philosophy Integrity	*Most important factors* Location convenience Time convenience Bank philosophy
Least important factors Time convenience Location convenience	*Least important factors* Location convenience	*Least important factors* Bank philosophy Ego enhancement	*Least important factors* Ego enhancement Expertise Bank philosophy	*Least important factors* Time convenience Pricing	*Least important factors* Integrity Expertise
Demographics 45–54 age College grad or better Upper income Professional/management Teachers Farm owners	*Demographics* 55+ age Newer residents Middle to upper income Retired	*Demographics* Under 35 age Lower income Blue collar Renters Newer residents	*Demographics* Below 44 age Lower to middle income Large families	*Demographics* Middle income	*Demographics* 55+ age Lower income Less educated Blue collar, sales/clerical Home owners Long-time residents
Financial attitudes Optimistic	*Financial attitudes* Pessimistic Reliance on savings Not new brand tryers	*Financial attitudes* Optimistic No strong need for savings	*Financial attitudes* Smart shoppers Above average users	*Financial attitudes* Ego Reliance on cash (if possible) Conscious of debt Savings reliance New brand tryers	*Financial attitudes*

Less reliant on savings Do not shop around Not price sensitive Considered heavy credit card users Neutral attitude toward banks *Banking habits* Below average use of savings and loans and credit unions Above average in number of savings accounts held Above average in number of loans made Satisfied with banking hours *Media habits* Below average in use of radio, TV and newspapers	Not heavy users of credit Favorable attitude toward banks *Banking habits* Above average use of credit unions Satisfied with banking hours *Media habits* Above average use of radio and TV	Average users of credit cards Not new brand tryers Not bargain hunters Nonsociable Unfavorable attitude toward banks *Banking habits* Below average use of all financial institutions except banks Above average number credit cards Above average in personal loans Dissatisfied with banking hours Drive-in Night depositories *Media habits* Below average use of media, especially TV	of credit cards Negative view of debt Unfavorable attitude toward banks *Banking habits* High multiple use of financial institutions Above average use of checking, savings, personal loans Below average number of credit cards Least satisfied with current banking hours	Neutral attitude toward banks *Banking habits* High multiple use of financial institutions Above average number of savings accounts Above average number of credit cards Below average number of personal loans Satisfied with current banking hours *Media habits* Above average use of radio and newspapers Below average use of TV	Pessimistic Reliance on bank savings Unfavorable attitude toward credit Reliance on cash Smart shoppers Neutral attitude toward banks *Banking habits* Above average use of banks Below average number of savings accounts, loans, credit cards Satisfied with banking hours (Saturday) Inside bank facilities *Media habits* High radio use

Source: D. H. Robertson and D. N. Bellenger, 'Identifying bank market segments', *Journal of Bank Research*, Winter 1977, pp. 276–83.

different covers in different regions which each feature a photo-
graph of a current college football star from each region, thus
appealing specifically to the interests of different geographic areas.

- **Geographic market measures** include examination of population
  density, climate-related factors, and standardized market areas.
  Geographic measures are especially important in the selection of
  specialized mass communications media. Most mass circulation
  media profile geographic coverage of standardized market areas in
  detail as well as providing media circulation by type of reader and
  other variables. Geographic market measures are used to determine
  relative sales potential in different geographic areas. In the UK
  there are a number of geo-demographic services available to the
  services marketer. These are mostly derived from census data, and
  use postcodes to locate households. They include ACORN (A
  Classification Of Residential Neighbourhoods). CACI (Consolid-
  ated Analysis Centres Incorporated) and PIN (Pinpoint Identified
  Neighbourhoods analysis). Such services combine household composition data with demographic data.

Benefit segmentation

The segmentation variables listed above focus on the personal attributes of the customer. Segmentation can also be carried out on the
basis of the customers' response. Figure 4.3 also shows variables which
can be broken down on the basis of measures of consumer response.
One of the most important ways of doing this is benefit segmentation.

Benefit segmentation assumes that the benefits that people are
seeking from a given product or service are the basic reasons why they
buy the product. This differs from psychographic segmentation which
focuses on *who* will buy a product. Identifying a segment seeking a
common benefit permits the service provider to develop a relevant
offering. For example, various benefits are sought within the retail
banking market. One segment seeks large, well known banks which
offer a full range of service for varying needs. Another segment looks
for advantageous loans with borrowing easily available at low interest.
A third segment may seek high savings interest with quick service and
a personal banking relationship. A fourth segment might seek a
one-stop bank with a wide variety of services, convenient hours and
quick service. A bank can direct its service to satisfying one or more of
these segments and gain a reputation for offering a distinct package.

Benefit segmentation is applicable to almost all services as it focuses
on the underlying reasons for purchasing them. For example, within
the education market consumers can be analyzed based on the primary
benefits they seek from the education experience. An example of

benefit segments used for categorizing prospective MBAs is shown in Table 4.3. These were identified from a survey of candidates from the USA.

Another example is offered by SAS, who realized that business travellers looked for convenient schedules and a punctual service. These benefits were not being adequately supplied by other carriers, and so they gained recognition amongst business travellers for their quality of service on these important service benefit dimensions. Benefit segmentation is a market-oriented approach to segmentation, seeking to identify customer needs and then to satisfy them.

Usage segmentation

Usage segmentation focuses on the type and extent of usage patterns. Consumers are typically divided into heavy users, medium users, occasional users or non-users of the service being considered. Many services marketeers are concerned with focusing on the heavy user segment, who may consume many times more of the service than the occasional user. This is the basis of many fast food restaurants who cater for high volume usage by providing speedy, low-cost food.

Banks and building societies are concerned with heavy, medium, light and non-users of their services. They wish to understand the nature, behaviour and identity of heavy users and attract them to their bank. Similarly banks and building societies may wish to discourage light users. In early 1992 the Halifax Building Society announced that it would introduce charges for investors who allowed their savings accounts to fall below £50 for long periods and customers with less than £250 in their accounts who made more than two counter withdrawals a month.

Airlines are focusing on business travellers who use their airlines more frequently than others. In the UK, British Airways has developed its Latitudes programme aimed at retaining frequent business travellers. Most major airlines have similar frequent user programmes, as do hotel chains such as Trust House Forte, Hilton and Sheraton, where various inducements are used to increase patronage.

Promotional response

Promotional response segmentation considers how customers respond to a particular form of promotional activity. This may include response to advertising, sales promotions, in-store displays and exhibitions. Users of mail order catalogues tend to be good users of credit cards and will have a higher response rate to other direct mail offerings. This information can be used by service companies to ensure that this

Table 4.3 MBA degree benefit segments

---

1. **Quality seekers** desire the highest-quality education available. They believe a first-rate education will benefit them throughout their business lives, ultimately leading to job advancement or career change
2. **Speciality seekers** desire a specialized education to become experts in their fields of interest. Concentrated programmes will fit their needs, and they will seek out institutions that offer them
3. **Career changers** want new job positions or employers and believe the MBA degree will give them the opportunity for career advancement and mobility. They have worked for several years and typically perceive themselves to be in dead-end jobs
4. **Knowledge seekers** want to learn and feel knowledge will lead to power. They believe a graduate MBA education will be an asset to any activity they undertake in their social, community, political or corporate lives
5. **Status seekers** feel that graduate MBA course-work will lead to increased income and prestige
6. **Degree seekers** believe the bachelor's degree is insufficient and that the MBA is essential to being job-competitive in today's business environment. They are active, self-oriented and independent
7. **Professional advancers** strive to climb the corporate ladder. They want professional advancement, higher income, job flexibility and upward mobility. They are serious, future oriented and want to build careers within their current corporate structures
8. **Avoiders** seek the MBA programmes which require them to invest the least effort. They feel all schools will give them essentially the same education. Their motivation is 'other directed' and they select low-cost, lower-quality programmes
9. **Convenience seekers** enrol in the MBA programmes that are located near their homes or jobs and have simple registration procedures. They are interested in any school with these characteristics and low cost
10. **Non-matriculators** want to take MBA courses without completing formal application procedures. They are attracted to schools that allow them to begin the MBA programme without formal application

---

Source: Based on G. Miaoulis and D. Kalfus, '10 MBA benefit segments', *Marketing News*, 5 August 1983.

segment receives frequent communication by direct mail, thus building a relationship with the customer as well as obtaining a high response rate to promotions.

With loyalty segmentation customers are categorized according to the extent of the loyalty they exhibit to the particular product or service being offered. Customers can be characterized according to their degree of loyalty in the channels of distribution or outlets. In retailing, for example, the high level of outlet loyalty experienced by retailers such as Marks and Spencer in the UK and Nordstroms in the USA presents considerable opportunities for increased sales. Nordstroms has built on this by developing long-term relationships with customers through their personal buyer service, where a customer's 'personal buyer' will keep records on customers and send them information on new merchandise, as well as merchandise itself.

Some customers are very loyal to the services organization they are currently with, even if they are not happy with the service they are receiving. Despite customer dissatisfaction in banking, loyalty remains high with about 75 per cent of customers remaining with the one bank most of their adult lives. Bank marketing departments often point out that you are more likely to change your marriage partner than your bank. Nevertheless, the market research firm NOP showed that over half a million UK bank customers changed their bank accounts over the six-month period to March 1991.

Customers are sometimes divided into four categories according to consumer loyalty patterns, 'hard-core loyals' (consumers who buy their brand all the time); 'soft-core loyals' (who are loyal to two or three brands); 'shifting loyals' (who shift from favouring one brand to another); and 'switchers' (who show little sustainable loyalty to one brand). The underlying reasons for these different behaviour patterns need further analysis.

Segmentation by service

One area which has received relatively little attention is the consideration of how customers respond to varying service offerings. This may be considered a subset of benefit segmentation, but it is of sufficient importance to be addressed separately. The various elements of customer service that can be offered, and possible differentiation in terms of service levels within these elements, represent a considerable opportunity to design service packages appropriate to different market segments.

Segmenting markets by service involves addressing the following issues:

- Can groupings of customers be identified with similar service requirements?
- Can we differentiate our service offering?
- Do all our products require the same level of service?

In a study of the instrument supplies industry, Peter Gilmour examined the response of five customer segments to a range of nine customer service elements.[1] The results of his study are partly summarised in Table 4.4, which shows the response of both the suppliers and the five customer segments, as well as the composite results for all customers. The results show some disparity between customers' and suppliers' perception of the importance of certain customer service elements, particularly in the areas of sales service and back up and efficient telephone handling of orders and queries. Table 4.4 also shows several important differences between market segments. For example, two government markets – government instrumentalities and secondary schools – showed very marked differences in the importance they attached to a wide range of service elements, including availability, after sales service and back up, ordering convenience, competent technical representatives, and demonstrations of equipment.

By explicitly measuring the perceived importance of different customer service elements across market segments, the supplier is much better placed to respond to that segment's identified needs and allocate the service offering appropriate to it. This particular study suggested that highly qualified technical representation was appropriate to servicing the government and hospitals segments but not the others, where a less technically qualified salesman would suffice. Highly efficient and responsive handling of orders was appropriate for private companies and secondary schools, but was less necessary for other customer segments.

Studies such as that outlined above suggest that policy decisions to increase or reduce customer service levels should not be made equally across the entire customer base or across service factors. Differentiation of the service requirements of different customer segments offers considerable potential for reducing customer service costs and/or improving levels of service.

Selection of best base(s) for segmentation

The types of segmentation outlined above are illustrative of the main forms of segmentation used by services companies. They are, however, by no means exhaustive.[2] To a large extent the identification of segmentation bases involves an element of creativity. Those marketing services should constantly be considering alternative ways of segmenting the market and seeking ways in which they can create differential advantage over their competitors. This stage of the segmentation process should result in the selection of the best base(s) for segmentation. The starting point is to list the potentially useful segmentation options. For example, an initial list developed by the partners of a large accounting firm included the following:

- Geographic location.
- Type of legal entity.
- Geographic scale (local/national).
- Stage in business cycle.
- Industry type.
- Stage in industry life cycle.
- Size.

Table 4.4 Average importance ratings for customer service elements for different market segments

	Suppliers	All customers	Private companies	Government instrumentalities	Secondary schools	Universities and CAEs	Hospitals
Availability of item	1	1	1	5	1	1	1
After sales service and backup	5	2	5	1	7	2	2
Efficient telephone handling of orders and queries	2	6	4	6	4	7	7
Ordering convenience	7	7	8	9	2	6	8
Competent technical representatives	3	5	5	2	8	5	3
Delivery time	5	4	2	6	5	3	5
Reliability of delivery	4	3	3	4	3	4	4
Demonstrations of equipment	8	7	7	3	9	7	5
Availability of published material	9	9	9	8	6	9	8

Source: P. Gilmour, 'Customer segmentation: differentiating by market segment', *International Journal of Physical Distribution*, vol. 7, no. 3, 1977, p. 146.

- Centralized versus decentralized.
- Management style/age/culture.
- Buying history.
- Profitability.
- Degree of risk.
- Current level of contract.
- Current advisers.
- Connector network.
- Aspirations.
- Growth rate.
- Sensitivity/vulnerability to economic factors.
- Ownership.
- Capitalization.
- Return on capital.

Such a list then needs to be evaluated and prioritized to determine the best bases for segmentation. Before proceeding to a more detailed analysis it is useful at this stage to consider, in broad terms, both the current emphasis being placed on these segmentation bases and to form some views of where segmentation emphasis should be re-directed. Figure 4.5 shows an example from a financial services firm and highlights initial views on the differences between the present and desired emphasis in segmentation.

Once a broad list of possible bases has been identified this is refined to develop a short list of segmentation bases for further consideration. As part of the process each segmentation base needs to be broken down into appropriate individual segments. In some cases this is straightforward and requires only relatively simple analysis of company records or patterns of demand: segmentation variables such as age, sex and geographic area fall into this category. Other segmentation variables based on psychographics may require considerable market research to identify both the nature of the segments and their demand characteristics.

One approach to choice of the best base(s) for segmentation involves listing the key segmentation bases and the various subdivisions into which segments can be broken down and developing a profile of each market segment to identify those areas which are worthy of more in-depth investigation. Figure 4.6 shows a simplified example based on an insurance broking company.

This step and the next one interact, as it is often only after examination of specific segment attractiveness that a decision can be made about choice of segmentation base.

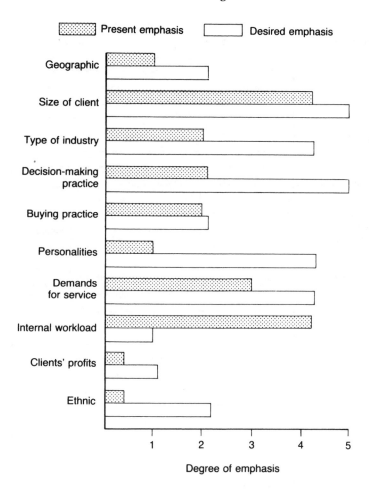

Figure 4.5 Market segmentation profile in a financial services firm

Identify and select target market segments

The identification and selection of a particular market segment for targeting with a distinctive service offering may depend on many factors, but the size of the segment, its special needs, the extent to which these needs are already being met by the service company or by competitors, and whether the service company has the resources available to meet the service requirements are particularly important.

There are various widely accepted criteria for determining if a market

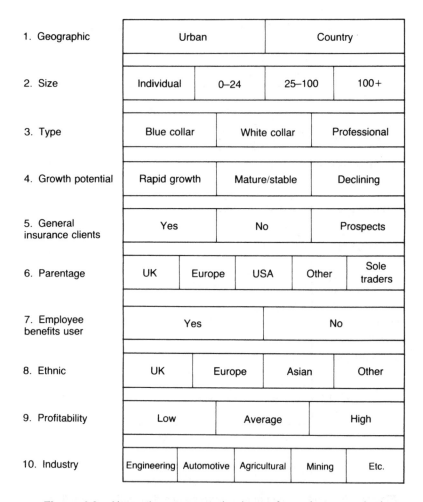

Figure 4.6 Alternative segmentation bases for an insurance broker

segment is viable. Firstly, the segment must be measurable in size and characteristics. For example, it can be difficult to use social class for segmentation purposes, as boundaries between classes are vague. Secondly, the segment must be meaningful, and capable of generating sufficient long-run profit to merit separate marketing attention. It must be reachable within budget confines. For example, it is not viable for a small regional law firm to target City-based financial institutions. Thirdly, the chosen segments must also be responsive to marketing effort. If the response of a segment to changes in marketing strategies is no different from that of other segments, there is no need to treat it separately. If, for example, all passengers on an airline had a similar service requirement, then it would not be necessary to offer first class, business class and economy travel.

One problem with segmentation is that a given person may be associated with different market segments at different points in time. Business executives may fly business class to a work commitment, whilst with their family they may select economy class. This mobility within segments could potentially cause problems for a service company seeking to serve more than one segment with the same personnel or equipment. For example, American Airlines noticed that its three-class service during summer months caused a fall off of business sales in later months. Business travellers who were taking their families on holiday were attracted to the low-priced, economy service. However, their experience affected their view of American Airlines business class service. American was forced to drop the three-tier service.

This illustration from American Airlines highlights the problem faced by service companies who may find it difficult to offer the same product to distinctly different segments. Manufacturers have an advantage, in that the same basic product can be sold to a variety of different customers with different packaging or distribution systems. However, a service is typically consumed at the point of delivery. A hotel offering quiet, sophisticated surroundings suited to the business traveller cannot accommodate noisy package tour groups during the week. However, business travellers mainly need facilities during the week, and the hotel may be underutilized over the weekend. This represents an opportunity to offer family weekend packages whilst retaining the business travellers during the week.

Choice of target market segments by service companies should be based on detailed review of existing and potential profitability of the segments. We will now consider the approach taken by two service organizations, a retail bank and a large accounting firm.

Some banks are now taking a rigorous approach to segmentation. Table 4.5 provides an example of a profitability analysis study of the retail financial services market in the USA based on lifestyle segmentation. The study examined in detail the number and percentage of household heads in each lifestyle category in terms of the following:[3]

- **Demographic profile,** including age of household head, occupation, education, home-ownership, number of full time wage earners in household, annual household income and net worth and average balances.

- **Service penetration:** by transaction accounts, regular savings accounts and time deposits. Details of credit services, credit cards used, trust-related services and electronic funds transfer services were included.

Table 4.5 Measurement of lifestyle segment profitability

	Total market	Bachelor stage	Young married stage	Young full nest stage	Older full nest stage	Older empty nest employed stage	Older empty nest retired stage
Number in sample	25 756	3818	2437	6994	4851	4835	2821
Average profit per household (US$)	598	287	309	323	690	906	1257
Average delivery costs required/used per household (US$)	187	158	202	187	213	190	164
Percentage of market represented by segment	100.0	14.8	9.5	27.1	18.8	18.8	11.0
Percentage of all profits in total market produced by segment	100.0	7.1	4.9	14.7	21.8	28.5	23.0
Percentage of all delivery costs required/used in total market required/used by segment	100.0	12.6	10.2	27.1	21.4	19.1	9.6
Ratio of profit produced by segment to weight of segment in total population	1.00	0.48	0.52	0.54	1.16	1.52	2.09
Dollars of profit produced by segment for each dollar of delivery costs required/used by segment	3.20	1.82	1.53	1.73	3.24	4.77	7.66

Source: 'Life cycle segmentation', *Compendium*, vol. 4, no. 3, 1983, p. 8.

- **Average dollar balances:** by transactions accounts, savings accounts, time deposits, instalment credit and revolving lines of credit.

The outcome of such a review, shown in Table 4.5, gives a measure of dollars profit produced after each dollar of delivery cost required to service that segment. In this example, the high potential profitability of the older empty nest segments is highlighted. However, not many service organizations go to this level of rigorous segmentation review.

Some professional service firms are now developing more focused approaches to segmentation. One large accounting firm followed an approach, outlined in Figure 4.7, based on industries. It began by identifying its current clients' industries and their usage of products and services over the past five years. Particular attention was paid to cross-selling patterns and the likely future growth in terms of use of its services. It then classified the clients into industry groups. With about a dozen classes at the top of the Standard Industrial Classification and hundreds at the lowest level it was clear that the firm would need to develop its own list by which to classify its clients. From a potentially

---

1. Identify existing clients by:
   - Industry
   - Use of products/services (volume and growth)
   - Pareto (80/20)

2. Use Standard Industrial Classification (SIC) code or similar to categorize existing clients

3. Sort clients by industry code and quantify level of industry activity

4. Profile:
   - Existing industry strength
   - Industry attractiveness
   - Develop industries priority list

5. Decide on target clients, e.g. by size, location, etc.

6. Set up industry teams:
   - Work with existing 'full service range' clients to improve expertise and range of services offered
   - Develop industry team and appropriate promotional material
   - Use expertise to cross-sell 'non-full service range' clients
   - Attack competitors' clients

7. Develop client retention programme (relationship management)

Figure 4.7 Summary of accounting firm segmentation strategy

long list some thirty segments or industry codes were decided on. Clients were then sorted by these industry codes and an overview made of these thirty segments to determine which companies were major players in them. A bank's economic department helped the firm to obtain necessary data so that they could quantify the existing level of industry activity for their firm and its major competitors.

The firm then profiled its existing industry strength as well as the relative attractiveness of the industry sector. An approach similar to the directional policy matrix (described in Chapter 7) was used for this purpose. From this analysis an industry priority list, consisting of about twelve industry segments, was prepared and specific target clients were then identified within each of the segments. Industry teams were then set up to identify and document 'best practices' being used with those existing clients to whom a full range of accounting and consulting services were being provided. For some industry groups research was undertaken to identify more clearly the services that clients in these groups wanted and this information was used to improve performance in serving them. This information was then fully documented. A series of industry teams were set up, promotional materials developed and training of staff in the teams was undertaken. The teams commenced with cross-selling of other services to existing clients and then developed an integrated long-term plan of attack on identified clients of their competitors. A client retention programme was also established.

Segmentation, positioning and marketing mix strategy

The segmentation process should result in one of four basic decisions being reached:

1. The service company may decide to target one segment of the market.
2. The service company may decide to target several segments and so will develop different marketing mix plans for each segment.
3. Management may decide not to segment the market but to offer the service to the mass market. This may be appropriate if the market is very small and a single portion would not be profitable. It also may be the case that the service company dominates the market so that targeting a few segments would not increase volume or profit.
4. Analysis may show that there is no viable market niche for the service offering.

Market segmentation will determine the basic segments of the market to be targeted with a particular service. The services offered to these segments then need to be positioned in the minds of the customers. The next chapter will consider this in detail. Positioning includes a consideration of competitors and this will help determine which segments should be focused on. For example, segments which may seem to be viable might be ignored if competitive products already dominated those segments in market share and in the minds of the customers: smaller banks such as the Cooperative Bank cannot compete with the major high street banks for users requiring convenient locations and frequent face-to-face banking transactions. They have focused on segments who rely more on credit cards and cash dispenser facilities, and use direct mail to build relationships with customers who do not see the need for face-to-face high street banking facilities.

Each individual market or segment may require a specific marketing mix to be designed for it. One approach that helps determination of the marketing mix is outlined in Figure 4.8, which shows an example of segmentation of the market for package holidays. This approach involves a number of steps including identification of:

- Priority market segments (four in this case).
- Characteristics and common buying factors (by market segment).
- Key success factors (for market as a whole).
- Relative importance of key success factor (in each segment).
- Market size and market share held in each segment (not shown in this example).

Understanding the relative priorities in each market segment in terms of the key success factors assists considerably in coming to a judgement about the appropriate marketing mix to be developed.

The design of the marketing mix will in part be developed as the selection of the target markets proceeds. For example, if a segment is price sensitive, then price levels will already have been considered within the decision to target the segment. A distinct strategy for all of the elements of the marketing mix will need to be developed for each segment. This is discussed in some detail in Chapter 6.

The relevance of market segmentation is now being increasingly recognized in the services sector. A number of studies have pointed to the importance of market segmentation. One study ranked 'problems in recognising, defining, understanding and segmenting markets' as the most important problem facing the senior executives surveyed. Another survey ranked segmentation as the third most important

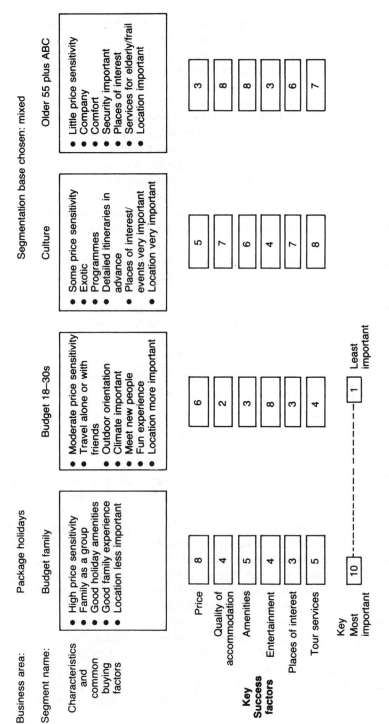

Figure 4.8 Importance of key success factors by market segment

marketing tool out of eighteen surveyed. However, despite the recognition of the importance of market segmentation, and the developments that have been made in market segmentation methodology, some service firms are still basing their marketing strategies and tactics on either a broad approach to the market, or a relatively unsophisticated approach to segmentation. Many service firms need to be more disciplined in their focus on their marketplace.

Segmentation is at the heart of marketing strategy and is concerned with the development of a market position that minimizes competitors' strengths whilst maximizing those of your own company. Segmentation and the associated steps of positioning provide the opportunity to tailor your service offer to better meet the needs of specific segments.

Notes

1. P. Gilmour, 'Customer segmentation: differentiating by market segment', *International Journal of Physical Distribution*, vol. 7, no. 3, 1977, pp. 141–48.
2. For a detailed discussion of other approaches see A. Weinstein, *Marketing Segmentation*, Probus Publishing Company, Chicago, 1987; and J.F. Engel, H.F. Fiorillo and M.A. Cayley, (eds.), *Marketing Segmentation: Concepts and applications*, Holt, Rinehart and Winston, New York, 1972.
3. 'Life cycle segmentation', *Compendium*, vol. 4, no. 3,1983, pp. 3–15.

5

Positioning and differentiation of services

The evolution of positioning

During the 1980s the strategic relevance of positioning started to become recognized amongst leading service organizations. Service companies are now identifying their key market segments and then determining how they wish consumers to perceive both their company and its products and services. Positioning is of particular significance in the services sector as it places an intangible service within a more tangible frame of reference. Thus the concept of positioning stems from a consideration of how a company wishes its target customer to view its products and services in relationship to those of its competitors and their actual, or perceived, needs.

The idea of positioning can be traced to the idea of identifying needs and then fulfilling them. This idea, which has existed in writings on marketing since at least the 1940s, was developed further with the concept of identifying improved ways of creating product appeal and the 'unique selling proposition'. Other writers have referred to related ideas including product differentiation, distinctive business proposition and market position analysis.

The concept of positioning also has origins in the increased recognition of the importance of corporate image in the 1960s. To many, David Ogilvy of advertising agency Ogilvy and Mather epitomized the 'image era'. His belief that every advertisement is a long-term investment in the image of a brand and his famous and highly successful campaigns for a wide range of manufactured products including Hathaway shirts, Schweppes soft drinks and Rolls Royce motor cars drew attention to the value of brand image.

The notion of a unique selling proposition which identified a unique product feature that was then emphasized to customers in the promotional campaign worked well where it *was* unique. Unfortunately technological advances often made so-called unique features short lived since they could be easily copied. In response to competitive imitation, advertising agencies such as Ogilvy and Mather developed image advertising as a means of differentiation. However, the enormous increase in advertising in the 1960s led to considerable duplication of messages and as a result it became increasingly difficult for a company to distinguish its image from that of others.

In the first book to be published on positioning Ries and Trout describe how marketing thought evolved from the product era of the 1950s to the image era of the 1960s and the positioning era of the 1970s.[1] They are credited with having developed the idea of positioning through a series of articles they wrote in 1972. Ries and Trout argue that we live in an 'over-communicated' society where huge sums are spent on advertising but only a tiny fraction of it gains our attention. Their concept of positioning is that it is '. . . not what you do to a product. Positioning is what you do to the mind of the prospect. That is, you position the product in the mind of the prospect.'

Much of the discussion about positioning in companies, advertising agencies and in journal articles uses 'positioning' in this restricted sense. This perspective of positioning suggests that positioning is largely a communications issue dealing with the psychology of positioning an existing product in the consumer's mind. It focuses on achieving a desirable position in the mind of the consumer and has little to do with the product. It sees changes in name, pricing or packaging as cosmetic changes aimed at securing this position in the consumer's mind.

We term this form of positioning 'communications positioning'; it is an important part, but only a part, of strategic positioning. Positioning can, however, be affected by all the elements of the services marketing mix, in addition to promotion. Thus price, distribution, people, processes, customer service and the product or service itself can all affect a firm's positioning. Service processes can be particularly relevant to positioning. As Lynn Shostack has pointed out, **processes** have characteristics which affect positioning and which can also be deliberately and strategically managed for positioning purposes.[2] The strategic positioning of services, then, involves a consideration of these other elements of the marketing mix. We define positioning as follows:

> Positioning is concerned with the identification, development and communication of a differentiated advantage which makes the organization's products and services perceived as superior and distinctive to those of its competitors in the mind of its target customers.

Positioning is thus concerned with differentiation and using it to advantageously fit the organization and its products or services, to a market segment. We can differentiate on the basis of subjective criteria which involve image and communication, or objective criteria which involve differentiation in terms of other elements of the marketing mix including product, processes, people, customer service, etc.

In this chapter we begin with a consideration of the means of competitive differentiation. The specific characteristics of services and how they impact on positioning are then examined. We then provide an overview of the process of positioning including the development of positioning maps. Alternative strategies in positioning are then considered.

Competitive differentiation of services

Positioning is heavily dependent on a firm's capability to effectively differentiate itself from its competitors by providing superior delivered value to its customers. Superior delivered value can be thought of in terms of the total value offered to a customer less the total cost to the customer. It has been suggested that these elements have the following components:[3]

- Total customer value:
  services value;
  product value;
  people value; and
  image value.

- Total customer cost:
  monetary price;
  time cost;
  energy cost; and
  psychic costs.

Customers make buying decisions on services based on superior delivered value in terms of an acceptable balance between cost, value and quality. Customers who are purchasing services buy what they need based on cost components, value-added components and quality components. Some illustrations are shown in Table 5.1.[4]

One technique for considering superior delivered value is the value chain. The value chain represents a means of identifying ways to create differentiation through value enhancement. The value chain developed by Michael Porter is shown in Figure 5.1. Value chain activities are

Table 5.1 Some cost, value-added and quality components for selected services

Service	Cost components	Value-added components	Quality components
Bank	Service charges; interest rates	Variety of services; easy to understand services	Financial stability; personal interest in customers
Discount store	Sales/clearances; low price	Easy return; cheque cashing	Selection; well-known brands; pleasant atmosphere
Family steak house	Low prices; coupons	Salad bar; menu for children	Taste of steak; atmosphere
Pizza restaurant	Specials; coupons; promotions; low prices	Fast service; home delivery take out; variety	Hot product; taste; consistent product
Psychiatric hospital	Low-cost treatment	Comfortable rooms; visitor accommodations	Experienced physicians; innovative treatment
Speciality tuneup clinics	Reasonable cost; specials	Car ready when promised fast service	Fixed right the first time; qualified mechanics
Supermarket	Low prices	Well stocked; cheque cashing	Clean; selection; speciality departments
Temporary secretarial service	Reasonable cost	Performance guarantee; follow up	Competence of temps; understands what we need

categorized into two types: primary activities (in-bound logistics, operations, out-bound logistics, marketing and sales, and service) and support activities (infrastructure, human-resource management, technology development, and procurement).[5] These support activities are integrating functions that cut across the various primary activities within the firm. It may also be useful to further subdivide specific primary activities within the value chain. For example, the marketing and sales activity can be expanded further into the constituent activities of marketing management, which include advertising, sales force administration, sales force operations, promotion, etc.

The generic value chain outlined in Figure 5.1 was derived largely from a consideration of manufacturing companies. Although it has broad applicability to services it is more useful to develop value chains which specifically reflect the tasks within a particular service sector. For example, in the management consulting sector the primary activities comprise the following:

- Decisions on service configuration.

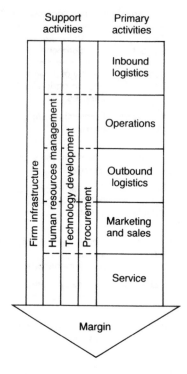

Figure 5.1 Generic value chain

- Marketing and sales.
- Data collection.
- Data analysis.
- Interpretation and recommendations.
- Reporting and communication.
- Interpretation, service and evaluation.

A consulting firm's value chain is shown in Figure 5.2.

For a retail financial service organization, such as a building society, the primary activities in the value chain include:

- Funding.
- Product innovation and design.
- Funds management.
- Customer administration.
- Marketing.

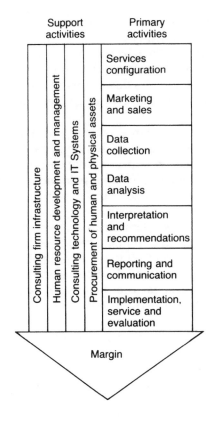

Figure 5.2   Management consulting firm's value chain

- Delivery channels.
- Servicing.

A bank operating in the corporate market defined its value chain's primary activities as:

- Product creation.
- Planning.
- Marketing.
- Selling.
- Single target selling.
- After sales service.

Superior delivered value grows out of the way in which firms organize and perform these discrete activities within the value chain.

Development of a specific value chain which identifies these activities for a specific service company is of much greater use than relying on the generic value chain. To gain advantage over its rivals a firm must promote this value to its customers through performing activities more efficiently than its competitors (lower cost advantage) or by performing activities in a unique way that creates greater buyer value (differentiation advantage).

The process activities within a value chain should not be considered in isolation. It is essential to consider the linkages where the performance of one activity has an impact on the cost or effectiveness of other activities. In a manufacturing company, improved product design may reduce the need for inspection and result in significantly reduced after-sales service costs. However, in a service firm boundaries between activities are often less clear. In services, activities such as marketing, operations and human resources cannot really be considered independently, and effective co-ordination and integration of them becomes more essential than with manufactured goods. Appropriate cross-functional coordination of linked activities can reduce the time needed to perform them. Reconfiguration of the value chain by relocating, reordering, regrouping or even carefully eliminating activities may represent an opportunity for major improvement in delivered value.

A critical role in a service organization is the examination of costs and performance in each value-creating activity within the value chain. Each element of the value chain represents an area which should be investigated thoroughly to identify existing or potential means by which the firm can achieve cost advantage or differentiation advantage. The objective of this examination is to identify improvement opportunities. To ensure differentiation is achieved, benchmarking of competitors' value chains and their performance is essential. The benchmarking process is described in Chapter 8.

The value chain concept may be used in several ways by a service firm as follows:

1. The firm can use it to gain a clear understanding of its own value chain and where it seeks to gain sources of differentiation or cost advantage to achieve superior delivered value to its customers.

2. It can use it to understand where it fits in the value chain of its customer. If the customer is a typical manufacturing company its value chain will be similar to that of the generic value chain described above. However, if the customer is a service business the firm will benefit from considering how the value chain for this services company differs from the generic value chain. For individual customers (as opposed to companies), a personal value chain could also be considered; however, relatively little attention

is given in the literature to an individual's value chains and more emphasis is usually placed on needs analysis.

3. It can be used to understand where it fits in the value chain of its suppliers and distributors.

4. To identify how competitors create value and how their activities compare to yours (competitive benchmarking).

The ultimate purpose of value chain analysis is to systematically identify appropriate means of differentiation for a firm so that it can provide superior delivered value to its customers. This differentiation then needs to be communicated to its customers through positioning.

Positioning and services

Positioning offers the opportunity to differentiate any service. Each service company and its goods and services has a position or image in the consumer's mind and this influences purchase decisions. Positions can be implicit and unplanned and evolve over a period of time or can be planned as part of the marketing strategy and then communicated to the target market. The purpose of planned positioning is to create a differentiation in the customer's mind which distinguishes the company's services from other competitive services. It is important to establish a position of value for the product or service in the minds of the target market, i.e. it must be distinguishable by an attribute, or attributes, which are important to the customer. These attributes should be factors which are critical in the customer's purchase decision.

There is therefore no such thing as a commodity or 'standard' service. Every service offered has the potential to be perceived as different by a customer. Buyers have different needs and are therefore attracted to different offers. It is therefore important to select distinguishing characteristics which satisfy the following criteria:[6]

- **Importance** – the difference is highly valued to a sufficiently large market.

- **Distinctiveness** – the difference is distinctly superior to other offerings which are available.

- **Communicability** – it is possible to communicate the difference in a simple and strong way.

- **Superiority** – the difference is not easily copied by competitors.

- **Affordability** – the target customers will be able and willing to pay for the difference. Any additional cost of the distinguishing characteristic(s) will be perceived as sufficiently valuable to compensate for any additional cost.

- **Profitability** – the company will achieve additional profits as a result of introducing the difference.

Each product or service has a set of attributes which can be compared to competitive offerings. Some of these attributes will be real, others will be perceived as real. A company wishing to position itself should determine how many attributes and differences to promote to target customers. Some marketers advocate promoting one benefit and establishing recognition as being the leader for that particular attribute. Others suggest that promoting more than one benefit will help in carving out a special niche which is less easily contested by competitors. The selection of the differentiating attribute(s) is most successful if it confirms facts which are already in the mind of the target market. Denying or fighting customers' perceptions of different offerings in the market is unlikely to be successful. A successful positioning strategy takes into account customers' existing perceptions of market offerings. It determines needs which customers value and which are not being met by competitors' services. It identifies which unsatisfied needs could be satisfied. The positioning strategy seeks to integrate all elements of the service, to ensure that the perceived position of the service is strongly reinforced.

Services have a number of distinguishing characteristics which have special implications for the positioning and selection of which attributes to emphasize. Three of the key characteristics of services, discussed in Chapter 1, make positioning strategies of particular importance in marketing a service. These are the intangibility, the degree of variability or heterogeneity in quality of a given service, and inseparability – the fact that the performance of a service will often occur in the presence of a customer. Easingwood and Mahajan have illustrated a range of positions that can be adopted based on these services characteristics (see Table 5.2), some of which are outlined below.[7]

The intangibility of services makes the marketing task for a service different from that for a product which can be physically identified touched and compared. A service often cannot be marketed by features which the consumer can readily identify and compare, it may therefore be hard to evaluate. For example, with financial or legal advice choosing between alternative sources is difficult when the benefits are intangible (e.g. the quality of advice). It is thus not easy to compare the physical attributes of competing services.

Positioning can permit an intangible service benefit to be represented tangibly. It can help the customer see an intangible benefit, by offering tangible evidence. For example, customers to a hotel expect an

Table 5.2 Some alternative positionings based on service characteristics

Response to special service characteristics	Basis of position
Intangibility • Offer a tangible representation	The reputation and special capabilities of the organization itself • Expertise position • Reliability position • Innovativeness position • Performance position
• Offer an augmented service	Augmentation of product offering • Product augmentation • Extra service
Heterogeneity • Superior selection, training and monitoring of contact personnel	People advantage
• Package the service • Industrialize the service production process	More attractive packaged offering A superior product through technology (i.e. faster, more reliable, better value for money)
Inseparability • Use multi-site locations • Customize the service • Offer a complete product line	Accessibility Extra attention given to individual requirements Satisfaction of more user needs within the sector

Source: C. J. Easingwood, and V. Mahajan, 'Positioning of financial services for competitive advantage', *Journal of Product Innovation Management*, vol. 6, 1989, p. 210.

intangible benefit – cleanliness; and this view can be reinforced by plastic covered glasses in rooms and a paper cover over the lid of a lavatory stating 'sanitized for your protection'. This helps the customer to associate cleanliness with the service offering, reinforcing the position that the hotel wishes to portray. Service companies often promote their reputations in an attempt to add tangibility. For example, they promote their reputation for expertise with a particular sector; Coutts Bank positions itself as a bank for the wealthy upper class.

Developing a positioning strategy may also assist identification of other tangible features which can be added to the service. The augmented service offer (see Chapter 6) will be more easily distinguished from other service offerings. For example, a positioning strategy for an insurance product which aims to be distinctive by its ease of take up for the customer, may include a step-by-step guide for prospective policy holders with sample forms which can be easily copied.

Services are also highly variable and rely to a great extent on input from company employees for their production. For example, in a restaurant the waiter is the main point of contact with the customer and his service performance will be a major factor in the way the establishment will be judged. His performance will vary at different times, and there will also be variance between his service and that of another waiter or waitress in the restaurant. As a result, the quality of the delivered service can vary widely.

Further, the quality of a small element of the total service offering may affect the perceived quality of the service as a whole. For instance, a poor check-out procedure from a hotel, may greatly affect the perceived quality of the overall experience of staying in it. The customer's perception of the quality of the service is therefore greatly affected by the quality of the staff who are responsible for delivery. An advantage can be gained by providing better trained and more highly responsive people. A positioning strategy may therefore include the distinctive characteristic of employing 'better people'. McDonalds recognized this advantage and established McDonald's Hamburger University where employees are trained to render a high quality standardized service and to limit the amount of variation in customer experience, giving a service which matches the customer's perception.

Services tend to be inseparable and are characterized by the fact that they are performed in the presence of the customer. A manufactured product is usually produced within a controlled environment, and there is an opportunity to control the quality and ensure compliance with customer expectations. Manufacturers are able to reject products which do not meet consistency and quality standards. However, a service frequently does not have these opportunities. Often a service will require customer presence both when the service is initially being delivered and then on an on-going basis. A service may require the customer to be present during most of the delivery process, as in the case of a patron in a restaurant or a passenger on an airline or train.

The distinctive features of the services outlined above provides the basis for competitive positioning strategy. There are may dimensions on which services can be differentiated. In Figure 1.3 in Chapter 1 we examined five alternative models for classifying services. Each of these represent an opportunity for creating differentiation of a services in some way. For example, there is the opportunity of customizing the service to meet the exact needs of the customer. This may have a danger, in that the modification process is often largely left to the front-line service provider. However, if customer needs can be closely matched, customer satisfaction will be greater. SAS recognized this in empowering their employees and allowing them to make their own decisions during service delivery. They positioned themselves as an airline that cares for its passengers and is responsive to their needs.

There are many examples of passengers who have been pleasantly surprised by the decision-making ability and empowerment of SAS staff, in contrast to the red tape of other airlines. Staff can decide, without reference to superiors, on upgrading passengers, resolving baggaging problems and special travel problems.

Having outlined opportunities to use the distinctive characteristic of services to position the offerings of a company, we will now turn our attention to the levels of positioning and how the positioning process can be formally addressed.

The levels of positioning

We are primarily concerned in this chapter with the positioning of goods and services delivered by service organizations. We will use the term 'positioning' or 'product positioning' to reflect this emphasis. Whilst most of the emphasis is placed on positioning from this perspective it should be recognized that the principles of positioning apply at other levels.

We can consider positioning at several levels:

- **Industry positioning** – the positioning of the service industry as a whole.

- **Organizational positioning** – the positioning of the organization as a whole.

- **Product sector positioning** – the positioning of a range or family of related products and services being offered by the organization.

- **Individual product or service positioning** – the positioning of specific products.

In addressing their company's position, service organizations may wish to consider where their **industry** is positioned. A frequent means of positioning used within public relations agencies is to identify the relative favourability and familiarity of different organizations. This can also be applied to industries. Figure 5.3 provides details of selected service industries based on research by MORI. This provides useful context for the consideration of the organizational and product positioning.

At the corporate level a credibility/visibility or favourability/familiarity framework such as that shown in Figure 5.3 can also be used for a company and its competitors. Regular monitoring can identify shifts in both the company and its competitors' positions.

Companies need not be concerned with all the levels listed above.

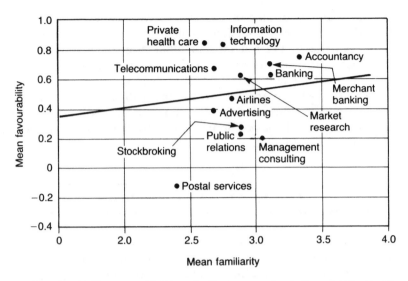

Source: Based on H. Thompson, 'Problems for the image makers', *Financial Weekly*, 20 August 1987, p. 17.

Figure 5.3   Positions of selected service industries

For some organizations, such as a car rental company or a restaurant, the positioning decision for the organization and the services provided may be very similar. However, for larger multi-business service organizations such as banks, all these levels may need to be considered.

Figure 5.4 illustrates the three levels we can address in the positioning of a bank. Positioning can be considered at the level of organizational positioning of the bank as a whole, product sector positioning (for example the family of lending or investment products), and the positioning of individual products and services within that sector. Two observations are worth making here. Firstly, that decisions relating to positioning of the organization and individual products should be clearly related and have some logic between them. Secondly, that brands can be created at either the product sector level or at the individual product level.

When we consider positioning of the product level we are usually concerned with the specific positioning for a target market segment. When we are concerned with positioning at the corporate level this usually, but not always, involves a consideration of segmentation.

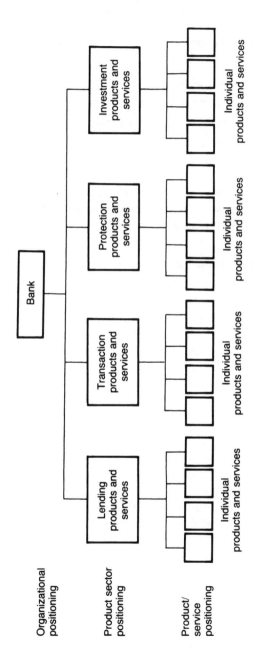

Figure 5.4 Levels of positioning for a bank

The process of positioning

Product positioning involves a number of steps including the following:

- Determining levels of positioning.
- Identification of key attributes of importance to selected segments.
- Location of attributes on a positioning map.
- Evaluating positioning options.
- Implementing positioning.

As explained in the previous chapter the process of product positioning has close linkages with market segmentation and developing a marketing mix. Each step is now examined.

Determine levels of positioning

We have already described how positioning can be directed at the product or service level, at 'product sector' levels, or at the corporate level. The first step in positioning is to determine which level(s) are to receive explicit positioning attention. Some examples will illustrate the choices that are made by some service organizations. The level or levels of positioning to be undertaken are usually fairly clear cut, although some organizations have placed different emphasis on these levels at different points in time. For example, some British clearing banks are currently reemphasizing corporate positioning, rather than product positioning.The Forte Group has recently decided to reposition Forte Crest, one of its hotel groups, as 'the definitive hotel for business'. About the same time they repositioned Forte Post-houses with a new lower room rate for the mid-market. Thus positioning for Forte is focusing on the product sector.

American Express introduced its platinum card in the USA in 1984 at a product level. It was positioned to appeal to very high net worth individuals. This was a controversial move when it was introduced. Industry experts queried the positioning of a new card that cost US$250 for the privilege of carrying around a new colour of plastic. The 100 000 people signing up showed this was a viable position.Separate positioning is undertaken for the green card, gold card, and optima products within the cards product sector of American Express.

Companies such as Club Med effectively position their organization as a whole on the basis of 'the Club Med experience'. Although they offer a 'product range' in their winter and summer brochures, emphasis is very much on an organizational positioning basis.

Identification of attributes

Once the level of positioning has been determined it is necessary to identify the specific attributes that are important to the chosen market segments. In particular, the way in which purchasing decisions are made should be considered. Individuals use different criteria for making a purchase decision of a service. The purpose for using the service may change the set of criteria, e.g. business insurance or personal insurance. The timing of the use of the service will also affect the choice of service (e.g. the choice of a restaurant will be different for an individual if it is for a weekday lunch or a Saturday night dinner).

A consideration of the decision-making unit is also relevant. For example, the decision may also be affected by whether a group or an individual will use the service, e.g. the amenities of a hotel may be more important for a family than for an individual. A hospital may be selected by either a patient or a doctor, with a different ranking of attributes being used in the selection process.

Customers make choices between alternative services based on perceived differences between them. These may not be the most important attributes of the service. An example of this is the fact that passengers using airlines rank 'safety' as the most important feature. But many airlines have similar standards of safety, so passengers' choice of airline will actually be based on other characteristics such as comfort, convenience of flight times and standards of food and beverage. Thus research needs to identify the salient attributes which determine the selection of a service. This will form the basis of the positioning.

First, research needs to be undertaken to identify the salient attributes and specific benefits required by the target market segment. A number of approaches can be used to identify salient attributes which can then be used to develop a positioning map. What is important here is the customer's perception of the benefits that are delivered by these relevant attributes. An express parcel service scoring high on the speed dimension is one that is perceived as fast. The reality is that other service providers in the express parcel industry may provide a faster service but may be perceived as being slower.

A range of analytical research techniques, most of them computer based, can be used to identify the salient attributes. These include perceptual mapping, factor analysis, discriminant function analysis, multiple correlation and regression analysis, and trade off and conjoint analysis. These tools are in the province of the market researcher, rather than the marketing manager, so will not be discussed further here. However, the reader interested in a technical discussion can refer to articles by Keon[8] and Wind[9] which discuss their relative merits.

Location of attributes on positioning map

The positioning process involves the identification of the most important attributes and location of various companies' services, for these attributes, on a positioning map. Where a range of attributes are identified, statistical procedures exist for combining these attributes into aggregate dimensions. Such dimensions are referred to by various names such as principal components, multi-dimensional scales, factors, etc., depending upon how the data were elicited and which statistical procedures were used. Usually two dimensions are used on positioning maps and these often account for a large proportion of the 'explanation' of the customer's preferences. For example, in a political marketing study, the analysis showed that two factors accounted for 86 per cent of the discrimination amongst 14 political figures.

Products or services are typically plotted on a two dimensional positioning map such as shown in the Figure 5.5. The positioning map can be used to identify the position of competitors' services in relation to the selected attributes. The analysis can be further developed by drawing separate positioning maps for each market segment. Customers in each market segment may perceive the service and its benefits differently, and different maps will show these different positions.

With some positioning techniques respondents are requested to evaluate the relative similarity of different competitors' services. The respondents are not told on which attributes to assess the similarity. Techniques such as multi-dimensional scaling can then be used to produce a positioning map that reflects the perceived extent of psychological distance between them. This technique does not explicitly identify the axes used and these need to be inferred, or derived from further research. Often a second group of respondents is used, to avoid possible bias, in determining what characteristics they use to evaluate the services offered. The positioning map can be used to identify potential gaps in the market including where there is a demand but little competition (if such a position exists). It should be noted that the existence of a vacant space in a positioning map does not necessarily infer a viable positioning.

Positioning maps can be based on either objective attributes or subjective attributes. The positioning map used in a study of UK national newspapers used objective variables of average age and average social class. Maps can also use a combination of objective and subjective attributes. A positioning study for a bank used a positioning map which positioned three banks on an objective dimension of 'best interest rates on loans' and a subjective attribute 'friendly/courteous service'.

In addition to identifying where different companies' products are positioned on the map we are also concerned with where are the areas

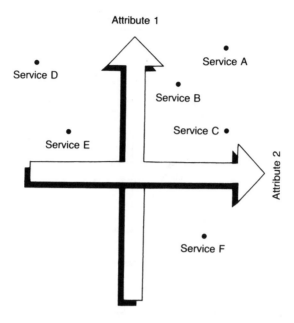

Figure 5.5 Illustrative positioning map

of core demand. In some cases there is a clear area of core demand such as shown in Figure 5.6. This figure, based on an example from Cambell Pretty Associates, shows positions of various occupations in the workforce based on two key attributes: level of esteem associated with the occupation, and level of interest associated with the occupation. In this example the area of core demand is clear – jobs which are relatively interesting and which have relatively high levels of esteem associated with them. The research showed that the client, the Australian Army Reserve, was positioned as an occupation of fairly high interest, but low esteem. The positioning task, then, was to create a communications and advertising campaign to reposition it in the area of core demand.

In other cases areas of core demand may not be so obvious, particularly where there are different groups with different preferences. Figure 5.7 shows a positioning study undertaken prior to the 1966 US presidential election and referred to above. A technique known as cluster analysis was used to identify groups with similar interests. The analysis identified eight clusters (or market segments) plus a student group. In this example political candidates, Humphrey, Kennedy and Johnson could have increased their acceptability to these segments by repositioning themselves by shifting perceptions of themselves upwards and to the right, modifying their position. Note

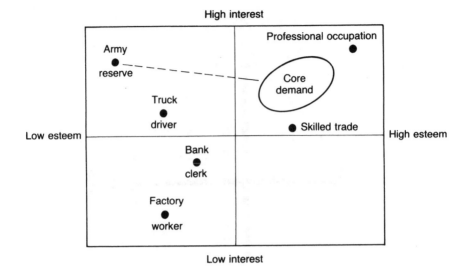

Source: Campbell Pretty Associates.

Figure 5.6 Positioning map of the occupations in the workforce

that in this case 'the product', i.e. the politician, is probably unchanged but the perception of 'the product' could be significantly altered by these politicians endorsing issues associated with 'conservatism' and 'reduced government involvement'.

Evaluating positioning options

Ries and Trout have suggested three broad positioning options:

- **Strengthening current position against competitors.** This often involves avoiding head-on attack. For example, Avis created a classic positioning with its campaign 'Avis is only No 2 in rent-a-cars, so why go with us? We try harder!' By acknowledging that Hertz was the largest company in the car rental business Avis presented a believable positioning proposition (we try harder), and also capitalized on people's natural sympathies for the underdog. Thus they used their number two position as an asset.

- **Identifying an unoccupied market position.** This strategy consists of identifying a gap in the market that was not filled by a competitor. United Jersey Bank, a small bank in New Jersey, positioned itself as 'the fast moving bank'. In competing against giant banks like Citibank and Chase Manhattan it attacked their

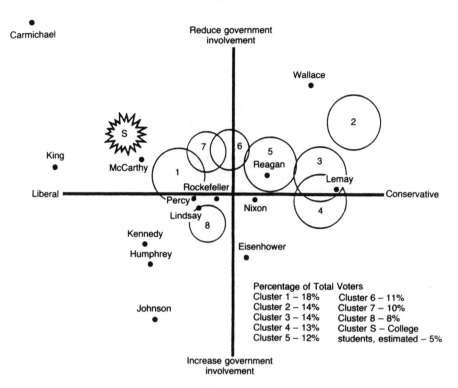

Source: R. M. Johnson, 'Market segmentation: A strategic management tool', *Journal of Marketing Research*, vol. 8, February 1971, pp. 13–18.

Figure 5.7 Positioning of US political figures and voters' preference clusters

weak point of being slower (or at least perceived to be slower) in arranging loans and dealing with their customers.

- **Repositioning the competition.** The Long Island Trust Company was a small bank operating in Long Island – a commuter area for New York City. The bank faced increased competition from large New York City banks such as Citibank, Chemical Bank and Chase, who had become firmly entrenched in Long Island following a new law which permitted unrestricted branch banking throughout New York State. Market research on six attributes showed that Long Island Trust was last on a list of six banks in terms of perception of number of branches, full range of services, quality of service and large capital base. By repositioning Long Island as the 'Long Island Bank for Long Island residents' the bank improved its ranking on all attributes. Following the campaign Long Island Trust was ranked first on the number of branches and large capital base, and fourth on full range of services and quality of service. This represented a significantly improved positioning for the bank.

Once a company had identified where it is positioned at present, it then needs to determine how to enhance or sustain its position relative to its competitors. Thomas Kosnik provides the following examples of these key characteristics of successful positioning:[10]

- **The positioning should be meaningful.** Apple Computers' image of a young, free spirited Silicon Valley company out to change the world worked well in the home and education markets, but has no relevance in the conservative corporate market. More recently Apple has focused marketing communication on the theme of problem solving for its customers.
- **The positioning must be believable.** Many companies claim to be all things to all people. For example, most of the Big Eight (now the Big Six) accounting firms claim to be able to undertake any management consulting project. Can they do an exceptional job on strategy consulting – compared to specialists like McKinsey & Company, Bain & BCG – and human resources – compared to specialists like Hay Associates? Interestingly the largest and most successful accounting firm to enter consulting has been Arthur Andersen, which for many years has focused mainly on one specific area – information systems.
- **The positioning must be unique.** Many companies in the computer industry claim they are unique by their leadership in technology. This is seldom the case for any one of the computer companies. Companies need to find a positioning where they can consistently outpace the competitors in serving a given market.

A wide range of approaches to differentiation are possible, twelve of which are shown in Table 5.3. Kosnik suggests that the following questions are relevant for considering which of these positioning alternatives is appropriate (they apply at either the corporate or the business level):

- Which one of these positions most differentiates our company or business unit?
- Which position is held by each of our major competitors?
- Which positions are of most value to each of our target market segments?
- Which positions are cluttered with lots of competitors claiming to hold the title?

Table 5.3 Alternative corporate positioning strategies

• Market share leader	The biggest
• Quality leader	The best/most reliable products and services
• Service leader	The most responsive when customers have problems
• Technology leader	The first to develop new technology
• Innovation leader	The most creative in applying it
• Flexibility leader	The most adaptable
• Relationship leader	The most committed to the customer's success
• Prestige leader	The most exclusive
• Knowledge leader	The best functional, industry or technical expertise
• Global leader	The best positioned to service world markets
• Bargain leader	The lowest price
• Value leader	The best price performance

Source: Based on T. J. Kosnik, '*Corporate Positioning*', Harvard Business School, Note 9-589-087, 1989, p. 13.

- Which are relatively free of competition?
- Which corporate or business unit positions provide the best fit with our company's product and product line positioning strategies?

Review alternative perspectives of positioning

The preceding discussion has focused on positioning of services from the perspective of how the customer perceives the company. A range of other perspectives on positioning should be taken into account including the following:

- The company's perception of itself.
- The company's perception of competitors.
- Competitors' perception of the company.
- Competitors' perception of themselves.
- The customers' perception of competitors.
- Competitors' perception of customers.
- The customers' perception of themselves.
- The company's perception of its customers.
- The customers' perception of the company.

A company's position is influenced by a group of competing companies and their customers. The network of perceptions between the company, its competitors and its customers is shown in Figure 5.8. These networks of perception can profoundly influence how companies develop their marketing strategies.

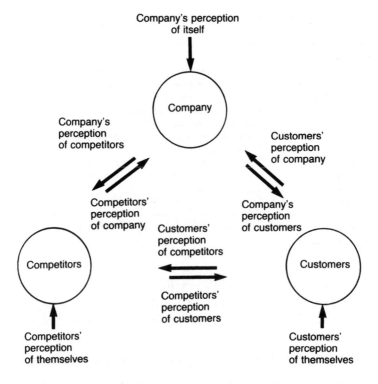

Figure 5.8 Networks of perceptions

It should be noted that companies often do not see themselves as their customers or competitors see them. Table 5.4 provides an illustration of the Big Eight chartered accounting firms in the late 1970s from the perspective of both how they see themselves, and how their competitors see them. Companies' positioning changes over time, and the positions of the chartered accounting firms have changed following a number of recent mergers.

Positioning at the corporate level is concerned with managing and communicating a differentiated position to enhance the visibility and credibility of the company. Companies must continually engage in a dialogue with their customers to support and enhance their position in the market.

Implementing positioning and the marketing mix

How a company and service is positioned needs to be communicated throughout all of its implicit and explicit interactions with customers. This suggests that all elements of the company, its staff, policies and image, need to reflect a similar image which together conveys the

Table 5.4 Competition and self-perception of the Big Eight accounting firms

Firm	How they see themselves	How competitors see them
Peat, Marwick, Mitchell & Co.	Aggressive but not in an unprofessional way. We have the best people. Biggest weakness: too decentralized	Trying to recover from past problems with SEC. Very aggressive. Price cutter. Expanding scope of practice
Coopers & Lybrand	Tough. We work harder. We've got a winner's kind of feeling. Our real strength is in the management team	Has changed a lot. Most aggressive of the eight in hustling business. Price cutter
Price Waterhouse & Co.	The premier accounting firm. We are to accounting what sterling is to silver. Our clients are the cream	Not very aggressive. Stuffy. Arrogant. Getting steamed up after losing some clients
Arthur Andersen & Co.	Tough. Aggressive. We speak with one voice everywhere. Not well known outside the US	Aggressive. Likes publicity. First firm to emphasize growth. No room for individual thought
Deloitte Haskins & Sells	Not as aggressive as most of the Big Eight. Technical leader in the profession. The auditor's auditor	Not very aggressive. Narrow in scope of services. Getting their act together. Strong auditors
Arthur Young & Co.	Tend to be less aggressive than others. Heavy emphasis on client service. We do not want to be the biggest	Not as aggressive as other Big Eight firms. Widely respected. Super-professional
Ernst & Ernst	A practical firm. Pragmatic. We put strong emphasis on quality service to our existing clients	Sleepy. Not growing fast except in certain industries. Not on the competitive edge. Loosest organization overseas
Touche Ross & Co.	We want to be the best. We're not as big as we want to be. We're not price cutters, but we are price competitors	Very aggressive in hustling business. Enamoured of size. Price cutter. Weak overseas

Source: Peter W. Bernstein, 'Competition comes to accounting', *Fortune*, 17 July 1978, p. 92.

desired position to the marketplace. This means that a company must establish a strategic positioning direction, which is followed through in all of its tactical marketing and sales activities.

This is not always the case, and there is often a conflict between a desired position and that which is actually being conveyed. For example, before the Lord King and Sir Colin Marshall era, British Airways promoted itself as a caring airline. However, customers' experience did not match this position. The company had to discontinue its advertising message 'we care for you', and make major changes within the company. This included a major refocus on how the passenger was perceived by employees. Staff had to actually care about the customer. To support this, the airline itself had to demonstrate a caring attitude to its employees. The successful repositioning of British Airways and its campaign Putting the Customer First was dependent on a coordinated and integrated internal and external marketing strategy.

A significant failure of a positioning strategy occurs when target customer segments do not recall a service offering and the service does not stand out from those of its competitors. A successful positioning strategy should make the service clearly distinguishable by features which are desirable and important to the target customer segment. This means that the positioning strategy should be examined from time to time to ensure that it does not become outdated and that it is still relevant to the target market segment.

The marketing mix is the key to implementing a positioning strategy. The design of the marketing mix to implement the positioning must be based on the key salient attributes relevant to the target segment. These attributes should be identified in the context of analysis of competitors, whose positions should be assessed to discover their vulnerability.

The marketing mix elements represent almost unlimited opportunities for positioning. As the next chapter is concerned with the market mix we shall present here only a brief example of how each element can support the positioning of a service firm.

- **The service product.** The product itself offers considerable opportunity to deliver the positioning. For example, Barclays' Connect card helps position the bank as innovative. The card fulfils a wide number of roles: cheque guarantee, cash withdrawal, Visa usage debited directly to the current cheque account, and a deposit card, to mention a few.

- **Price.** Retailers and hotel chains are examples of organizations with a good understanding of the role of price, and associated quality, in positioning. The recent repositioning of the various Forte Group hotel brands into different price and quality offers is an example of this.

- **Service availability and location (place).** Some banks are positioning themselves to be more accessible to the customer. This is achieved by use of technology – making ATMs widely available, as well as improved banking hours.

- **Promotion.** Promotion and positioning are inextricably bound together as it is the advertising and promotional programmes which communicate positioning. Positioning themes or 'signatures' such as the following can help reinforce the desired positioning:

    Morgan Guaranty, 'the big bank of big business';
    IBM, 'fast, reliable service, every customer, everyday, everytime';
    American Airlines, 'we built an airline for the professional traveller';
    Midland Bank, 'the listening bank';
    British Rail, 'we're getting there';
    Federal Express, 'absolutely, positively overnight delivery';
    British Airways, 'the world's favourite airline';
    Sainsbury, 'good food costs less at Sainsbury's'.

- **People.** People are essential to delivery of positioning. For Avis to deliver the 'we try harder' positioning they had to ensure that every employee was actually trying harder to serve the customer, or was supporting someone who was serving the customer. British Airways spent several years on Putting the Customer First, and related initiatives aimed at training and improving people performance, before it attempted to communicate the positioning as shown in the recent customer care TV commercials.

- **Processes.** Processes are essential to delivering the position. If large queues develop in a bank or supermarket, or an ATM network ceases to function, no amount of communication or well intentioned people will overcome the breakdown. Processes are also fundamental to repositioning. Repositioning can be achieved through structural change in processes, involved changing (either increasing or decreasing), complexity and divergence of the service offer.

- **Customer service.** Customer service influences customers' perceptions greatly. It can thus be used as a weapon to create competitive advantage that is not easily copied. This represents an important means of creating differentiation in the company's positioning strategy.

Positioning thus guides the development of the marketing mix. All the elements of the marketing mix can be utilized to influence the customer's perception and hence the positioning of the product or organization concerned. The marketing mix can be used to develop a coherent totality that creates the positioning in the customer's mind.

The importance of positioning

Positioning involves both launching new brands into the marketplace (new brand positioning), and repositioning old brands. It is concerned with the differentiation of products and services and ensuring that they do not degenerate into a commodity. To maximize its potential a company should position itself in its core market segments, where it is objectively or subjectively differentiated in a positive way over competing offerings.

Positioning is particularly important for services in the market of the 1990s. As a result of competitive pressure the consumer is becoming increasingly confused by the huge offering of services within each market sector. These offerings are communicated by a vast number of advertising messages promoting different features of the services. The key to a successful positioning strategy is to promote the feature which the company is best at and which exactly matches the needs of the customer.

Because of intangibility and other features associated with services, consumers find that differentiation of services can be more difficult and complex. Successful positioning makes it easier for the customer to see a company's services as being different from others and exactly what is wanted.

Positioning is a strategic marketing tool which allows managers to determine what their position is now, what they wish it to be and what actions are needed to attain it. It permits market opportunities to be identified, by considering positions which are not met by competitors' products. It therefore helps influence both product development and the redesign of existing products. It also allows consideration of competitors' possible moves and responses so that appropriate action can be taken. The concept is often considered at the product level although it is also relevant at the product sector and organizational level. Positioning involves giving the target market segment the reason for buying your services and thus underpins the whole marketing strategy. It also offers guidelines for development of a marketing mix with each element of the mix being consistent with the positioning.

Notes

1. A. Ries and J. Trout, *Positioning: The Battle for Your Mind*, Warner Books, New York, 1981.
2. G.L. Shostack, 'Service positioning through structural change', *Journal of Marketing*, vol. 51, January 1987, pp.34–43.
3. P. Kotler, *Marketing Management*, Prentice Hall, Englewood Cliffs, 1991, p. 290.
4. T.C. Ragland, 'Consumer define cost, value and quality', *Marketing News*, 25 September 1989, p. 20.
5. M.E. Porter, *Competitive Advantage*, The Free Press, New York, 1985.
6. P. Kotler, *op cit*, p. 301.
7. C.J. Easingwood and V. Mahajan, 'Positioning of financial services for competitive advantage', *Journal of Product Innovation Management*, vol. 6, 1989, pp. 207–19.
8. J.W. Keon, 'Product positioning: trinodal mappings of brand images, ad images, and consumer preference', *Journal of Marketing Research*, vol. 20, November 1983, pp. 380–92.
9. Y.J. Wind, *Product Policy: Concepts, Methods and Strategy*, Addison Wesley, Reading, Mass., 1982, Chapter 4.
10. T. Kosnik, *'Corporate positioning: how to assess and build a company's reputation'*, Harvard Business School, Note 9-589-087, 1989.

6

The services marketing mix

The marketing mix elements

The marketing mix concept is a well established tool used as a structure by marketers. It consists of the various elements of a marketing programme which need to be considered in order to successfully implement the marketing strategy and positioning in the company's markets. The discipline of considering the integration of the elements of the marketing mix, as well as the individual various elements, helps ensure that there is consistency within the marketing strategy as a whole.

Traditionally, most marketeers have considered four basic components or elements of a marketing mix: product, price, promotion and place. However, within services marketing, as explained earlier, it is useful to extend this list to include other key ingredients. A consideration of each element of the marketing mix and how they fit together forms the basis of a marketing programme.

This chapter considers the role of each element of the marketing mix for services. We consider examples of different services and the importance and contribution of different elements of the marketing mix, showing how they can provide a source of competitive advantage for a services firm. The chapter concludes with a discussion on the interaction of the marketing mix elements.

An entire book on services marketing could have been written solely around a discussion of the marketing mix elements. Although this chapter is considerably longer than others, the space available to discuss the marketing mix is limited. Accordingly, we provide more detailed references, which relate to the services marketing mix elements, for the reader to refer to.

Essentially the marketing mix represents the factors which need to be considered when determining a service firm's marketing strategy. For example, in marketing a law firm the following elements should be considered: What particular legal services it offers to the target market segment(s) it has selected; the pricing strategy that is appropriate to those services; how it will promote itself and communicate with its market; the processes it will adopt; the appropriate service levels it will offer to its clients; the delivery system of the legal services; and the type and expertise of the people who will be involved in providing them.

The starting point for making any decisions about marketing mix depends both on how the service is to be positioned and the market segments to be addressed. The advantage of using a marketing mix framework is that it permits the fit between the various elements to be considered. Each element within the marketing mix has an impact on all the other elements. For example, a City law firm can command much higher fee rates than a provincial law firm. It must employ highly qualified lawyers who can provide the level of expertise which is required by target clients in large City institutions. The type of delivery system must also be consistent and might include expensive offices, client entertainment and lawyers who understand the businesses of their clients. Quality of customer service, measured by clients in terms of prompt efficient and effective service is also vital within the competitive environment of legal services. All these elements impact on one another, and a marketing mix needs to be assembled so each of the elements reinforces and supports the other parts of the marketing mix.

There has been much debate as to what should be included within the framework of the marketing mix for services. A number of authors have added to the list of the four basic components of the 4Ps product, place price and promotion. In Chapter 2 we introduced the marketing function and briefly described the justification for expanding the traditional marketing mix of four elements into an expanded mix of seven elements including product, price, promotion, place, people, processes and customer services. It should be noted some authors include physical evidence as an additional P; however, we consider this to be subsumed under the product element of the marketing mix.

The original list of 4Ps helps as a memory device, but terms such as 'place' are not a good description of the distribution task (for a manufactured good) or service location and channels (for a service). Our list does not include all elements starting with a P; however, 'proactive customer service' can be used for consistency, if desired. This serves to emphasize how customer service has an active strategic role to play in the marketing mix.

Having outlined the elements of the marketing mix for services we will now consider each of them in more detail. The underlying concept in developing each of these elements is to use them to support each other, to reinforce the positioning of the product and to deliver appropriate service quality to achieve competitive advantage.

The service product

In discussing products and services there is often a confusion over terminology, so it may be useful to repeat a point made earlier. A **product** is an overall concept of objects or processes which provide some value to customers; **goods** and **services** are subcategories which describe two types of product. Thus the term 'product' is frequently used in a broad sense to denote either a manufactured good or product, and a service.

In fact customers are not buying goods or services – they are really buying specific benefits and value from the total offering. We term this total offering to customers 'the offer'; it represents those benefits that customers derive from the purchase of goods or services. In Chapter 1 we examined the nature of services, and outlined how 'the offer' can be subdivided into four categories including a prime good, a tangible good with accompanying services, a major service with accompanying minor goods and services, and a prime service. Most services (or goods) are not pure; thus the use of the term 'the offer' or 'the offering' can avoid some of the problem of semantics. In practice, in different service industries, the terms, product, service or service product are all used. Even within the same service organization such terms may be used interchangeably.

An offer can be visualized as an atom with the nucleus or core in the centre surrounded by a series of both tangible or intangible features, attributes and benefits which cluster around the core product. These include packaging, advertising, financing, availability, advice, warranty, reliability, etc. It has been suggested the offer can be viewed at several levels, which include the following:[1]

- **The core or generic product.** This consists of the basic service product, e.g. a bed in a hotel room for the night.

- **The expected product.** This consists of the generic product together with the minimal purchase conditions which need to be met. When customers buy an airline ticket they expect, in addition to a seat on the aeroplane, a range of additional elements, including a comfortable waiting area, prompt in-flight service, good quality meals, clean lavatories and arrival on time.

- **The augmented product.** This is the area which enables one product to be differentiated from another. For example, IBM have a reputation for excellent customer service although they may not have the most technologically advanced core product. They differentiate by 'adding value' to their core product in terms of reliability and responsiveness.
- **The potential product.** This consists of all potential added features and benefits that are or may be of utility to buyers. It includes the potential for redefinition of the product to take advantage of new users and the extension of existing applications. This could involve building in switching costs which can make it difficult or expensive for customers to switch from their existing service provider.

Thus a service product is a complex set of value satisfactions. People buy services to solve problems and they attach value to them in proportion to the perceived ability of the service to do this. Value is assigned by the buyers in relationship to the benefits they receive. Augmentation of the expected product represents a means of creating product differentiation and thus added value from the customer perspective.

This framework reconciles the marketeer's view of a product, seen in terms of various inputs and processes needed to produce it, and the consumer's view of the product as being a set of utilities which supply various benefits. This is shown in the example of the personal computer market in Figure 6.1. The core product for a computer is a machine that permits input, processing, storage and retrieval of data. This is the minimum requirement for such a product. The expected product will also have service support, warranty, a recognizable brand name and attractive packaging. The augmented product may include the supply of free diagnostic software, a generous trade in allowance, user clubs and other product augmentations which are valuable to personal computer buyers. The potential product may consist of future applications including use as a systems controller, facsimile machine or a music composer.

It is essential to recognize that all customers are not the same. Customers' requirements for different configurations of benefits, features and attributes will vary by market segment. The brand name itself also becomes an important element of the augmented product. Brands can be a major determining element in the purchase of services and an important means of adding differentiation at the augmented product level.

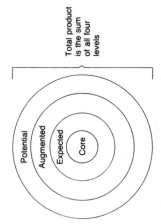

Potential
Augmented
Expected
Core

Total product is the sum of all four levels

Product level	Customer's view	Marketer's view	Personal computer example
Core product	Customer's generic need which must be met	Basic benefits which make product of interest	Data storage, processing, speed of processing, retrieval
Expected product	Customer's minimal set of expectations	Marketer's product decisions on tangible and intangible components	Brand name, warranty, service support, the computer itself
Augmented product	Seller's offering over and above what customer expects or is accustomed to	Marketer's other mix decisions on price, distribution and promotion	Diagnostic software, trade-in allowance, base price plus options, dealer network, user clubs, personal selling
Potential product	Everything that potentially can be done with the product that is of utility to the customer	Marketer's actions to attract and hold customers regarding changed conditions or new applications	Use as a system controller, facsimile machine, music composer, and other areas of application

Figure 6.1   The total product concept

Source: B. Collins, 'Marketing for engineers', in D. Sampson (ed.), *Management for Engineers*, Longman Cheshire, Melbourne, 1989, p. 372.

Branding and differentiation

The three levels beyond the core or generic product represent opportunities to provide added value to customers. Whilst this added value may be solely at the emotional level it is nevertheless real to the customer. Value is added through the creation of strong brand names and the owners of the brands can command premium prices for them. Branding has an important role in helping customers be assured of uniform service quality.

Two decades ago branding was mainly the domain of consumer goods, today it has become much more common in services. Considerable efforts have been made to establish distinctive brands in virtually every service sector, as shown in Table 6.1. This suggests that the company brand is typically the primary brand in services. It has been

Table 6.1   Well known brands in various service sectors

Passenger Transport	*Hospitality*
British Airways: Club World, Super Shuttle	Trusthouse Forte: Travelodge, Posthouse,
British Midland: Diamond Service	Exclusive Hotels
Virgin Atlantic Airways: Upper Class	Accor: Formula One, Ibis, Novotel, Sofitel
British Rail: Intercity, Network SouthEast,	Mount Charlotte: Thistle
Sleeper	Marriott
Pullman	Ladbroke: Hilton International, Hilton
Avis	National
Hertz	
	Financial Services
Freight Transport/Distribution	Midland Bank: First Direct, Vector, Orchard,
Royal Mail: Registered, Recorded, Special	Meridian
Delivery, Datapost	Guardian Royal Exchange: Freedom,
British Rail: Red Star, Rail Freight	Choices
Federal Express	
DHL	*Retail*
	Next: Next Directory
Travel Trade	Burton: Principles, Harvey Nichols
British Airways: First, Four Corners	House of Fraser: Harrods
Midland Bank: Thomas Cook	W.H. Smith: Do-It-All, W.H. Smith,
Pickfords	Paperchase,
Lunn Poly	Our Price, Waterstones
	Kingfisher: Woolworths, B&Q, Comet
Food and Beverage	
McDonald's	*Leisure*
Grand Metropolitan: Burger King	Scottish & Newcastle: Center Parcs
Trusthouse Forte: Harvester, Happy Eater,	Alton Towers
Welcome Break, Wheelers, Gardner	Disney
Merchant	
Whitbread: Pastificio	

Source: J. Dobree and A. S. Page, 'Unleashing the power of service brands in the 1990s', *Management Decision*, vol. 28, no. 6, p. 21.

argued that in the future the company brand will become the main discriminator and that consumers' choice will depend less on evaluation of the functional benefits of a product or service and more on their assessment of the company and the people behind it.[2]

Differentiation for a brand is achieved by adding value to the basic core service product. Figure 6.2 illustrates this concept; it suggests that the core product may represent 70 per cent of the cost of providing the service but may only have 30 per cent of the total impact on the customer. By contrast the augmented product or product surround may represent perhaps 30 per cent of the cost but may account for 70 per cent of total customer impact. The research findings on service quality support this view.

The topic of service quality is discussed in Chapter 8. However, we should make the point here that perceived service quality depends more on reliability, responsiveness, assurance and empathy than on tangibles. This means that service marketers should give increased attention to how they can differentiate the product surround and enlarge it. The larger the product surround the greater the probable differentiation of a company's brand offering from those of its competitors.

The American Express green card is a good example of a strong service brand. In the USA, its major market, in strict product terms it compares unfavourably with Visa or Access/Mastercard in the following ways:

- American Express offers no convenient option of paying off part of its bill monthly. The entire balance is required upon receipt of the statement.

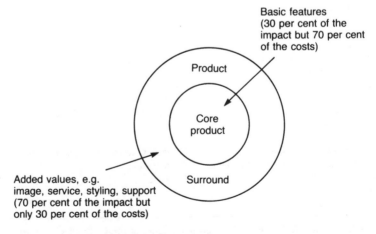

Figure 6.2 The product surround concept

- Only a quarter of the number of merchants world wide that take Visa/Mastercard accept American Express.

- Emergency cash is available to American Express holders at only 20 per cent of locations at which it is available to the Visa or Mastercard holder.

- The American Express yearly fee, in the USA, of U$55, is more than that of either Visa or Mastercard; many cards do not charge any annual fees.

Consumers are willing to pay more for a less useful, less convenient credit card. Despite these shortcomings, American Express has turned its green card into a highly successful brand. By positioning the green card as a 'travel and entertainment card' they have created a distinctive product surround which no other card has achieved.

A key issue which needs to be considered in the context of differentiation and brands is the brand to commodity continuum. This applies equally to both goods and services. This continuum is shown in Figure 6.3. At one extreme the service product consists of a speciality – often a highly differentiated brand – and at the other extreme a commodity. When a totally new product is introduced it is, by definition, a speciality. Over time, as new competitors emerge, there is a tendency as it moves through the product lifecycle for it to move towards commodity status. This 'speciality to commodity slide' results in considerably reduced product image and differentiation, lowered

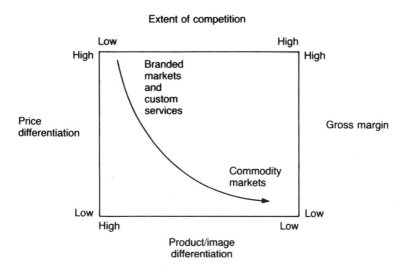

Figure 6.3 The brand to commodity continuum

prices and increased competition. Competition in commodity markets is primarily based on prices and terms. By contrast, competition in speciality branded services and goods is based on the other elements of the marketing mix and submixes including customer service, advertising, brand name, guarantees, packaging, warranties, etc. Service firms need to consider how to halt (or reverse) this transition to ensure service products remain differentiated, rather than slide into the commodity category.

This speciality to commodity slide is not inevitable. In a chapter entitled 'No such thing as a commodity', Peters and Austin[3] point out a wide range of examples of firms which have differentiated essentially identical generic products through the development and expansion of this product surround by providing physical evidence supporting the differentiation. Some dry cleaning services have recognized this and offer specialist dry cleaning services such as 'premier service', 'gold service' or 'orchid service'. By paying a higher price and receiving the cleaned garment in superior or differentiated packaging, customers perceive higher quality service. In reality, the only difference may be a more detailed inspection procedure after the standard dry cleaning process has been completed.

Berry and Parasuramen have suggested some key questions service managers should address with respect to their company's branding:[4]

1. Are we proactive in presenting a strong company brand to our customers (and other stakeholders)?
2. How does our company name rate on the tests of distinctiveness, relevance, memorability and flexibility?
3. Do we use to full advantage branding elements other than the company name?
4. Is our presented brand cohesive?
5. Do we apply our brand consistently across all media?
6. Do we use all possible media to present our brand?
7. Do we recognize the influence of the service offering on brand meaning?
8. Do we base our branding decisions on research?
9. Are we respectful of what exists when we change our brand or add new brands?
10. Do we internalize our branding?

Addressing these questions should help avoid the speciality to commodity slide. They also provide a platform for elements of physical evidence to be added which reinforce the brand and product surround.

Physical evidence

This is the service firm's physical environment where the service is created and where the service provider and customer interact, plus any tangible elements that are used to communicate or support the role of the service. In a service business, the marketeer should seek to compensate for the intangibility dimension by providing physical clues to support the positioning and image and enhance the product surround.

Some writers argue that physical evidence should form a separate element of the services marketing mix.[5] However, whilst its importance is undoubted, so too is that of advertising and personal selling. Just as advertising and personal selling are subelements of the promotion element of the marketing mix, so we consider that physical evidence should be viewed as a subelement of the product element of the mix. However, perhaps the more relevant issue is that the significance of physical evidence should be recognized, and attention directed to it, regardless of whether it is viewed a subelement of product (or even of promotion), or a marketing mix element in its own right.

Physical evidence can be divided into two types: essential and peripheral. Essential evidence represents the key decisions made by the service provider about the design and layout of a building, the type of aeroplanes to be used by an airline, the ambience of a reception room at a doctor's surgery. These can be used to add significantly to the product surround.

Peripheral physical evidence has little value on its own. A railway ticket has no independent value in itself, but represents a right to experience the service at a later point in time. Peripheral evidence adds tangibility to the value of the service provided the customer segment to which it is directed values it. For example, in 1989, British Airways proposed the following additions to its Club World: expedited clearance of customs and immigration formalities, fresh fruit, mineral water on every mealtray, healthier food and a cold course option, automatic choice of a vegetarian meal, sleep-over neck cushion for each seat, speedier baggage handling, and where practical a chauffeur-driven car option to be provided at every destination at a subsidized price. These additions were based on market research on what customers expected from an airline's business class.

Physical evidence helps with the positioning of a service firm and gives tangible support to the expected service experience. Banks have traditionally built highly elaborate and decorative facades and banking chambers to give the impression of substance and solidity. Today banks and building societies spend large amounts of money on creating branding, decor, architecture, layout, furnishings, uniforms and selection of corporate colours that reinforce their desired image and positioning. Supermarkets have the smell of freshly baked bread close to the front entrance to attract customers and airlines have a carefully integrated corporate look on every item, from the ticket to the aeroplane itself.

Where services are performed at the location of the service organization, physical evidence has an essential role to play. Familiarity is often a factor used by service franchise operators to provide reassurance, by physical evidence, of what the customer can expect. For example, customers of Holiday Inn hotels and McDonald's restaurants have a clear idea of what they can expect and are familiar with the type of facilities offered and how they should be used when they visit a new location.

Service product decisions

Service organizations will often wish to offer a range of services. For example, banks can provide a wide range of financial services for different customer segments. A bank which focuses on corporate clients will offer a different range of products from one focusing on private investors. A hotel catering for business customers may be full during the week satisfying this segment's needs, but may decide to offer weekend discounts to attract families and holiday clients. This helps satisfy its objectives of focusing primarily on the business customer, but also achieving higher average levels of occupancy.

Decisions on the range of services to be offered need to be considered in the context both of the companies' positioning strategy and the competitors' services offerings. New services to be offered should also be consistent with the competence of the firm to deliver them.

A service organization has a range of strategic growth options available to it when considering service product decisions. These can be considered using the product/market matrix, known as the Ansoff matrix, which we briefly introduced in Chapter 3. This matrix can be used to consider four fundamental growth options for the service provider. It represents a framework for reviewing how to improve the sales of the existing service products, or to develop new product and/or market opportunities. An example of such a review for a management consulting firm is shown in Figure 6.4. Each of these four growth options will now be discussed in more detail.

Market penetration

Market penetration is concerned with how to exploit your current position in the marketplace better. This can be achieved by more

	Existing products	New products or services
Existing markets	*Market penetration* ■ Repeat business ■ Increased frequency ■ Depth consulting	*Product or service development* ■ New products & services ■ New image ■ Consultant involvement on boards
New markets	*Market development* ■ Industry groups ■ Segmented growth ■ Internationalization	*Diversification* ■ Venture capital ■ New businesses ■ Acquisitions

Figure 6.4 Growth options for a management consulting firm

focused segmentation, a more clearly defined positioning strategy, or through better application of the marketing mix elements. Essentially it is concerned with gaining greater productivity from the marketing mix elements and building market share at the expense of competitors.

Two aspects, customer retention and increasing frequency of use, are of particular importance. Customer retention strategies aim at keeping customers – this is discussed in some detail in Chapter 8 and can be assisted by using devices such as frequent flyer programmes and loyalty clubs. Increasing frequency of usage involves encouraging customers to use your services more frequently. For example, British Rail has been very successful with offering off-peak discounted fares to a wide range of groups from students to pensioners to stimulate additional use of its services.

New product/service development

New service development, or new product development for service businesses, is a relatively new area for research attention.[6] Christopher Lovelock has suggested six categories of service innovation, including the following:[7]

- **Major innovations.** These innovations represent major new markets. Examples include Dyno-rod (drain/sewer unblocking services); Federal Express and DHL (overnight distribution); cellular telephones and Open University (distance education). The risk and reward profile of such major innovations are typically large.

- **Startup businesses.** These are new and innovative ways of addressing the current needs of customers and increasing the range of choices available to them. Examples include Prontoprint (stationery and printing through retail outlets); Interflora (florist directory and distribution internationally); and video cassette hire. Some innovations could fit either of the above two categories.

- **New products for the market currently served.** This allows the service provider to use the customer base to the best advantage and cross-sell other products. The growth in sophistication of databased marketing has greatly aided this approach. For example, the Automobile Association established a core range of products related to car breakdown services. The customer base is now offered a range of other car-related services, including car insurance, travel insurance and map books. From this the database offers were extended to include a holiday planning service and travel books. Their product extension has expanded into an interlinked range of services using the customer base to maximum advantage.

  Technological change has increased the range of opportunities for innovation and creativity, and is also responsible for creating a market for products and services which consumers may not have considered that they require. For example, automated teller machines, electronic mail and desk top publishing have each resulted from technological development and created consumer demands which previously did not exist.

- **Product line extensions.** These offer customers greater variety of choices within existing service lines. This is typical of a business in maturity, which already has a core market segment which the service provider seeks to maintain. For example, City law firms serving the corporate clients have found increasing demand from clients in offering advice on environmental law. This supplements the commercial legal services already provided, but is in response to both new EC legislation and companies' desire to be perceived as being environmentally conscious.

- **Product improvements.** This usually consists of altering or improving the features of existing service products. British Rail's newer faster trains, British Airways/Air France's Concorde, and Fidelity's twenty-four hour service centres are examples of such improvements.

- **Style changes.** These involve cosmetic alternations or enhancement of tangible elements of the service product. The development of a new corporate image, or the introduction of uniforms for bank counter staff are examples of style changes.

Market development

An alternative strategy to service development is to undertake market extension, which seeks new groups of buyers with a firm's current service offerings. For example, many banks have opened international offices in order to attract foreign clients. Similarly, management consulting firms have extended their markets by opening branch offices internationally. This strategy is often a higher risk than either of the other two strategies, and may require in-depth market research to ensure that the needs of international customers are understood and met competitively. Many service firms have not given sufficient consideration to the different needs of different customers in these circumstances. Market extension can be more safely adopted if the service is to be used by existing customers in the different market. For example, a strategy consulting firm may open an overseas office where an existing client already has established operations. This client can be the basis of business for the new office, whilst new clients are being developed.

Diversification – new services to new markets

This is the riskiest strategy, as a service firm is not building on any of its existing strengths. It is most typically adopted within a mature service industry where growth cannot be achieved in any other way. For example, airlines such as SAS have attempted to provide combined airline, hotel and limousine services. On the whole these attempts have not been judged to be successful. In reality it is hard to achieve success as each business has very different critical success factors. The lack of success of retail bank diversification into stockbroking and merchant banking is a testimony to the difficulties inherent in diversification.

A distinctive feature of services is the role that both the customers and the service providers play in the development of new services. Operation staff are often brought into the decision-making process of new service development. It is these people who will have to provide the service and so their opinions are often sought in order to gain valuable market information. They are also in contact with the customers and provide a valuable feedback system on customer requirements. It is therefore the simultaneity of service production and consumption which leads to this important distinction in new service development in comparison with new product development.

Managing the service offer

Grönroos outlines four steps that the services marketer needs to manage in providing a service offer:[8]

- **Developing the service concept** – the basic concept or intentions of the service provider.

- **Developing a basic service package** – the core service, facilitating services and goods, and supporting services and goods.

- **Developing an augmented service offering** – the service process and interactions between the service provider and customers, including the service delivery process. It includes a consideration of the accessibility of the service, interaction between the service provider and the customer, and the degree of customer participation.

- **Managing image and communication** – so that they support and enhance the augmented service offer. This is the interface between the promotion and product marketing mix elements.

A consideration of these steps makes clear some of the linkages with other elements of the marketing mix. Once the basic service offer has been established attention can then be directed at development of pricing, promotion, distribution and other ingredients of the marketing mix.

Pricing the service

Price plays a pivotal part in the marketing mix of a service because pricing attracts revenues to the business. Pricing decisions are significant in determining the value for the customer and play a role in the building of an image for the service. Price also gives a perception of quality. Pricing decisions are often made by adding a percentage mark up on cost. This approach, however, loses the benefits which a pricing strategy can offer within the marketing strategy. Service firms, at least within deregulated markets, need to use pricing more strategically to help gain competitive advantage.

Pricing decisions have an impact on all parts of the supply/marketing channels. Suppliers, sales people, distributors, competitors and customers all are affected by the pricing system. Further, pricing affects buyers' perceptions of the service offered. For example, a hotel chain servicing the tourist package holiday market will offer cheap prices and its customers will have a lower expectation of service quality than for a premium priced hotel.

Pricing decisions for services are particularly important given the intangible nature of the product. The price charged for a service signals to customers the quality of the service that they are likely to receive. Thus, a restaurant that places its menu in its window for prospective customers to view is giving customers information about what they can expect in terms of quality of food and servicelevels as well as cost.

Special pricing considerations also apply to services by virtue of the immediacy of delivery and the importance of availability. Thus pricing decisions for services may involve premium pricing at maximum demand times and discounted pricing in order to attract additional customers when demand is low. This has given rise to complicated pricing of services within the package holiday market, railways and airlines, entertainment and leisure services, media advertising services and many utilities.

Branding allows homogeneous services to be differentiated and allows a premium pricing strategy to be adopted. American Express is a good example in that it has successfully segmented the credit card market and has created new service forms for these segments. American Express was the first to adopt premium 'gold' cards which allowed the company to charge higher membership fees. When credit card companies began to offer their own 'gold' cards American Express developed a new market segment by offering the superpremium 'platinum' card for its most exclusive group of customers.

The decision on the pricing of a new service must take into account many relevant features. The most important of these is that the pricing decision must be consistent with the overall marketing strategy. The charging of different prices in different markets may also need to be considered. In addition, the specific price to be charged depends on the type of customer to whom the service is sold. Value is not determined by price but by the benefits the buyer perceives the new service to offer relative to its total acquisition cost, and the price of alternative services which are competing with it.

A service company will very often sell a range of services. It may decide to offer bundles of these services at special prices. Package holidays – which offer travel, hotel, transportation, sports facilities and equipment –, entertainment and insurance are examples of this. In these areas pricing needs to be carefully considered in order to obtain the maximum potential profit and revenue from each customer.

A simple cost-plus price structure loses many of the advantages which can be gained by a researched and managed pricing policy. Services have an intrinsic value for the customer and it is this rather than the cost of performing the service that a pricing policy needs to consider. Pricing needs to be viewed from a market-oriented perspective.

Pricing objectives

The alternative pricing methods or approaches for services are similar to those used for goods. The pricing method to be adopted should start with a consideration of pricing objectives. These might include the following:

- **Survival** – in adverse market conditions the pricing objective may involve forgoing desired levels of profitability to ensure survival.
- **Profit maximization** – pricing to ensure maximization of profitability over a given period. The period concerned will be related to the lifecycle of the service.
- **Sales maximization** – pricing to build market share. This may involve selling at a loss initially in an effort to capture a high share of the market.
- **Prestige** – a service company may wish to use pricing to position itself as exclusive. High-priced restaurants and Concorde are examples.
- **ROI** – pricing objectives may be based on achieving a desired return on investment (ROI).

These represent some of the more common, but by no means all, pricing objectives. The decision on pricing will be dependent on a range of factors including:

- Positioning of the service.
- Corporate objectives.
- The nature of competition.
- Lifecycle of the service(s).
- Elasticity of demand.
- Cost structures.
- Shared resources.
- Prevailing economic conditions.
- Service capacity.

Three of these elements, the demand, costs and competition require further elaboration.

Demand

Service companies need to understand the relationship between price and demand and how demand varies at different pricing levels. This may vary by market segment. A useful concept to help understand this relationship is the 'elasticity of demand'. This concept helps service managers understand whether demand is elastic (a given percentage change in price produces a greater percentage change in demand) or inelastic (a significant change in price produces relatively little change in levels of demand). These different characteristics of demand are shown in Figure 6.5. Pricing levels are especially important if demand for the service is elastic. Demand for many services is elastic, including airlines, railways, cinemas and package tours. Demand for other services such as cheque books, medical care and electricity is more inelastic.

Costs

Services marketers need to understand the costs of providing services and how these vary over time and with level of demand. Two major types of cost, fixed costs and variable costs, need to be identified. In addition some costs may exhibit mixed behaviour and are semi-variable. Fixed costs are those which do not vary with the level of output. They remain fixed over a given period and include buildings, furniture, staff costs, maintenance, etc. Variable costs vary according to quantity of the service provided or sold. They include part-time employees' wages, expendable supplies, electricity, postage, etc. It should be noted that some costs have elements which are partly fixed and partly variable. For example, these include telephone costs and salaried staff used for overtime work.

Many service businesses, such as airlines, have high levels of fixed costs because of the expense of the equipment and staff needed to operate them. In financial services fixed costs can represent more than 60 per cent of total costs.

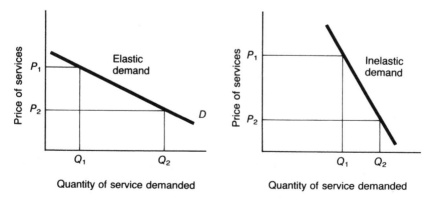

Figure 6.5 Elastic and inelastic demand for services

Total costs represent the sum of the fixed, variable and semi-variable costs at a given level of output. Service managers need to understand how cost behaviour will vary at different levels of service output. This has important implications for decisions to expand capacity, as well as for pricing.

The experience curve is a useful tool to help managers understand cost behaviour in a service industry. The experience curve is an empirically derived relationship which suggests that as accumulated sales or output double, costs per unit (in real terms) typically fall by between 20 and 30 per cent. Many financial service organizations have moved from paper-based processing which offers no real economies of scale, to mechanization and electronic processing which offer considerable potential for scale economies. Figure 6.6 shows an experience curve for electronic banking compared with paper processing of cheques.

In banking the use of automatic teller machines (ATMs) has had a profound effect on lowering costs. Although the cost of installing an ATM can be high, once installed the per transaction cost is considerably less than using a human bank teller in the transaction. In the US

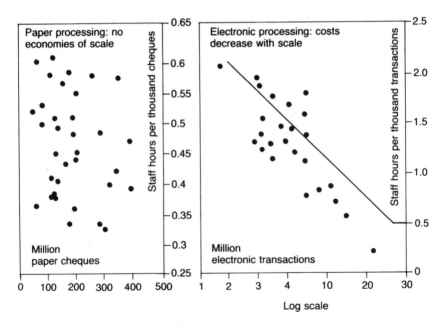

Source: D. F. Channon, *Global Banking Strategy*, Wiley, New York 1988, p. 307, based on material from Boston Consulting Group.

Figure 6.6   Experience curve for electronic banking

volumes of ATM transactions have increased from an average of 4000 transactions per month in 1978 to an average of 6500 transactions per month in 1983; and whilst wage costs have been rising with inflation, the cost of ATMs has fallen in real terms by about 7–10 per cent per annum.[9] Thus the experience curve helps understand the potential for using scale and mechanization to improve a service firm's cost position.

Competition

The costs and pricing behaviour of competitors is a further important element that needs to be reviewed. In addition to seeking information about the prices of key competitors in each major segment, the cost position of major competitors needs to be considered. An understanding of competitors' costs helps the service manager make an assessment of competitors' capacity to alter their pricing structure. For example, some organizations such as Citibank have sought to gain competitive advantage in their US retail operations by achieving the lowest cost position in clearing transactions.

Service firms should attempt to benchmark their competitors to determine their costs, prices and profitability. This can be done by a variety of techniques including competitive shopping and market research and should include a price–quality comparison of each major competitor's offer. The strength of competitors in profitability, cost position and market share terms in each segment can then be factored into the pricing decision.

Pricing methods

Once the basic pricing objectives have been considered and a review made of demand, cost, competitors' prices and costs, and other relevant factors, the services marketeer needs to consider the method by which prices will be set. Such methods vary considerably in the services sector and typically include the following:

- **Cost-plus pricing,** where a given percentage mark up is sought.
- **Rate of return pricing,** where prices are set to achieve a given rate of return on investments or assets. This is sometimes called 'target return' pricing.
- **Competitive parity pricing,** where prices are set on the basis of following those set by the market leader.
- **Loss leading pricing,** usually applied on a short-term basis, to establish a position in the market or to provide an opportunity to cross-sell other services.

- **Value-based pricing,** where prices are based on the service's perceived value to a given customer segment. This is a market-driven approach which reinforces the positioning of the service and the benefits the customer receives from the service.

- **Relationship pricing,** where prices are based on considerations of future potential profit streams over the lifetime of customers.

Relationship pricing

It is clear that cost-plus based pricing is unacceptable as customers are interested in their own costs, not those of their suppliers. Costs in many service businesses can be extremely hard to estimate as companies offer a range of services which typically make use of the same resources.

We would argue that relationship pricing is the appropriate form of pricing where there is an on-going contact between the service provider and the customer. Relationship pricing follows closely the market-oriented approach of value-based pricing but takes the lifetime value of the customer into account. It is based on value considerations of all the services provided to the customer and makes an assessment of the potential profit stream over a given period of time – often the customer's lifetime. Whilst value-based pricing which emphasizes benefits drives this pricing philosophy, it allows the firm to use loss leader, competitive or marginal costing at appropriate points in time, on relevant services, for both strategic and tactical purposes.

The value-based relationship approach to pricing is aimed at helping position the service and reflects the fact that customers are willing to pay extra for the perceived benefits provided by both the core product and the product surround (Figure 6.2). This concept is shown in Figure 6.7 and reflects the notion that customers will pay a premium for perceived benefits, and especially those supplied by the product surround in terms of brand image, brand values and service quality. The size of the price premium is not meant to be to scale in Figure 6.7; in fact, the premium provided by the surround could be greater than the core product.

One approach firms are using to enhance their product surround and achieve premium prices is the unconditional service guarantee. "Bugs" Burger Bug Killers (BBBK) are a pest extermination company based in Miami. It charges up to 600 per cent more than some of its competitors and has a high market share of clients with severe pest problems. The company's service guarantee to clients in the hotel and restaurant sectors promises:[10]

1. You don't owe one penny until all pests on your premises have been eradicated.

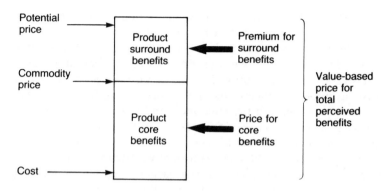

Figure 6.7 Value-based pricing

2. If you are ever dissatisfied with BBBK's service, you will receive a refund for up to 12 months of the company's services – plus fees for another exterminator of your choice for the next year.

3. If a guest spots a pest on your premises, BBBK will pay for the guest's meal or room, send a letter of apology, and pay for a future meal or stay.

4. If your facility is closed down due to the presence of roaches or rodents, BBBK will pay any fines, as well as all lost profits, plus US$5 000.

The large price premium charged for their services and the unconditional service guarantee does not imply staggeringly high costs. In 1986 BBBK paid out only US$120 000 in claims, on sales of US$33 million.

As with other marketing mix elements, the pricing of services also needs to take into account the delivery mechanism, which we shall now address.[11]

Place: service location and channels

The location and channels used to supply services to target customers are two key decision areas. Location and channel decisions involve considering how to deliver the service to the customer and where this should take place. This has particular relevance to services as very often they cannot be stored and will be produced and consumed at the same point. 'Place' also has importance as the environment in which the service is delivered, and how it is delivered, are part of the perceived value and benefits of the service.

The diversity of services makes generalization about place strategies difficult. In Chapter 1 we described several alternative means of classifying services, including how the service is delivered. Addressing this issue involves considering the nature of the interaction between the service provider and the customer, and the decision about whether the service organization needs single or multi-site locations.

Service marketeers should seek to develop appropriate service delivery approaches that yield competitive advantage for their firms. We will now review some of the issues relating to location and channels that need to be considered when seeking to develop such delivery approaches.

Location

Location is concerned with the decisions a firm makes about where its operations and staff are situated. The importance of location for a service depends upon the type and degree of interaction involved. In Chapter 1 we distinguished between three types of interaction between the service provider and the customer:

- The customer goes to the service provider.
- The service provider goes to the customer.
- The service provider and customer transact business at arm's length.

When the customer has to go to the service provider, site location becomes very important. For a service business such as a restaurant, location may be one of the main reasons for patronage. In this type of interaction, service providers seeking growth can consider offering their services at more than one location.

The optimum location of services for a multi-site operator becomes a critical decision in businesses such as car rental, restaurants, motels, banks and retailers. Such organizations take great care in selecting appropriate sites on the basis of potential customers in the catchment area and location of competitors' sites. A number of sophisticated computer models have been developed which can be used to assess the desirability of various site alternatives.

Where the service provider can go to the customer, site location becomes much less important provided it is sufficiently close to the customers for good quality service to be received. In some circumstances the service provider has no discretion in going to the customer as certain services must be provided at the customers' premises. This is the case with a wide range of maintenance services such as lift repair, pest control and cleaning services. In other cases service providers have discretion in whether they decide to offer their services at the customer's or their own premises. Some garages now offer car tune up and servicing at the customer's home or office, as do hairdressers and TV repair firms. Some dry cleaning and laundry firms have built up highly profitable businesses by dispensing with the need for expensive multiple high street locations and locating their operations in a low cost area and providing a pick up and delivery service.

However, when the customer and service organization transact at arm's length location may be largely irrelevant. In such cases, provided efficient mail or electronic communications are in place, we are not concerned with where the physical locations are of suppliers of services such as electricity, telephone or insurance. In some cases certain services offered by the service provider can be provided at arm's length but others need physical interaction between the service provider and customer. A bank can provide routine home banking services or ATM machines at a remote location but a customer may wish to arrange a mortgage in person with a manager at the bank premises.

Some express parcel companies and airlines have developed innovative ways of achieving economies of scale with a single physical plant location. The 'hub and spoke' strategy used by firms such as Federal Express (and many US airlines) involve all parcels going to Memphis for overnight sorting, even if they are only going from, say, one location in New York to another.

The importance of location varies according to the service concerned. Cowell has neatly summed up some of the key considerations that should be addressed by the service marketeer as follows:[12]

1. What does the market require? If service is not provided in a convenient location will purchase of the service be postponed or use delayed? Will poor location lead to do-it-yourself decisions by the customer? Are accessibility and convenience critical factors in service choice (e.g. bank choice)?

2. What are the trends within the sector of service activity in which the service organization operates? Are competitors reaching out into markets (e.g. distance learning in education)? Could some competitive advantage be obtained by going against the norms operating in the subsector?

3. How flexible is the service? Is it technology based or people based? How do these factors affect flexibility in location and relocation decisions?

4. Does the organization have an obligation to locate in convenient sites (e.g. public services like health care)?

5. What new systems, procedures, processes and technology can be harnessed to overcome the weaknesses of past location decisions (e.g. growth of banking by post)?
6. How critical are complementary services to the location decision? Are customers seeking service systems or service clusters? Does the location of other service organizations reinforce any location decision taken (e.g. services can reinforce each other in attracting custom)?

A consideration of these questions will help the service marketer with the location decision.

Channels

The second type of decision relates to who participates in the service delivery in terms of both organizations and people. There are three kinds of participant:

- The service provider.
- Intermediaries.
- Customers.

Traditionally it has been argued that direct sales are the most appropriate form of distribution for services. Whilst this form of distribution is common in some service sectors (e.g. professional services), companies in other areas of the service sector are increasingly seeking other channels to achieve improved growth and to fill unused capacity.

Many services are now being delivered by intermediaries. These can take a variety of forms such as advertising agencies which act as brokers for a number of related services including media buying, print and production. Travel agents act as middlemen for airlines, hotels and leisure services. A recruitment agency provides a service as an intermediary between employer and employee.

The broad channel options for services are outlined in Figure 6.8 and include:

- **Direct sales,** e.g. accounting and management consulting services.
- **Agent or broker,** e.g. insurance broker, estate agent and travel agent.
- **Sellers' and buyers' agents or brokers,** e.g. stockbrokers and affinity groups.
- **Franchises and contracted service deliverers,** e.g. fast food, car services and dry cleaning.

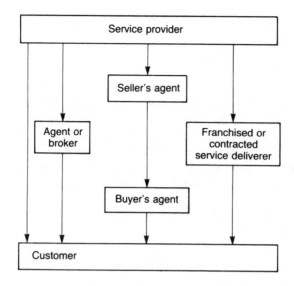

Figure 6.8   Channel options for service companies

This illustrates that although many services are intangible and inseparable and direct sales may be the appropriate channel, services can be distributed by a considerable number of other channel options. Indeed those above can be added to and we can identify other channels such as the wholesaler in merchant banking in the financial services sector, and package tour wholesalers in the travel sector. In the financial services sector a range of distribution options are being used. These include the following:

- Direct face-to-face sales.
- Use of tied or untied sales representatives.
- Direct mail.
- Telemarketing and home banking.
- Computer networked distribution.
- Professional service firms, e.g. estate agents and consultants.
- Cable TV.

One approach to considering your channels and how they compare with those of your competitors is suggested by Light.[13] His framework has these main sectors:

- The channel participants and their relationships.

- The various functions that participants perform using material and technological supports.
- The service they create.

Figure 6.9 shows this framework for the American Agency System Insurance Company, a home owners' insurance company. This shows the participants in the distribution channel (the service firm, the intermediary and the customer), and key aspects of the relationship between them. It also depicts the numerous functions that are allocated between the participants and the material and technological supports.

This framework can be used to do the following:

- Illustrate differences between a company's distribution and that of its competitors.
- Create alternative channel strategies by varying the type of intermediaries or the allocation of functions between participants.
- Understand relative power, conflict and cooperation between channel participants.
- Understand structural shifts within the industry (e.g. the move towards direct response marketing).

It can also be used to help configure the design variables within each major sector. These include:

- The number of intermediaries.
- The type of intermediary.
- The allocation of value-adding functions among channel participants.
- The material and technological support that participants use.
- The service itself.

Design of these channel variables needs to be considered in conjunction with location decisions.

Location and channel choice

The choice of both distribution and channels for services largely depends on the particular requirements of the market and the nature of the service itself. Technology has, in some instances, changed the advantage to be gained by proximity of a service to the customer market. For example, electronic banking has removed some of the need for banks to be located on high streets and also the requirement for long opening hours to deliver their services. Many banking transac-

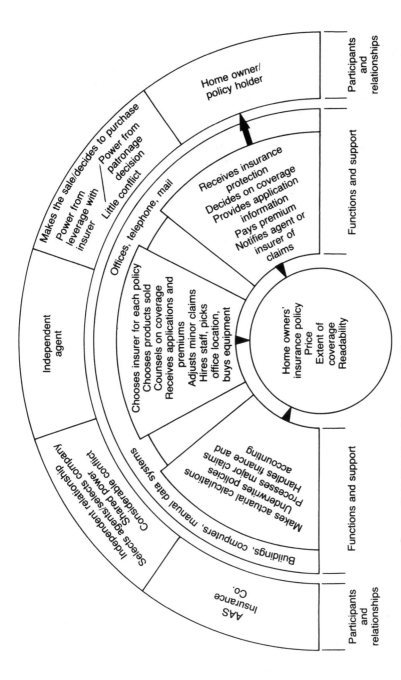

Figure 6.9 shows a semicircular framework diagram with the following labels:

Outer ring (top): Home owner/policy holder — Participants and relationships

Functions and support (upper right): Receives insurance protection; Decides on coverage; Provides application information; Pays premium; Notifies agent or insurer of claims

Left outer segments: Makes the sale/decides to purchase; Power from patronage decision; Power from leverage with insurer; Little conflict; Offices, telephone, mail

Independent agent segment: Chooses insurer for each policy; Chooses products sold; Counsels on coverage; Receives applications and premiums; Adjusts minor claims; Hires staff, picks office location, buys equipment

Center circle: Home owners' insurance policy; Price; Extent of coverage; Readability

Lower functions and support: Makes actuarial calculations; Underwrites policies; Processes major claims; Handles finance and accounting; Buildings, computers, manual data systems

Lower outer segments: Independent agents' relationship; Shared power; Selects; Considerable conflict; AAS Insurance Co. — Participants and relationships

Figure 6.9 A framework for reviewing service distribution channels

Source: D. H. Light, 'A guide for new distribution channel strategies for service firms', *Journal of Business Strategy*, vol. 7, no 1, Summer 1986, p. 59, based on material from SRI International.

tions can now be performed easily without personal contact. Technology has allowed changes in the location decision in many service industries, but the decision on where and how to distribute services is often still dependent on the needs of the customer.

Some services are required in clusters of associated services and products and so proximity to other service offerings can play a major role. This is particularly the case in services for businesses where provision of a fast and integrated service requires not only proximity to the client but also access to other business services. This applies to some communications and business agencies.

Service delivery channels are often the service providers. This highlights the importance of the selection of the appropriate delivery channel. If a franchised delivery system is chosen, then the choice of franchisee is of great importance to ensure the quality of the service. Stringent requirements are therefore often applied to franchisees to maintain the standard of service. Training of service deliverers is thus vital to provide consistency of quality. This poses a particular problem to those services where service providers may have relatively low qualifications and may not remain in one job for long (e.g. the hotel and catering trade).

Promotion and communication of services

The promotion element of the services marketing mix forms a vital role in helping communicate the positioning of the service to customers and other of the key relationship markets described in Chapter 2. Promotion adds significance to services; it can also add tangibility and help the customer make a better evaluation of the service offer.

The promotion of services encompasses a number of major areas. These areas, known as the communications mix or promotions mix, include the following elements:

• Advertising.
• Personal selling.
• Sales promotion.
• Public relations.
• Word of mouth.
• Direct mail.

The choice of the communications mix for services involves decisions on such issues as whether to advertise, use personal selling or generate publicity through greater public awareness by such means as through editorials, publications and press activity. The choice of medium is determined by decisions on how to create the most favourable awareness amongst the target audience.

The communications programme

Promotion is the means by which the service organization communicates with its target markets. Within the communications mix there are a wide variety of alternative communications and promotions tools which can be used in a communications programme. The steps to integrating them within a promotion and communication programme consist of several key tasks. These include:

1. **Identification of target audience.** This will have been broadly defined in the market segmentation process. At this point a clear specification of the target audience to whom promotional actions are to be directed should be undertaken.

2. **Determine promotion objectives.** Promotional goals fall under the three broad headings: to inform, to persuade and to remind. The key to development of an effective and integrated communication programme is to identify the communications objectives that the service firm seeks to achieve. The main objectives of communications include:

   helping to reinforce the positioning;
   developing and enhancing the brand and its image;
   informing customers about the service and its relevant attributes;
   persuading customers to buy the service; and
   reminding customers about the service on an on-going basis.

3. **Development of the message.** A number of customer response models have been developed. One of the most common is the AIDA model which suggests the buyer moves through from stages of attention, interest, desire and action. Development of the message involves consideration of which of these AIDA tasks are to be emphasized. This will depend on how well a company's services are known and customers' perceptions of them. Development of the message involves a consideration of four issues:

   message content – what to say;
   message structure – how to say it logically;
   message style – creating a strong presence; and
   message source – who should develop it.

4. **Selection of communications mix.** This involves determining the appropriate communications tools. These may involve:

> personal communication, e.g. sales activity, word of mouth and interaction during service delivery; and
> non-personal communications, e.g. mass communications techniques including advertising, point of sale and brochures, and the service environment.

One of the key promotion issues a service company has to consider is the relative emphasis on the different communications mix elements. Should advertising or personal selling be the dominant promotions tool? In considering this issue the readers may wish to consider both the degree to which their company's offer possesses the key characteristics of a service (Figure 1.2 in Chapter 1) and where it fits in service classification systems (Figure 1.3 in Chapter 1). Other issues which affect the communications mix include the degree of competition, and sector constraints which exist within, for example, some professional service areas.

It has been argued that several factors impact on the communications mix and the emphasis placed on different elements within it. These include whether:[14]

- The service is in the profit or non-profit sector.
- Constraints exist, as in some professions.
- Competitive intensity is high or low.
- The geographic spread is large or small.
- The custom within a specific service sector dictates promotional practice.
- Managers are sophisticated or not.

Guidelines for services communications

George and Berry have identified six guidelines for services advertising which really are applicable to most elements of the communication mix. These apply to a wide range of service industries, but not, because of the heterogeneous nature of services, to all of them.[15]

- **Provide tangible clues.** A service is intangible in the sense that a performance rather than an object is purchased. Tangible elements within the product surround can be used to provide tangible clues.
- **Make the service understood.** Services may be difficult to grasp mentally because of their intangibility. Tangible attributes of the service can be used to help better understand the service offered.

For example, Legal and General use an umbrella to symbolize the shelter and protection offered by their insurance policies.

- **Communications continuity.** This is important to help achieve differentiation and present a unifying and consistent theme over time. The black horse used by Lloyds Bank and the McDonalds and Disney logo, signage, symbolism, packaging and advertising provide good examples of such continuity.
- **Promising what is possible.** Service firms need to deliver on their promises. If a promise such as fast delivery cannot be consistently met it should not be made at all. British Rail's 'We're getting there' advertising campaign suffered when operations could not deliver a significant perceived improvement in their services.
- **Capitalizing on word of mouth.** The variability inherent in services contributes to the importance of word of mouth. Word of mouth is a vitally important communications vehicle in services, as evidenced by the way we seek personal recommendations for lawyers, accountants, doctors, hairdressers and bankers.
- **Direct communications to employees.** In high contact services advertising should be directed at employees to build their motivation and *esprit de corps*, as well as to customers. The notion behind this is closely tied to internal marketing which we will discuss shortly under the 'people' element of the marketing mix.

Having described the basic elements of the communication programme and guidelines for services communications we will now discuss each of the main categories within the communications mix.

Advertising

Advertising is one of the main forms of impersonal communication used by service firms. The role of advertising in services marketing is to build awareness of the service, to add to the customer's knowledge of the service, to help persuade the customer to buy, and to differentiate the service from other service offerings. Relevant and consistent advertising is therefore of great importance to the success of the marketing of the service.

Advertising has a major role in helping deliver the desired positioning for the service. As discussed earlier, because the core product is intangible it is difficult to promote, service marketers therefore frequently choose tangible elements within the product surround for promotion. Thus airlines promote the quality of their cuisine, the width and pitch of their seats, and the quality of their in-flight service.

In recent years the advertising of services, especially financial services, telecommunications and retailing, has grown dramatically and services now account for a large component of total advertising expenditure. Several issues are of special importance in advertising, including selection of media, the determination of advertising goals and methods for determining the advertising budget.

The principal media include TV, radio, cinema, newspapers, magazines, direct mail, posters and outdoor advertising, and telephone. Each of these have specific advantages and disadvantages that should be considered by the service marketer. Selection of media involves taking the following four main factors into account:[16]

- **Characteristics of the medium** including geographical coverage, types of audience reached, frequency, potential for use of colour, sound and movement, and power to reach special target segments in a credible manner.

- **Atmosphere of the medium** which involves ensuring that the medium reinforces the image the organization is seeking to project.

- **Coverage of the medium** in terms of number of people reached, and their characteristics.

- **Comparative cost** which specifies cost to reach a specific audience size such as cost per thousand viewers or readers.

Selection of the appropriate media and determining the balance between them is essential to obtain the most effective return on advertising expenditure. A consideration of the specific advertising goals to be accomplished will facilitate this process.

The determination of advertising goals is a most important requirement for effective advertising. Some of the more common advertising goals, in order of ease of measurement, and, interestingly, in inverse terms of importance, are as follows:

- **Exposure** – this means the members of the target audience who were exposed to the medium, whether they actually saw the advertisement or not.

- **Awareness and attitudes.** Advertisers would feel happier if they knew the target audience actually read their advertisement and to what extent favourable attitudes were created or reinforced. Obviously, these goals are much more difficult to measure than exposure, particularly with intangible products like services.

- **Resultant desired behaviour.** The advertiser would like to learn what effect the advertising had on their target market and to what degree purchasing behaviour resulted from this advertising.

Several approaches are commonly used by advertisers in deciding advertising budgets. These include the 'affordable' method (how much can the organization afford); the 'percentage of turnover' method (a given proportion of the overall budget is set aside for advertising); the 'competition parity' method (an amount designed to effectively compete in a given competitive area); and the 'objective and task' method. The objective and task method suggests that advertisers should decide on their budget by firstly defining their advertising objectives and, secondly by determining the advertising task, and its cost, to achieve those objectives. It is suggested this is the most appropriate method to use, and it is one which has strong appeal amongst more sophisticated advertisers. However, it is necessary to evaluate the trade off between the benefits in achieving the objectives and the cost of their achievement.

The advertising activity must also be integrated with other elements of the communications mix. For example, it should help form a positive image which supports the activities of the service company's sales staff and increase their prospects of obtaining a sale when they meet a customer.

Personal selling

Personal selling has a vital role in services, because of the large number of service businesses which involve:

* Personal interaction between the service provider and the customer.
* The service being provided by a person not a machine.
* 'People' becoming part of the service product.

Many customers of service firms have a close and on-going relationship with the service providers. Under these circumstances selling has a pivotal role in the communications mix. In certain services selling is the preeminent element in the communications mix.

Selling of services has, despite the differences outlined above, many aspects in common with the selling of goods, including target prospect identification, sales call planning, preparation of presentations, handling objections, closing a sale. Sales force management issues are also similar.

Personal selling has a number of advantages over other communications mix elements. These include the following:

* **Personal contact.** Three customer contact functions have been identified – selling, servicing and monitoring. A framework for considering the personal contact function, based on work carried out by Kotler, is shown in Table 6.2. These personal contacts

Table 6.2 Personal contact functions in services

Function	Responsibilities	Examples
Selling	To persuade potential customers to purchase services and/or to increase the use of services by existing customers	Insurance agent; stockbroker; bank calling officer; real estate salesperson
Service	To inform, assist and advise customers	Airline flight attendant; insurance claims adjuster; ticket agent; bank branch manager
Monitoring	To learn about customers' needs and concerns and report them to management	Customer service representative; repair person

Source: E. M. Johnson, E. E. Scheuing and K. A. Gaida, *Profitable Services Marketing*, Dow Jones-Irwin, Homewood, Illinois, 1986, p. 212.

should be managed to ensure that the customer's satisfaction is increased or maintained at a high level.

- **Relationship enhancement.** The frequent and sometimes intimate contact in many service businesses provides a great opportunity to enhance the relationship between the seller/service provider and the customer. The objective here is to move the customer up the relationship marketing ladder described in Figure 2.5.

- **Cross-selling.** Not only can the sales person close the sale, but the close contact frequently provides the opportunity for cross-selling other services. The sales person is also in a good position to communicate details of other services he or she can offer to customers. This involvement between, say, the bank officers and the customers provides a chance for them to sell to the holders of current accounts a range of services including a mortgage, insurance, savings accounts and stockbroking services.

Two potential problems in certain service businesses (such as professional services) are the lack of training and resistance to selling. In professions such as accounting and law little effort is typically given in firms to the development of selling and presentation skills. In other professions such as insurance broking and estate agency it is more common. A sales management structure supported by a programme of sales training can do much to improve professionals' capacity to improve billings.

The problem of resistance to selling is common in the services sector. Customer contact staff may resist selling and claim it is not part of their job. Many partners in professional firms abhor the thought of selling and frequently employ marketing professionals in the hope of avoiding becoming involved in selling and marketing. A programme to develop a marketing orientation, which we address in Chapter 8, can do much to alleviate this problem.

Seven guidelines have been suggested for selling services which include the following:[17]

1. **Orchestration of the service purchase encounter** by identifying buyer needs and expectations, applying appropriate technical and presentational skills; management of impressions; and eliciting positive customer participation.

2. **Facilitation of a quality assessment by the customer** by establishing standards of expected performance; and using expectations as a basis for judging service quality.

3. **Making the service tangible** by helping buyers determine what they should be looking for (evaluative criteria); educating buyers on alternative services (comparative analysis); and educating buyers about the uniqueness of the service (differential advantage).

4. **Emphasis on organization's image** by assessing customer's awareness levels of the generic service and the sales representative; and communicating relevant image attributes of the service, firm and the sales representatives.

5. **Use of references from external sources** to encourage satisfied customers to become involved in a word of mouth campaign, and help develop and manage favourable publicity for the service company.

6. **Recognition of importance of customer contact personnel** by sensitizing all staff to their role in the satisfaction of customers, and minimizing the total number of people interacting with each specific customer.

7. **Recognition of customer involvement during the service design process** and the customer's capacity to help generate specifications and test concepts.

Personal selling is thus an essential element of the communications mix in most service businesses. Whilst advertising can create knowledge of the firm, targeted and effective personal selling and motivated staff are needed to bring in the revenues. This process can be assisted by integrated support of other elements in the communications mix.

Sales promotion

A number of activities can be undertaken which aim at providing incentives to encourage sales. Patronage awards schemes such as green stamps, and British Airways' Airmiles and Latitudes programmes, and other frequent user programmes are further examples of promotions activity. Point of sale promotion includes brochures, information sheets and other materials made available to customers.

Sales promotion tools can be aimed at three audiences:

1. **Customers** – free offers, samples, demonstrations, coupons, cash refunds, prizes, contests and warrantees.
2. **Intermediaries** – free goods, discounts, advertising allowances, cooperative advertising, distribution contests, awards.
3. **Sales force** – bonuses, awards, contests and prizes for best performer.

The Institute of Sales Promotion estimates that expenditure on sales promotion activity throughout the UK is worth £6 billion annually. This is a remarkable achievement for an industry that was, until recently, more famous for cheap give aways and retailer incentive schemes that bordered more on bribery than any credible, marketing-led activity.[18] Traditionally, sales promotion has been used mainly in the fast moving consumer goods market. However, in the past ten years we have seen a trend for many service firms, and particularly financial services, to use sales promotion.

Until fairly recently, the atmosphere at any branch of one of the 'big five' banks was at best restrained and at worst depressing. Today all of the major operators in retail banking offer tailor-made incentives to virtually all of their target markets, courtesy of their sales promotion agencies. Students opening accounts receive free banking and personal organizers, while younger teenagers receive similar give aways plus magazines offering added interest and prizes. All this is aimed at making the banks more approachable and in tune with their potential customer's aspirations.

Promotions are not always well coordinated with marketing object-ives and other components of the communications mix. To help develop, implement and test a promotions programme the following steps should be taken:

1. Decide the objectives of sales promotion and how they will support other communications and marketing mix elements.
2. Determine the balance of promotions activity between customer, intermediaries and sales force.
3. Decide the sales promotion tools to be used.
4. For each element of sales promotions programme:
   a   determine the amount of the incentive;

b   establish conditions for involvement;
c   decide on the length of the promotion;
d   choose the distribution method for promotion; and
e   schedule the promotion timetable.

5. Agree the sales promotion budget.

6. Pre-test the sales promotion programme.

7. Launch the sales promotion programme.

8. Evaluate the sales promotion programme.

Public relations

Public relations (PR) is defined by the British Institute of Public Relations as 'The planned and sustained effort to establish and maintain goodwill between an organisation and its publics'. These 'publics' are all the groups of people and organizations which have an interest in the service company. These publics are broadly equivalent to the six markets described in Chapter 2, particularly the influence markets. However, publics can be more diverse and may include individuals or bodies which do not have direct influence over the service organization's activities, but with whom the organization nevertheless wishes to communicate. An example of the main publics of a university or college is shown in Figure 6.10.

Public relations is a growing industry and is likely to increase in importance in the future. Within the UK it is estimated that the PR industry employs around 20 000 PR professionals with about half being in PR departments in organizations and about half in PR agencies. Overall it is about a £800 million industry.

PR is concerned with a number of marketing tasks. These include the following:

• Building or maintaining image.

• Supporting the other communication activities.

• Handling problems and issues.

• Reinforcing positioning.

• Influencing specific publics.

• Assisting the launch of new services.

A service organization's 'image' is made up of the collective experiences, views, attitudes and beliefs held about it. We have already discussed corporate image in the context of positioning in Chapter 5. Public relations can use a range of communications approaches to improve or maintain the image of a service organization. Overall the

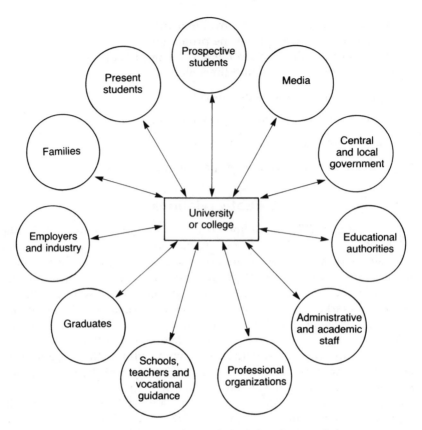

Figure 6.10 Main publics for a university or college

objective with image is to ensure that an organization is viewed more favourably, and is more familiar, than competitors in the market segments it serves.

A wide range of tools can be used in the design of a PR programme. These could include:

- Publications, including press releases, annual reports, brochures, posters, articles and employee reports.
- Events, including press conferences, seminars, speeches, conferences.
- Investor relations aimed at gaining support of investors and analysts.
- Stories which create media coverage.
- Exhibitions including exhibits, displays.
- Sponsorship of charitable causes and community projects.

As with other elements of the communications mix a PR programme should follow a process which consists of the specification of objectives, determining the mix of PR activities to be undertaken, implementing an integrated programme, and evaluating the results.

Word of mouth

One of the most distinctive features of promotion in service businesses is the greater importance of referral and word of mouth communications. This highlights the importance of the people factor in services promotion. Customers are often closely involved in the delivery of a service and then talk to other potential customers about their experiences. They are glad to offer advice on service providers and, indeed, some businesses are specially established in order to offer such services. Research points to personal recommendations through word of mouth being one of the most important information sources. Where people are the service deliverers personal recommendation is often the preferred source of information. Thus word of mouth can have a more important impact than other mass or personal communications mix elements in a number of service businesses, including professional and health care services.

Grönroos has outlined a communications pattern that illustrates the role word of mouth and referrals have to play:[19]

- Expectations/purchases.
- Interactions.
- Experiences.
- Word of mouth/referrals.

An existing, or a new, customer has certain expectations. Once the decision to purchase has been made the customer begins interacting with the service provider and discovers the technical and functional quality of the service being supplied. As a result of the experiences that follow from these interactions and the judgements made about service quality, the customer will or will not return. Positive or negative word of mouth communication will then influence the extent to which others use the service.

The multiplier effect from word of mouth varies from industry to industry and situation to situation. However, negative experiences tend to have a greater impact then positive experiences. Customers who are dissatisfied tend to tell more than twice as many people of their poor experiences as those who are satisfied relate good experiences. Thus negative word of mouth communication can significantly reduce the effectiveness of advertising and other elements of the communications mix, and positive word of mouth can result in less expensive formal communications programmes being needed.

Direct marketing

Direct marketing is the final element of the communications mix that we will consider. There are six main areas of direct marketing, as follows:

- Direct mail.
- Mail order.
- Direct response.
- Direct selling.
- Telemarketing.
- Digital marketing (using electronic media).

In recent years more sophisticated approaches to direct marketing have been adopted. Direct mail and telemarketing, in particular, have benefited from geo-demographic services such as ACORN (A Classification Of Residential Neighbourhoods) and PIN (Pinpoint Identified Neighbourhoods). ACORN segments the country into eleven distinct housing socio-demographic types. PIN uses census data and produces profile maps of geographic areas. These developments have allowed direct marketers to focus much more specifically on areas where they can achieve the greatest return from direct marketing expenditure.

Activities have not been restricted to consumer marketing. Direct marketing is also recognized as a low cost and effective method for communicating with corporate customers. A major reason for this is the increasing cost of reaching corporate markets through a direct sales force.

Companies such as British Telecom, American Express, Royal Mail and most banks and airlines are using direct marketing to build profitable business with their customer base. Developments in electronic media, telecommunications and computers are now presenting greater opportunities for developing an integrated programme of direct marketing activities. These can be used in conjunction with each other to reinforce the personal selling, advertising and other promotional elements. Many service firms are starting to take advantage of the benefits of a coordinated direct marketing programme.

People in services

The importance of people to services marketing has already been stressed. The success of marketing a service is tied closely to the selection, training, motivation and management of people. There are many examples of services failing or succeeding as a consequence of the ineffective or effective management of people.

One of the best known and most dramatic examples is the turn-around of British Airways during the 1980s. Faced with declining profits, greater customer complaints, employee dissatisfaction and increased competition, British Airways launched a series of programmes to refocus on the people within the organization. Employees were involved in the process of turning the company around through the development of increased awareness of the critical importance of the customer. Employees were trained to develop new attitudes towards customers by emphasizing that the airline was in business to satisfy their needs.

In turn, the company made employees feel wanted and cared for, building on the principle that those who are looked after will pass on this caring attitude. The success of this new direction for the airline brought increased profits matched by greater customer and employee satisfaction. The high level of profitability achieved by British Airways in 1992, in the midst of a major recession, highlights the effectiveness of their strategy.

Similar schemes which reflect the importance of people in services are used by the Disney Corporation. Employees are rigorously trained to understand that their job is to bring satisfaction to customers. Employees are part of the 'cast' at Disney and must at all times ensure that all visitors ('guests') to their theme parks have an enjoyable experience. Strict dress and conduct rules are maintained in order that employees conform to standards.

The importance of people within the marketing of services has led to great interest in internal marketing. This recognizes the importance of attracting, motivating, training and retaining quality employees by developing jobs to satisfy individual needs. Internal marketing aims to encourage effective behaviour by staff which will attract customers to the firm. The most talented people will be attracted to work in those companies which are seen to be good employers.

Attempts to view the employees of an organization as an element of a service organization's marketing mix have been notably absent from academic marketing literature until recently. While the expression 'our employees are our greatest asset' is increasingly being heard among companies, it is clear that this statement is often a platitude. By recognizing the contribution people make to acquiring and keeping customers, within the overall marketing mix, the service company's competitive performance will be substantially enhanced.

Differing roles of people

An essential aspect of viewing people as an element of the marketing mix is to recognize the different roles in which people affect both the marketing task and customer contact. Judd has developed a categorization scheme based on the degree of frequency of customer contact and the extent to which staff are involved with conventional marketing activities. This categorization results in four groups: contactors, modifiers, influencers and isolateds, as shown in Figure 6.11.[20]

- **Contactors** have frequent or regular customer contact and are typically heavily involved with conventional marketing activities. They hold a range of positions in service firms including selling and customer service roles. Whether they are involved in planning or execution of marketing strategy they need to be well versed in the marketing strategies of the firm. They should be well trained, prepared and motivated to serve the customers on a day-to-day basis in a responsive manner. They should be recruited based on their potential to be responsive to customer needs and be evaluated and rewarded on this basis.

- **Modifiers** are people such as receptionists, credit department and switchboard personnel; while they are not directly involved with

	Involved with conventional marketing mix	Not directly involved with marketing mix
Frequency or periodic customer contact	Contactors	Modifiers
Infrequent or no customer contact	Influencers	Isolateds

Source: V. C. Judd, 'Differentiate with the 5th P', *Industrial Marketing Management*, vol. 16, 1987, pp. 241–7.

Figure 6.11 Employee influence on customers

conventional marketing activities to a great degree, they neverthe-less have frequent customer contact. As such they need to have a clear view of the organization's marketing strategy and the role that they can play in being responsive to customers' needs. They have a vital role to play especially, but not exclusively, in service businesses. Modifiers need to develop high levels of customer relationship skills. Training and monitoring of performance are especially important here.

- **Influencers**, while involved with the traditional elements of the marketing mix, have infrequent or no customer contact. However, they are very much part of the implementation of the organiza-tion's marketing strategy. They include those with roles in product development, market research, etc. In recruitment of influencers people with the potential to develop a sense of customer respons-iveness should be pursued. Influencers should be evaluated and rewarded according to customer-oriented performance standards and opportunities to enhance the level of customer contact should be programmed into their activities.

- **Isolateds** perform various support functions and have neither frequent customer contact nor a great deal to do with the conventional marketing activities. However, as support people their activities critically affect performance of the organization's activities. Staff falling within this category include purchasing department, personnel and data processing. Such staff need to be sensitive to the fact that internal customers as well as external customers have needs which must be satisfied. They need to under-stand the company's overall marketing strategy and how their func-tions contribute to the quality of delivered value to the customer.

This suggests that people form an important part of the differentiation in a service organization which can create added value for the customer. By viewing people as a separate element of the marketing mix, the appropriate level of attention can be directed to maximizing the impact of their activities and motivating and rewarding them to make the desired contribution.

Internal marketing

It is increasingly being recognized in service firms that in order to be successful at marketing to the external customer, internal marketing to the staff is essential. In Chapter 2 we explained two key main aspects of internal marketing:

- Every employee and every department within an organization both have roles as internal customers and internal suppliers. To help ensure high quality external marketing, every individual and department within a service organization must provide and receive excellent service.

- People need to work together in a way that is aligned with the organization's stated mission, strategy and goals. This is obviously a critical element within high-contact service firms where there are high levels of interaction between the service provider and customer.

The idea behind internal marketing is to ensure that all members of the staff provide the best possible contribution to the marketing activities of the company and successfully complete all telephone, mail, electronic, and personal interactions with the customer in a manner that adds value to the service encounter.

A pilot study in internal marketing suggests that **formalized** internal marketing programmes in the UK are still fairly rare. Respondents were asked in semi-structured interviews to describe the internal marketing programmes established in their organizations. Specific questions were asked in relation to the length of time an internal marketing programme had been running, whether the programme was formal, if it had a name, the job title of the person in charge of internal marketing, whether this was a full-time or part-time appointment and the number of staff involved in internal marketing, and who they reported to. Respondents were additionally asked to describe the critical success factors of the internal marketing programme and to describe modifications to the programme, employee perceptions and potential future developments.

Some initial findings from the pilot study suggest the following points:[21]

- Internal marketing is generally not a discrete activity, but is implicit in quality initiatives, customer service programmes and broader business strategies.
- Internal marketing comprises structured activities accompanied by a range of less formal *ad hoc* initiatives.
- Communication is critical to successful internal marketing.
- Internal marketing performs a critical role in competitive differentiation.
- Internal marketing has an important role to play in reducing conflict between the functional areas of the organization.
- Internal marketing is an experiential process, leading employees to form their own conclusions.

- Internal marketing is evolutionary: it involves the slow erosion of barriers between departments and functions. It has an important role in helping with the balancing of marketing and operations – a problem that is discussed under the processes element of the marketing mix.

- Internal marketing is used to facilitate a spirit of innovation.

- Internal marketing is more successful when there is commitment at the highest level, when all employees cooperate, and an open management style prevails.

Internal marketing in all its forms was recognized as an important activity in contributing to the people element of the marketing mix and in developing a customer-focused organization (see Chapter 8). In practice, internal marketing is concerned with communications, with developing responsiveness, responsibility and unity of purpose. The fundamental aims of internal marketing are to develop internal and external customer awareness and remove functional barriers to organizational effectiveness.

There are many examples of high performing companies who use internal marketing to their best advantage. SAS recognized the importance of treating employees in a caring way which customers would, in turn, appreciate. Employees are encouraged to be involved in decision making to achieve the greatest level of customer satisfaction. Thus staff are empowered to make decisions appropriate with particular customer requirements. SAS employees are trained to develop a responsibility towards the customer which is also apparent in the relationship between the company and its employees.

Likewise many retail companies have also given a high priority to internal marketing. Marks and Spencer attracts and retains high calibre personnel who become wedded to the company philosophy. All staff are trained to understand that quality is of the greatest importance for success of the company. This is reflected through all elements of their organization: in the office and store environment, in the dress code for employees, in the staff canteen and in all employee contacts with customers.

Internal marketing is at an early stage of development and one where practitioners lead academic research. While little has been codified about internal marketing practice it is clear that a consideration of internal markets is essential. Where internal marketing is concerned with the development of a customer orientation, the alignment of internal and external marketing ensures coherent relationship marketing.[22] It further plays an important role in employee motivation and retention. This area is one which should receive considerable attention over the next decade.

Processes

The processes by which services are created and delivered to the customer is a major factor within the services marketing mix as services customers will often perceive the service delivery system as part of the service itself. Thus decisions on operations management are of great importance to the success of the marketing of the service. In fact, continuous coordination between marketing and operations is essential to success in most services businesses.

All work activity is process. Processes involve the procedures, tasks schedules, mechanisms, activities and routines by which a product or service is delivered to the customer. It involves policy decisions about customer involvement and employee discretion. Identification of process management as a separate activity is a prerequisite of service quality improvement. The importance of this element is especially highlighted in service businesses where inventories cannot be stored. Banks provide a good example of this. By reconfiguring the way they deliver service through the introduction of automatic teller machines (ATMs) banks have been able to free staff to handle more complex customer needs by diverting cash only customers to the ATMs.

While the people element is critical in the services marketing mix, no amount of attention and effort from staff will overcome continued unsatisfactory process performance. This is an area where the 'smile training' approach to customer service adopted by many companies is fundamentally flawed. If the processes supporting service delivery cannot, for example, quickly repair equipment following a breakdown or provide a meal within a defined period, an unhappy customer will be the result. This suggests that close cooperation is needed between the marketing and operations staff who are involved in process management. By identifying processes as a separate marketing mix element, we recognize its importance to service quality.

If the service operation runs efficiently, the service provider will have a clear advantage over less efficient competitors. For example, a hotel reservation system which ensures that a regular customer is always given a specified room will be seen as being efficient. If there is confusion in the reservation process the customer is likely to be more critical of other services offered by the hotel.

The immediacy of production of services can be used to advantage in the tailoring of the services product to meet customer needs. For example, one holiday tour company may offer low cost trips of fixed duration to specific locations for the economy customer. Another company may offer to meet specific customer requirements of time of travel, accommodation requirements, entertainment needs and other personal specifications. The appropriate processes will depend on the market segment which has been selected, positioning decisions, and the needs of the customer.

Decision-making processes are also of relevance. Some service providers give their service deliverers the autonomy to make decisions. For example, the billing of legal services is largely within the hands of the principal working on the case. A law firm will have charge out rates for individuals within the firm but these will vary according to the real and perceived complexity of the case where value-based billing is used. It is therefore at the discretion of a principal working on the case as to the appropriate fee level to be billed. Other service providers have little room for flexibility in pricing decisions. A waiter will bill a customer for food at a published price. If the customer is dissatisfied then he or she will often have to refer to a manager or supervisor.

It can be seen from the above examples that processes of delivery and decision making are of great significance for the successful marketing of a service. Generally it can be seen that for more specialized services higher degrees of decision making are entrusted to the service provider. This allows greater customization of service. Less specialized services have a more standardized delivery system with low levels of decision making at the point of customer contact.

The choice of process can therefore be a source of competitive advantage for a services company. An airline which empowers its employees to upgrade an aggrieved businessman travelling on a low capacity flight will gain a favourable response. A restaurant which is able to cook a low fat meal on request, and to suit particular dietary requirements has a differential advantage over one which has a fixed menu.

In reviewing the role of processes two issues are worthy of particular attention: how processes can be seen as structural elements that can be altered to help achieve positioning strategy; and how marketing and operations should be managed to achieve synergy between them.

Processes as structural elements

Lyn Shostack has suggested that processes are structural elements that can be engineered to help deliver a desired strategic positioning. She points out that a process-oriented approach involves the following:[23]

- Breaking down the process into logical steps and sequences to facilitate its control and analysis.

- Taking into account the more variable processes, which may lead to different outcomes, because of judgement, choice or chance.

- Deviation or tolerance standards which recognize that processes are real time phenomena which do not perform with perfect precision, but function within a performance band.

Processes can be considered in two ways: in terms of **complexity** and in terms of **divergence**. Complexity is concerned with the nature of the steps and sequences that constitute the process, while divergence refers to the executional latitude or variability of the steps and sequences.

Services processes can be analyzed according to their complexity and divergence. Thus the keeping of account books for a corner shop is relatively low in divergence and complexity, hotel services may be low in divergence but high in complexity, and a general surgeon's work is high in both complexity and divergence. The processes in services can be depicted by developing service blueprints which reduce the processes to interactive steps and sequences. Service blueprinting is discussed in more detail in Chapter 8.

Processes can be changed in terms of complexity and divergence to reinforce the positioning or establish a new positioning. The four options are as follows:

- **Reduced divergence.** This tends to reduce costs, improve productivity and make distribution easier. It can also produce more uniform service quality and improved service availability. However, negative effects may include a perception of limited choice and a rejection of the highly standardized service.

- **Increased divergence.** This involves greater customization and flexibility which may command higher prices. This approach suggests a niche positioning strategy based less on volume and more on margins.

- **Reduced complexity.** This usually means a specialization strategy. Steps and activities are omitted from the service process and this tends to make distribution and control easier.

- **Increased complexity.** Greater complexity is usually a strategy to gain higher levels of penetration in a market by adding more services. Supermarkets, banks and building societies tend to follow this approach.

Each of the above options has their advantages and disadvantages, as well as providing opportunities to alter customers' perceptions and positioning.

Figure 6.12 provides an illustration of medical services and positional shifts that could be adopted by a general practitioner to achieve less complexity and divergence (eliminating minor operations and surgical procedures), greater complexity (retailing medical supplies and drugs)

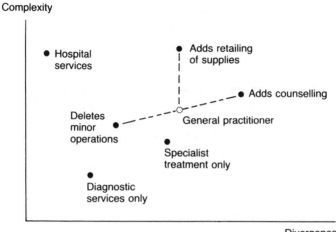

Complexity

• Hospital services

• Adds retailing of supplies

• Adds counselling

Deletes minor operations •

General practitioner

• Specialist treatment only

• Diagnostic services only

Divergence

Source: Based on G. L. Shostack, 'Service positioning through structural change', *Journal of Marketing*, vol. 51, January 1987, p. 41.

Figure 6.12   Positional shifts through structural change

or greater divergence (adding counselling services). It should be noted that changes in processes may also require a change in people. Thus processes and people are closely linked together as mix elements.

Processes have characteristics that can be deliberately and strategically managed within the marketing mix with the purpose of reinforcing or changing the positioning. Alteration of complexity and divergence is analogous to some elements of product design in the product marketing function for goods. Processes are thus a marketing mix element which can have a substantial role in reinforcing positioning and in product development.

Balancing marketing and operations

The configuration of appropriate levels of complexity and divergence for processes in order to achieve a desired strategic position has been described in the previous section. Once this has been decided it is essential to ensure a balance is achieved between market and operations perspectives.

In many manufacturing firms marketing takes a limited interest in operations other than ensuring that a satisfactory supply of products are achievable within a given cost structure. Within services, marketeers should be vitally concerned with the operations and service delivery processes. This balance becomes especially important in services which involve a high level of customer contact such as hotels, restaurants and airlines. However, many service businesses are frequently dominated by the operations function.

Lovelock points out that whilst many services firms are seeking to develop an effective marketing function to act as a bridge between the organization and the environment in which it operates, the introduction of a marketing orientation may be resisted by operations executives who see marketing as a costly add-on function.[24] They see marketing as being confined to consumer research and communications activity and resent it when marketers seek to become involved in product design and service delivery. Lovelock also provides an insightful perspective into seven key operations issues confronting high contact service firms, which are:

- Productivity improvement.
- Standardization versus customization.
- Batch versus unit processing.
- Facilities layout and design.
- Job design.
- Capacity management.
- Managing queues.

Table 6.3 summarizes these issues and shows the typical orientations of marketing and operations managers for each of them.

Each operational issue affects both market and operations. As service firms have traditionally been dominated by the operations function, the marketing staff are often relatively new to the function and do not have a full understanding of processes and operations. Marketeers need to take the initiative and fully understand the implications of the cost benefit trade offs of changes in processes and their impact on both the marketing and operations area. However, this is a necessary but not sufficient approach; the people element needs to be considered at the same time.

This is illustrated by Au Bon Pain, a chain of bakery cafes on the east coast of the USA.[25] The company made major changes in processes in an attempt to improve performance and staff turnover. Managers were empowered to make significant alterations to processes, procedures, store layout and other policies in order to develop service quality and marketing activities aimed at building stronger relationships with frequent customers.

These changes in processes have led to significant changes in people. Staff turnover in one of the Boston stores has dropped to 10 per cent per annum for entry level jobs versus an industry norm of about 200 per cent. Absenteeism has plummeted and sales soared as customers

Table 6.3 Operations and marketing perspectives on operational issues

Operational issues	Typical operations goals	Common marketing concerns
Productivity improvement	Reduce unit cost of production	Strategies may cause decline in service quality
Standardization versus customization	Keep costs low and quality consistent; simplify operations tasks; recruit low-cost employees	Consumers may seek variety, prefer customization to match segmented needs
Batch versus unit processing	Seek economies of scale, consistency, efficient use of capacity	Customers may be forced to wait, feel one of a crowd, be turned off by other customers
Facilities layout and design	Control costs; improve efficiency by ensuring proximity of operationally related tasks; enhance safety and security	Customers may be confused, shunted around unnecessarily, find facilities unattractive and inconvenient
Job design	Minimize error, waste, and fraud; make efficient use of technology; simplify tasks for standardization	Operationally oriented employees with narrow roles may be unresponsive to customer needs
Management of capacity	Keep costs down by avoiding wasteful underutilization of resources	Service may be unavailable when needed; quality may be compromised during high-demand periods
Management of queues	Optimize use of available capacity by planning for average throughput; maintain customer order, discipline	Customers may be bored and frustrated during wait, see firm as unresponsive

Source: C. Lovelock, 'Seeking synergy in service operations: seven things a marketer needs to know about service operations', *European Management Journal*, vol. 10, no. 1, March 1992, p. 24.

develop an on-going relationship with counter staff. Productivity has increased greatly and employee head count has been considerably reduced. Under the Partner–Manager programme at Au Bon Pain employees can earn double the industry average wages and a manager of an outlet can earn as much as US$160 000 a year. A complete shift has occurred in the type and quality of employee, and word of mouth creates strong demand for jobs at all levels in the chain.

The above example illustrates the critical interplay between processes, marketing and human resources. A clear understanding of configuring processes in terms of complexity and divergence, and a balance of marketing and operations activities, are key inputs for improving service systems. The reader wishing to explore this area further should refer to the references for this chapter.[26]

Customer service

A major differentiating factor for services companies is the quality of customer service. Customers are becoming more sophisticated in their requirements and are increasingly demanding higher standards of service. Many major services companies have woken up to the need to improve customer service in order to compete in today's highly competitive service environment.

In the marketing literature customer service is often seen to be part of the 'place' marketing mix element and to be concerned with the distribution and logistics component of that element. This view of customer service as the outcome of the distribution and logistics functions seeks to explain its significance in terms of the way in which services are delivered and the extent to which customers are satisfied, especially in the context of reliability and speed of delivery.

We consider, however, that several arguments support the choice of customer service as a broader and separate element of the marketing mix. These include the following:

- **Changing customer expectations.** In almost every market the customer is now more demanding and more sophisticated than he or she was, say, thirty years ago.

- **The increased importance of customer service.** With changing customer expectations, competitors are seeing customer service as a competitive weapon with which to differentiate their sales. The issue and importance of customer service has been commented on by many writers.

- **The need for a relationship strategy.** To ensure that a customer service strategy that will create a value proposition for customers is formulated, implemented and controlled it is necessary to give it a central role and not one that is subsumed in the various elements of the marketing mix.

On the basis of the criteria discussed in Chapter 2 for including ingredients as elements in the core marketing mix of a firm, these arguments give strong support to including customer service as a primary element.

A wider view of customer service

Companies often have different perspectives on customer service. Studies have shown that a range of views exists as to the definition of customer service. These include, in a service context:[27]

- All the activities required to accept, process, deliver and fulfil customer orders and to follow up on any activity that has gone wrong.

- Timeliness and reliability of delivering products and services to customers in accordance with their expectations.

- A complex of activities involving all areas of the business which combine to deliver the company's products and services in a fashion that is perceived as satisfactory by the customer and which advances the company's objectives.

- Total order entry and all communications with customers, all invoicing and total control of defects.

- Timely and accurate delivery of products and services ordered by customers with accurate follow up and enquiry response including timely delivery of invoice.

These alternative views illustrate the extent to which the meaning of customer service varies considerably from one company to another.

Our view of customer service is that it is broader than any of these definitions and that it is concerned with the building of bonds with customers and other markets or groups to ensure long-term relationships of mutual advantage which reinforce the other marketing mix elements. Customer service can thus be seen as an activity which provides time and place utilities for the customer and which also involves pre-transaction and post-transaction considerations relating to the exchange process with the customer. Some of the key elements are shown in Figure 6.13. The provision of high levels of customer service involves understanding what the customer buys and determining how additional value can be added to the offer.

Customer service is now starting to be seen in this wider context. For example, one major study views it as a separate mix element and sees the logistics function as being subsumed within the customer service activity. The results of this study show the relative importance of customer service contrasted with other elements of the marketing mix including advertising, promotion, and sales effort. Although the study focused on manufactured goods it was clear that service was a major component in these businesses examined. Customer service was generally considered important by most respondents. Overall, it was rated ahead of advertising, promotion and sales effort in terms of importance and ranked third behind product and price.[28]

However, because of the inseparability and intangibility characteristics of services that we have already discussed, customer service in service businesses is usually more important than it is in manufacturing companies. Leading service firms are recognizing that warranties, unconditional service guarantees and free phone-in advice centres such

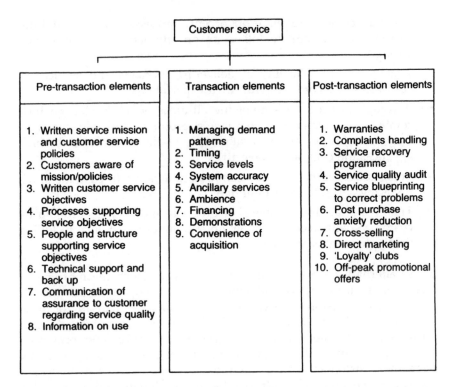

Figure 6.13 Illustration of elements of customer service

as General Electric's are critical to creating differential advantage in services marketing.

The concept of relationship marketing was explained in Chapter 2. Service companies are now realizing the importance of building upon their existing client base, increasing their understanding of client needs and creating additional cross-selling opportunities to tie their customers more closely to them. In order to do this employees need to be trained to take a pride in providing the best possible customer service to match the client's requirements. Services have a particular advantage in that very often there is close personal contact between the service provider and customer. This represents an opportunity to provide excellent customer service; but it also provides an opportunity for a poorly trained employee to destroy the relationship between the customer and the company.

Customer service strategy

Christopher has outlined four key steps in creating a customer service strategy:[29]

1. **Identifying a service mission.** We have already discussed the development of mission statements in some detail in Chapter 3. A service company should articulate its service commitment and values either within its corporate mission (for example, see DHL's mission statement in Figure 3.6) and/or in a separate customer service mission statement which reflects the company's philosophy and commitment to customer service.

2. **Setting customer service objectives.** This involves answering questions such as:

    How important is customer service compared with the other marketing mix elements?
    Which are the most important customer service elements?
    How do these vary by market segment?

    In considering levels of performance in setting these objectives, service companies need to consider the importance of service quality variables such as reliability, responsiveness, assurance, empathy and tangibles. These elements of service quality are discussed in more detail in Chapter 8.
    Customer service objectives need to be considered in the context of pre-transaction, transaction and post-transaction activities. This involves understanding what customers value, and their cost base, and developing a value proposition superior to that of competitors.

3. **Customer service strategy.** As discussed in Chapter 4, most markets consist of market segments which seek different combinations of benefits (see Table 4.4 for an example). As not all customers require the same level of service, segmentation can be a powerful means of creating appropriate service packages for each relevant market segment.
    Christopher's approach to developing a service-based strategy consists of four parts:

    identify service segments;
    identify most important products and customers;
    prioritize service targets; and
    develop the service package.

    Market research can be used to identify the key components of customers service and their relative importance, and develop service segments. Pareto analysis[30] can then be used to focus on the most important products and/or customers and specific service targets can then be prioritized. Finally, an appropriate service package can be developed which aims at offering benefits of greater value to customers than those of competing products. These benefits may be real or perceived.

4. **Implementation.** Once the most effective service package has been developed for each segment the company wishes to pursue it should then become part of an integrated marketing mix. For service-sensitive sectors such as airlines the service attributes can be used as part of the promotional campaign. British Airways and SAS are good examples of service organizations 'using service to sell'.

A service company should focus especially on customer service and keep customer satisfaction levels under constant review. Usually there is a need for a complaint system which allows unhappy customers to be identified and corrective action taken. Above all else, a service company needs to stay in touch with the changing needs of its customers in terms of customer service.

Many service companies have recognized the importance of customer service as a competitive weapon. Disney Corporation recognized the importance of customer service from the very beginning of its theme park operations. Customers visiting theme parks are treated with care by all Disney personnel to ensure they have the best possible experience during their visit. All staff at Disney, from the highest executives to the street cleaners, are trained in dealing with customers. This ensures high standards of service and instils a willingness to provide outstanding customer service at all levels.

Little has been written about customer service as a separate element of the marketing mix and in part this has been because it has been subsumed in the other elements of the mix. However, the increasing importance of customer service is obvious both from an observation of what is happening in service businesses and a study of the focus of current academic research on services. Customer service has emerged as having an important role within relationship marketing and thus deserving explicit examination as a marketing mix element in its own right.

Developing a marketing mix strategy

We have now considered seven elements of the services marketing mix. Each of these marketing mix elements interact with each other and they should be developed so that they are mutually supportive in obtaining the best possible match between the internal and external environments of the organization. In developing a marketing mix strategy service marketers need to consider the relationships between the elements of the mix.

It has been pointed out that there are three degrees of interaction between the marketing mix elements:[31]

- **Consistency**, where there is a logical and useful fit between two or more elements of the marketing mix.
- **Integration**, which involves an active harmonious interaction between the elements of the mix.
- **Leverage**, which involves a more sophisticated approach and is concerned with using each element to best advantage in support of the total marketing mix.

Thus effective relationship marketing is based on the choice and design of marketing mix elements that are mutually supportive and leveraged together so that synergy is achieved. This implies that people, processes and customer service should be seen as crucial additional elements of services marketing mix.

Each of the elements of the marketing mix and their subelements need to focus on supporting each other in terms of consistency, integration and leverage, reinforcing the positioning and delivery of the service quality required by the market segment (or segments) that are targeted. This is illustrated in Figure 6.14.

In developing a marketing mix strategy we need to consider the impact of each marketing mix element on the market segments selected. This implies ensuring that there is:

- A fit between the marketing mix and each target segment.
- A fit between the marketing mix and the company's strategic capabilities, emphasizing its strengths and minimizing the impact of its weaknesses.
- A recognition of competitors' capabilities, which involves evading their strengths and capitalizing on their weaknesses.

To achieve this an effective marketing plan should outline how the marketing mix strategy is to be developed and implemented. This involves organizing marketing resources, deciding levels of marketing expenditure and determining the expected results; it will be the topic of our next chapter. However, before concluding this chapter, some comment should be made on how the marketing mix and marketing planning process can be applied to other market areas.

While virtually all the literature on marketing is concerned with the relationship between a company and its customers, we outlined in Chapter 2 how marketing has a role to play in the other market areas. Members of supply markets, referral markets, employee markets, internal markets and influence markets may need to be served in the

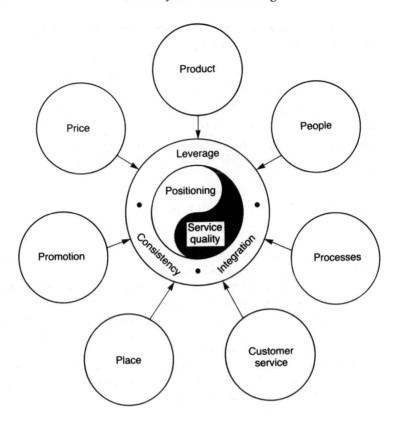

Figure 6.14 The synergistic services marketing mix

same way as customer markets. Many of the concepts described in this chapter and the next also apply to establishing and maintaining relationships with all these key markets. The concept of relationship marketing involves both a consideration of the six market areas and the creation of a bond with each market through the delivery of value satisfaction, as represented by the quality of the on-going relationship as well as the quality of service supplied. Thus consideration should be given to whether a marketing mix and marketing plan should also be developed for these other market areas.

Notes

1. T. Levitt, *The Marketing Imagination*, The Free Press, New York, 1983.
2. S. King, 'Brand building in the 1990s', *Journal of Marketing Management*, vol. 7, 1991, p. 6.

3. T. Peters, and N. Austin, *A Passion for Excellence*, Random House, New York, 1985.
4. L.L. Berry and A. Parasuramen, *Marketing Services: Competing through quality*, The Free Press, New York, 1991, p. 131.
5. B.H. Booms and M.J. Bitner, 'Marketing strategies and organization structures for service firms', in J.H. Donnelly and W.R. George, *Marketing of Services*, American Marketing Association Proceedings Series, Chicago, 1981, p. 48.
6. For further details see C.J. Easingwood 'New product development for service companies', *Journal of Product Innovation Management*, vol. 4, 1986, pp. 264–75; D.W. Cowell, 'New service development', *Journal of Marketing Management*, vol. 3, no. 3, 1988, pp. 296–312; and F.A. Johne and P.M. Pavlidis, 'Product development success in banking: a review of the literature', City University Business School, Working Paper no. 118, May 1991.
7. C.H. Lovelock, 'Developing and implementing new services' in W.R. George and C.E. Marshall, (eds.), *Developing New Services*, American Marketing Association, Chicago, 1984, p. 45.
8. C. Grönroos, *Service Management and Marketing*, Lexington Books, Lexington, Mass., 1990, pp. 73–82.
9. D.F. Channon, *Global Banking Strategy*, Wiley, New York, 1988, p. 308.
10. J.L. Heskett, W.E. Sasser and C.W.L. Hart, *Service Breakthroughs*, The Free Press, New York, 1990, p. 89.
11. For further discussion on pricing of services see: J.P. Guiltman, 'The price bundling of services: a normative framework', *Journal of Marketing*, vol. 51, April 1987, pp. 74–85; J. Dearden, 'Cost accounting comes to services industries', *Harvard Business Review*, vol. 56, September-October 1978, pp. 132–40; and G.M. Moebs and E. Moebs, *Pricing Financial Services*, Dow Jones-Irwin, Homewood, Illinois, 1986.
12. D. Cowell, *The Marketing of Services*, Heinemann, London, 1984, p. 199.
13. D.H. Light, 'A guide for new distribution channel strategies from service firms', *Journal of Business Strategy*, vol. 7, no. 1, Summer 1986, pp. 56–64.
14. J. Rathmell, *Marketing in the Service Sector*, Winthrop Publications, Cambridge, Mass., 1974, pp. 92–103.
15. W.R. George and L.L. Berry, 'Guidelines for the advertising of services', *Business Horizons*, vol. 24, no. 4, July–August 1981, pp. 52–6.
16. M. Christopher and M. McDonald, *Marketing: An introduction*, Pan Books, London, 1991.
17. W.R. George, J.P. Kelly and L.E. Marshall, 'Personal selling of services', in L.L. Berry, G.L. Shostack and G.D. Upah (eds.), *Emerging Perspectives on Services Marketing*, AMA Proceeding Series, Chicago, 1983, pp. 65–7.
18. This discussion is based on *The Director*, November 1988.
19. This section is based on Grönroos, *op. cit.*, pp. 158–60.
20. V.C. Judd, 'Differentiate with the 5th P: People', *Industrial Marketing Management*, vol. 16, 1987, pp. 241–7.
21. D. Helman and A. Payne, *Internal Marketing: Myth versus reality*, Cranfield School of Management Working Paper, Cranfield, SWP 5/92, 1992.
22. See: N. Piercy and N. Morgan, 'Internal marketing: making marketing happen', *Marketing Intelligence and Planning*, vol. 8, no. 1, 1990 and Grönroos, *op. cit.*, pp. 221–39.

23. This section is based on: G.L. Stostack, 'Service positioning through structural change', *Journal of Marketing*, vol. 51, January 1987, pp. 34–43.

24. C. Lovelock, 'Seeking synergy in service operations: seven things marketers need to know about service operations', *European Management Journal*, vol. 10, no. 1, March 1992, pp. 22–9.

25. This example is based on L.A. Schlesinger and J.L. Heskett, 'Breaking the cycle of failure in services', *Sloan Management Review*, vol. 32, no. 3, Spring 1991, pp. 25–6.

26. R.B. Chase and R.H. Hayes 'Beefing up operations in service firms', *Sloan Management Review*, Fall 1991, pp. 15–26; and W.E. Sasser, R.P. Olsen and D.D. Wyckoff, *Management of Service Operations*, Allyn and Bacon, Boston, Mass., 1978. See also references 23–5 above.

27. B.J. La Londe and P.H. Zinszer, *Customer Service: Meaning and measurement*, NCPDM, 1976.

28. B.J. La Londe, M.C. Cooper and T.G. Noordewier, *Customer Service: A management perspective*, Council of Logistics Management, 1988.

29. This section is based on M. Christopher, *The Customer Service Planner*, Butterworth-Heinemann, Oxford, 1992, Chapter 3.

30. For explanation see *ibid.*, pp. 37–9.

31. B. Shapiro, 'Rejuvenating the marketing mix', *Harvard Business Review*, September–October 1985, pp. 28–33.

7

Marketing plans for services

The marketing planning process

There has been growing emphasis on, and acceptance of, marketing planning over the past ten years. However, sadly there is little evidence of companies actually adopting, on a widespread basis, organized procedures to help them plan their marketing approach. Research suggests that British industry continues to be dominated by financial, rather than marketing, planners. The blame for the failure of many companies to become marketing oriented is firmly placed on companies using short-term, financially dominated objectives. This leads to an overemphasis on short-term sales performance and profit ratios, reflecting current market conditions, rather than a planned long-term growth strategy.

However different the concepts of physical product and the intangible service may be they are both ways of satisfying particular needs and wants. In this chapter we present a general model of marketing planning which is applicable to the service sector, we discuss specific issues and concepts relevant to service planners, and comment on the extent to which marketing planning has been adopted in service firms. In the chapter we will concentrate on the development of marketing plans for customers, although as pointed out in Chapter 2, the marketing planning approach is appropriate for developing marketing plans for all of the six relationship markets.

A number of authors have developed approaches to marketing planning; some are highly academic and are based on marketing theory, whilst others have attempted to identify demonstrated best practices in a wide range of companies, linking these to the theoretical concepts that have been developed in both strategic and marketing planning.

One approach that has proved robust in both industrial, consumer and services markets is the marketing framework developed by Malcolm McDonald.[1] This framework is used widely in both service and industrial firms in the work done through the International Marketing Planning Centre at Cranfield.

Our emphasis will be on a three-year strategic marketing plan rather than a one-year tactical plan. The planning framework has four phases which in turn break down into ten major steps. This framework follows closely that of McDonald. The major phases consist of the following:

- Strategic context.
- Situation review.
- Marketing strategy formulation.
- Resource allocation and monitoring.

These four phases together with the associated steps are shown in Figure 7.1. Although the process is shown as individual steps, many of the steps are interrelated and the process is interactive. Also the degree to which each step should be emphasized in a given service firm will depend on the size and nature of the organization.

We shall now review each of these steps.

Strategic context

The first phase of marketing planning has two steps: defining the mission and identifying corporate objectives. These are derived directly from the strategic planning process. It is necessary to identify the strategic context of the marketing plan to ensure that specific marketing objectives and strategies are directed towards the overall corporate goals of the company, rather than possibly suboptimal goals of the marketing department.

Mission

We have already explored the development of mission statements in detail in Chapter 3. The purpose of the mission statement is to give the various stakeholders of the service business a clear sense of purpose and direction. The mission statement is an important device for coordinating activities in a service organization. It provides a framework to enable staff operating in diverse parts of the organization

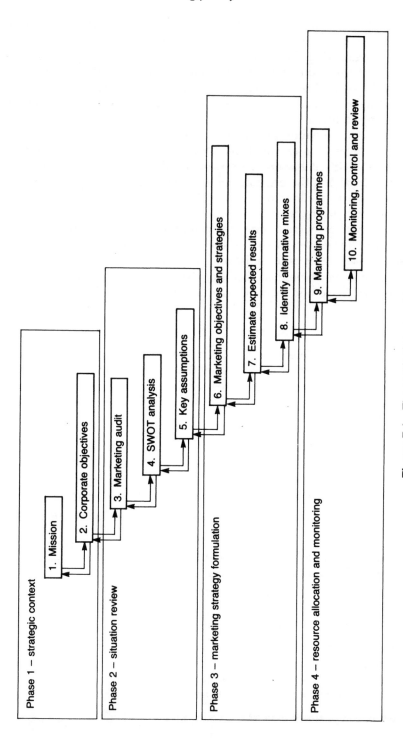

Figure 7.1 The marketing planning process

to work together in a coordinated manner towards the achievement of the overall objectives and philosophy of the enterprise. It must be stressed again that the usefulness of a mission to an organization is dependent upon the commitment that the various stakeholders, and especially internal ones, have to the mission. They can only have this commitment if the mission has been communicated clearly so it means something to them.

Whilst determination of the mission usually occurs at the corporate planning level, it is essential that this is considered in the marketing plan so that the subsequent steps of the marketing plan are focused towards achieving the organization's overall purpose. In organizations which have not adopted a formal corporate planning system, the planning activity may be marketing led, i.e. a marketing plan may be the first part of overall company planning activity. In this case the mission is developed as part of the marketing plan. If a corporate or strategic plan exists and a mission has been developed as part of this process, it is recommended that the mission is reviewed to ensure it is customer focused and meets the requirements outlined in Chapter 3.

Corporate objectives

Once a mission statement has been developed corporate objectives need to be addressed. The purpose of the corporate objectives is for the stakeholders to measure the success of the mission. Peter Drucker has identified a number of key areas in which objectives need to be set. These include the following:[2]

1. **Market standing:**
   sales and market shares by product and market segment;
   customer service levels; and
   availability of services.

2. **Innovation** – new products and services required to achieve market objectives.

3. **Productivity** – of employees and capital.

4. **Physical and financial resources:**
   buildings, equipment, processes and technology;
   capital; and
   raw materials and components.

5. **Profitability:**
   to replace assets;
   for innovation and expansion; and
   to reward risk taking and attract new capital.

6. **Manager performance and development.**

7. **Worker performance and attitude.**

8. **Public responsibility.**

Service companies need to consider in which specific areas objectives should be set for their organization. For example, in banking, objectives might be set in the following areas:

- Profits.
- Growth.
- Funds attracted.
- Market share.
- Shareholder value.
- Services mix.
- Productivity.
- Image.
- Operations.
- Diversification.
- Management development.
- Staff levels.
- Technology.
- Relationship markets.

The emphasis at this level is on corporate strategic objectives, not more tactical ones that relate to marketing or operations. To compete effectively in the market clear objectives should be set out in the areas outlined above. Corporate objectives should be attainable but require the organization to stretch itself.

Service companies approach the setting of objectives in different ways. British Airways' corporate objectives are shown in Table 7.1. In the early 1980s, British Airways regarded itself as an airline with the primary function of flying planes. It was led by objectives which stressed technical efficiency, ignoring the objective of trying to satisfy passengers needs in the best possible way. A major turnaround in profitability was brought around, in part, by modifying the objectives of the company to recognize that instead of being in the business of flying airplanes, British Airways was in fact in the business of satisfying passenger requirements.

Objectives may be qualitative (as in the case of British Airways' objectives in Table 7.1), quantitative or a combination of both. For broad statements of intent that are made public – such as in an annual report – qualitative objectives may be justifiable. However, for internal

Table 7.1   British Airways' corporate objectives

---

1. To provide the highest levels of service to all customers, passengers, shippers, travel agents and freight agents
2. To preserve high professional and technical standards in order to achieve the highest levels of safety
3. To provide a uniform image worldwide and to maintain a specific set of standards for each clearly defined market segment
4. To respond quickly and sensitively to changing needs of our present and potential customers
5. To maintain and, where opportunity occurs, expand our present route structure
6. To manage, operate and market the airline in the most efficient manner
7. To create a service- and people-orientated work environment, assuring all employees of fair pay and working conditions and continuing concern for their careers.

---

company purposes objectives should be established on the basis of actual targets to be achieved within a specific time period. Note that some organizations such as British Airways have a hierarchy of objectives. The top level strategic objectives may lack specific quantification and can be adopted as more permanent goals that are publicly communicated in conjunction with the mission. In support of these broad strategic objectives, closely related and specific quantified objectives, to be achieved within a given time frame, need to be set. For example, one financial services company expressed corporate objectives which included:

- **Profit** – doubling group earnings by 1996.

- **Growth** – trebling group revenues by 1997.

- **Innovation** – launching at least one major new product or service every two years which will represent at least 10 per cent of total sales revenue within two years of launch.

- **Corporate Image** – achieving unprompted awareness improvement, as measured by external research, from 30 per cent to 50 per cent by 1995.

- **Services** – increasing consultancy and value added services from 15 per cent to 25 per cent of total revenues by 1995.

- **Staff** – containing staff turnover to less than 60 per cent of industry average for the sector.

The setting of corporate objectives alongside the mission statement provides an opportunity to test the appropriateness of both the corporate objectives and the mission statement. The corporate objectives, in addition to comprehensively covering the areas identified, should also enable evaluation of whether the corporate mission is being achieved. Thus the mission statement and corporate objectives are tightly interlinked. Each key element of the mission statement should be covered by a corporate objective. In most cases these will be quantified so that the extent to which they are accomplished can be objectively assessed.

The marketing planning process starts with these two steps derived from the strategic planning process. These are the direct responsibility of top management rather than the marketing function. Nevertheless a marketing plan cannot be written properly until these elements of the overall corporate strategy are defined.

Service companies with relatively homogeneous services operating in a local market need to develop only one marketing plan at the corporate level, whilst those companies with considerable diversity of services and markets need to develop divisional or subunit marketing plans, which are then integrated into an overall marketing plan. Clear objectives, both corporate and marketing, are key elements of the marketing plan. The basic purpose of the marketing plan is to provide an integrated framework for implementing the marketing strategy and sub-programmes, in order to achieve these specified objectives.

Situation review

The situation review phase consists of three steps: the marketing audit, situation analysis and the identification of key assumptions in the marketing plan.

Marketing audit

The purpose of the marketing audit is to gather all the data necessary to determine how the business can succeed in each marketing segment in which it chooses to compete. The data collected are usually split between the external appraisal of the environment in which the company operates, and an internal assessment. Both sets of data need to be related to the current situation and the likely future trends. The categories of analysis for a marketing audit are shown in Figure 7.2 and include:

- Environmental analysis.
- Competitive analysis.
- Market analysis.
- Company analysis.

The external appraisal involves both an analysis of the general environment and the specific environment of the company's markets. The environmental influences are out of the control of any company. Each area will obviously affect different industries in different ways, presenting a variety of opportunities and threats. The specific environment relating to the industries and markets with which the firm is associated, requires a detailed knowledge of market trends, customers and competitors.

The marketing audit involves a comprehensive and systematic examination and analysis of the four categories outlined in Figure 7.2. Whilst most of the major headings within these categories are included in this figure, a service organization will need to develop its own relevant list of headings. Each of these headings can then be further subdivided into constituent parts. For example, the economic variable can be subdivided into elements such as inflation, income, prices, savings, credit restrictions, etc. For more detailed marketing audit check-lists see Wilson,[3] Naylor and Wood,[4] and McDonald.[5]

A marketing audit should be selective but comprehensive. Remembering the Pareto principle will help: 20 per cent of the data will give 80 per cent of the information needed for a satisfactory marketing audit. Not all marketing audit factors will be relevant. For example, for a bank operating in the UK, religion will have little relevance. However, for a bank operating in Northern Ireland religion might have some relevance; and for a bank operating in Saudi Arabia an understanding of the implications of Islamic laws as they relate to banking is critical.

An internal assessment should look at the company from a general view but each individual market segment or each service should be assessed on its own merits. In Chapter 4 we described a range of criteria by which market segmentation could be undertaken. These included segmentation by:

- **Common characteristics:**
  demographics and socioeconomics;
  psychographics; and
  geography.

- **Consumer responses:**
  benefits;
  promotional response;
  loyalty; and
  service.

Market segmentation is a critical part of marketing planning as it is focused on the achievement of differentiation. Its purpose is to target a

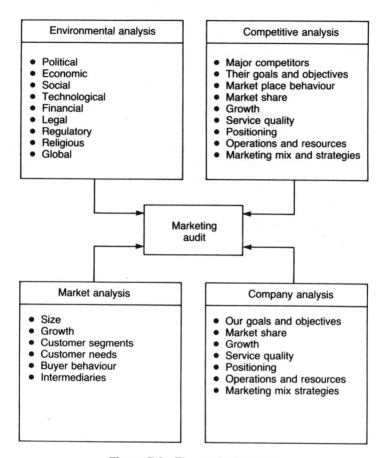

Figure 7.2 The marketing audit

group of consumers who are most likely to be attracted to the company's services. Marketing planning is the key to successfully reaching this target segment. This gives direction and focus to the marketing activity and permits marketing objectives and strategies to be developed and measured with respect to each target segment.

There are many analytical tools and techniques which can be used to look at both services and customers in a logical, structured manner. Several of the most important of these are the following:

- The product/service lifecycle.
- The Boston Consulting Group matrix.
- The multiple factor portfolio matrix.

We will now examine each of these.

Lifecycle analysis

The concept of lifecycles in marketing is usually applied to products. The same broad principle applies to services. The lifecycle concept suggests that if a product is introduced to the market successfully, then the buying momentum will increase over time. Consumers will try the product or service and will then often repeat their purchase decision. They will also pass on information about the product to others who will in turn test the product. However, the market will eventually reach its peak. As the market matures, more firms will enter the marketplace and price wars will be common as competition develops for market share. Eventually some firms will be forced out of the market, with only the most competitive producers surviving. The market will gradually decline as alternative products are offered and fashions change. The market may be sustained for a small volume, with few producers, although this will often be difficult as economies of scale can be lost. An illustrative lifecycle for a product or service is shown in Figure 7.3, together with the typical contribution to company profitability at each stage.

The study of lifecycles in services has been relatively limited to date. One study of multi-site service firms life cycles identified five stages, as follows:[6]

1. **Entrepreneurial stage** – where an innovator offers a service at a limited (often one) number of locations.

2. **Multi-site rationalization** – where successful service entrepreneurs add a limited number of locations.

3. **Growth** – where a period of rapid expansion occurs, often through the purchase of competitors or franchising or licensing arrangements.

4. **Maturity** – where growth is reduced through factors such as changing demographics, increased competition, or changing customer tastes.

5. **Decline/regeneration** – there is either successful extension of the service concept or the service firm enters a stage of decline and degeneration.

The concept of lifecycles is useful but it should be kept in mind that not all products or services follow this pattern indiscriminately. The concept is helpful as a descriptive model in trying to understand the dynamics of markets; it has less value as a predictive model.

In considering lifecycles we also need to differentiate between the service category, the service subcategory and the service brand. For example, if we take the overnight accommodation market (a service category) it may have a considerably different lifecycle from that of

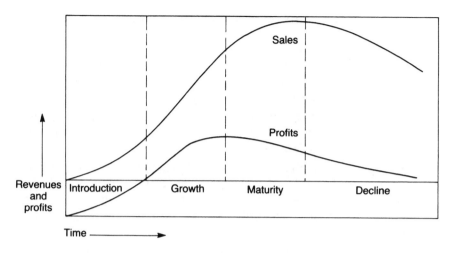

Figure 7.3 Lifecycle for a product or service

business hotels or motels (a service subcategory). Individual brands, e.g. Stakis Country Club Hotels (a service brand) within a category may also exhibit their own individual lifecycle behaviour.

The stage where the service firm is in its lifecycle needs to be considered carefully and the firm should be aware of different issues and problems it may encounter during the different lifecycle stages. This process can focus attention on future sales patterns and will have a bearing on the elements within the marketing mix.

The Boston Consulting Group matrix

Service firms need to consider how the different products and services they offer should be managed to ensure that they will meet their objectives, by balancing sales growth, cash flow and risk. As the various services offered grow or decline and as the markets change, then the overall nature of the company's portfolio will change. A portfolio model to assist in this has been developed by the Boston Consulting Group (BCG). Portfolio models present, in the form of a matrix, the external and internal environment of the firm. The difference between the BCG portfolio approach and the multiple factor portfolio approach is in the factors used to measure market attractiveness and business strength (or competitive position). The BCG matrix is based on the assumption that two factors, market growth rate and relative market share, are the critical factors in determining business success, whilst the multiple factor matrix uses many factors to describe market attractiveness and competitive position.

The BCG portfolio model uses market share as a proxy for competitive position, and growth rate of a business as a proxy for market attractiveness. The matrix consists of four boxes and is shown in Figure 7.4.

- The lower left box, known as a 'cash cow', represents the position of a service business having a high market share and low growth rate. Such businesses generate high positive cash flows.
- The lower right box represents a low market share and low growth rate – designated a 'dog' business. Such a service business, will generate little net cash flow.
- The upper right box, designated a 'question mark', is a service business with a low relative market share in a high growth rate industry. Such businesses consume large amounts of cash and generate only small amounts, so tend to have a strong negative cash flow.
- Finally, the upper left box represents a business with a high growth rate and a high market share – a 'star'. Such service businesses tend to generate and consume large amounts of cash so have a relatively neutral cash flow.

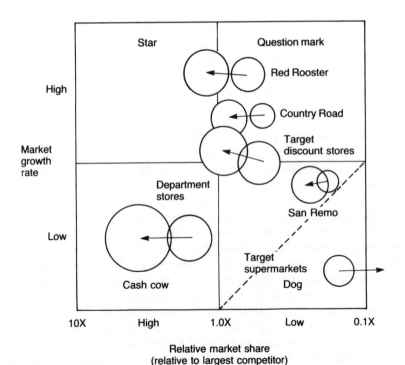

Figure 7.4 Illustrative portfolio matrix for a retailer

Proponents of the BCG matrix propose that certain generic strategies should be considered in the management of a company's portfolio of businesses. They suggest that the positive cash flow from cash cows should be used to selectively fund question mark businesses to enable their successful transition to the left hand side of the matrix to become stars. Over time such star businesses mature and their growth rate decreases; star businesses then become cash cow businesses which can be used to fund more businesses in the question mark category. They also suggest that dog businesses should be divested. Considerable caution is needed, however, in determining whether or not it is appropriate to follow a generic strategy.

Figure 7.4 shows an illustrative representation of a portfolio matrix for the Myer Group, an Australian retailer, in the early 1980s. Following the suggested sequence, one possible strategy for Myer would have involved taking funds from its cash cow businesses, its department stores, and using them to develop its newly acquired businesses such as Red Rooster, Country Road and Target discount group. Target supermarkets, a dog business, was divested from Myer's portfolio. The matrix presents both the position of these businesses when the analysis was undertaken and the projected position several years ahead.

The multiple factor portfolio matrix

A number of multiple factor portfolio matrices have also been developed. The best known are those developed by McKinsey and Co/General Electric and by Shell (the directional policy matrix). These approaches are often described as the 'market attractiveness/business strength matrix'. These portfolio approaches are more complex than the BCG matrix and are based on a view that the factors determining market attractiveness and competitive position in different markets vary considerably and that factors have to be chosen using criteria appropriate to specific markets. Illustrative factors which could be used for determining market attractiveness and competitive position are shown in Table 7.2. The position in which a product is placed on the matrix is based on factors that reflect competitive position and market attractiveness, the relative weighting and scores allocated to each factor. It should be noted that in addition to factors that are scored quantitatively, like those in Table 7.2. social, political or legal factors may also have to be acceptable on a pass/fail basis.

The overall scores are then plotted along the axes of the matrix and their positions can be used to consider the appropriate strategy. As with the BCG matrix, generic strategies or guidelines of invest/grow, selective funding, or divest/harvest are suggested as shown in Figure 7.5. Some managers may consider that the multiple factor approach

Table 7.2 Ranking market attractiveness and competitive position

		Weight	Rating (1–5)	Value
	Overall market size	0.20	4	0.80
	Annual market growth rate	0.20	5	1.00
	Historical profit margin	0.15	4	0.60
	Competitive intensity	0.20	2	0.60
Market	Technological requirements	0.15	4	0.60
attractiveness	Inflationary vulnerability	0.05	3	0.15
	Environmental impact	0.05	3	0.15
	Total	1.00		3.90
	Market share	0.10	4	0.40
	Share growth	0.15	2	0.30
	Service quality	0.10	4	0.40
	Brand reputation	0.10	5	0.50
	Network	0.05	4	0.20
Competitive	Promotional effectiveness	0.05	3	0.15
position	Operations capacity	0.05	3	0.15
	Operations efficiency	0.05	2	0.10
	Relative cost position	0.15	3	0.45
	Staff availability	0.15	3	0.45
	Managerial personnel	0.05	4	0.20
	Total	1.00		3.30

adds unnecessary additional complexity, whilst others may regard it as more realistic and practical than the BCG approach.

Portfolio approaches enable managers to consider their appropriate objectives and strategies for the business in accordance with its potential. At the same time, portfolio approaches have limitations and should be used with caution. Amongst the problems identified in using them are the difficulties of defining business boundaries, and the support the portfolio concept gives to the idea that market share is always positively correlated with return on investment. This ignores the reality of the high return on investments achieved by small niche players in many markets. On balance, portfolio models have a positive part to play in marketing planning, if the dangers are understood. Portfolio techniques are especially helpful in undertaking the marketing audit and presenting data from it in a summary form.

SWOT analysis

Once all the data from the marketing audit have been amassed it is necessary to evaluate the company's internal position in relationship to its particular strengths and weaknesses, compared with the opportunities and threats presented by the external environment. This analysis

	Strong	Medium	Weak
High	Protect position • Invest to grow at maximum rate • Concentrate effort on maintaining strength	Invest to build • Challenge for leadership • Build selectively on strengths • Reinforce vulnerable areas	Build selectively • Specialize around limited strengths • Seek ways to overcome weaknesses • Withdraw if indications of sustainable growth are lacking
Medium	Build selectively • Invest heavily in most attractive segments • Build up ability to counter competition • Emphasize profitability by raising productivity	Selectivity/manage for earnings • Protect existing programme • Concentrate investments on segments where profitability is good and risk is relatively low	Limited expansion or harvest • Look for ways to expand without high risk; otherwise, minimize investment and rationalize operations
Low	Protect and refocus • Manage for current earnings • Concentrate on attractive segments • Defend strengths	Manage for earnings • Protect position in most profitable segments • Upgrade services • Minimize investment	Divest • Sell at time that will maximize cash value • Cut fixed costs and avoid investment meanwhile

Market attractiveness

Business strength

Fig. 7.5 Multiple factors matrix – generic strategies

is well known as SWOT (strengths, weaknesses, opportunities and threats) analysis and provides a familiar, easily understood, and structured device for developing ideas for the future. The purpose of the SWOT analysis is to separate out the meaningful data in the marketing audit and to discover what management must do to best satisfy its customers in each market segment in which it chooses to compete.

The fundamental objective of SWOT analysis is to identify those trends, forces and conditions which have a potential impact on the formulation and implementation of the company's marketing strategies. This is a most important step for two reasons. Firstly, any change in the external environment can have a profound impact on a company's markets. By anticipating and taking action the company will be better placed to take advantage of these changes. Secondly, it provides an opportunity to establish which are the most important aspects to evaluate. The total amount of environmental information that could be collected in the marketing audit is enormous, and clearly the company must identify those aspects which are of the greatest significance and make a decision as to how much detail and accuracy is required. This stage lays the foundations for identifying the key marketing objectives and strategies.

Many writers refer to the fact that certain factors within the company can be viewed as both strengths and weaknesses, and that certain motherhood phrases are easily used, although they do not mean anything. In this situation we need to take our analysis further; we need to ask more questions to find out exactly which aspects are strengths and which are weaknesses. If it seems difficult to determine whether a factor is a strength or a weakness, the factor can usually be subdivided into a series of bullet points which can be grouped into those relating to strengths and those relating to weaknesses.

The same processes should be used to view the opportunities and threats in the environment which are relevant to the particular areas or segments chosen. This part of the analysis usually leads to the identification of information and market research needs.

When all four areas of the SWOT have been identified there must be a decision about what they mean, and what actions are needed to enhance or deal with the particular aspects. Table 7.3 shows a simplified and partial SWOT analysis for an off-shore bank. It provides a framework for dealing with the SWOT analysis, and ensuring action. SWOT analysis that does not suggest either specific objectives to be set or actions to be taken is of limited use.

Table 7.3 Partial SWOT analysis for a bank

SWOT element	Which means	So actions needed are
Strengths		
• Highly qualified personnel	Better competence, efficiency and professionalism	1) Promote capability to customers 2) Staff retention programme 3) Incentive package for high achievers
• Larger deposit base	Better cost base Higher average deposit	1) Leverage our cost base 2) Automate faster to reduce costs further 3) Emphasize upper and middle tier in bank positioning
Weaknesses		
• Low branch management discretion	Constant time wasting in referring back to head office	1) Develop improved credit scoring at branches 2) Better training and communications equipment 3) Wider delegation to branch managers 4) Approval hot line at head office
• No overseas representation	Lost business in key areas	1) Urgent feasibility study for Toronto, New York, Los Angeles and Sydney

Table 7.3 *continued*

SWOT element	Which means	So actions needed are
Opportunities		
• New industrial development	Increased bank lending in commercial area	1) Recruit new industrial team 2) Initiate industrial development seminar for branch managers 3) Representation on government and industrial bodies
• Exploit customers' financial needs	More income from investment and taxation advisory services Attraction of new customers to bank	1) Initiate study of new business opportunities 2) Survey of banks in four designated countries 3) Market research to confirm initial service concepts 4) Introduce new services
Threats		
• Increased competition	Loss of market share	1) Strengthen marketing department 2) Develop a marketing plan 3) Improve customer service 4) Emphasize no hidden charges 5) More aggressive advertising
• Key staff loss	Need to counter aggressive poaching by private sector firms and foreign financial institutions	1) Improve pay/conditions 2) Introduce staff satisfaction survey 3) Lobby to move outside civil service pay structure 4) Internal marketing initiative

Key assumptions

The last step in the situation review stage is the identification of key assumptions. The purpose of key assumptions is to identify, from the situation review, those factors that will be critical to the success or failure of the marketing strategy. We need to consider key assumptions as a whole, and also as they relate to each market segment.

Key assumptions are an estimate of the future operating conditions for the marketing plan. They may influence both its formulation and implementation. They represent your estimate of conditions that may occur. Key assumptions might include the following:

- Changes in gross national product.
- Interest rates.

- Inflation rates.
- Status of economy.
- Anticipated demand levels.
- Regulatory changes.
- Etc., etc.

It is useful to categorize key assumptions under general headings, such as the general economy, the service sector, the company's markets, etc. Emphasis should be placed on those key areas which are likely to influence the achievement of marketing objectives.

When key assumptions are identified, we suggest that they should be presented in two columns. The first column lists the key assumptions under appropriate headings. The second column lists 'implications for marketing plan'. This forces the marketing planner to consider what key assumptions mean for the plan. Key assumptions that are critical, and which could change, may need to form the subject of contingency plans, which will be discussed later in this chapter.

Marketing strategy formulation

The next phase of the marketing plan is marketing strategy formulation. This is perhaps the most important aspect of the whole process. The first step of this phase is setting the marketing objectives and strategies. It is necessary to set realistic and achievable objectives for the company's major services in each of its markets. If this phase is not carried out comprehensively then all plans and strategies will lack the cohesion and focus necessary to make them successful. This is followed by development of marketing strategies, estimating expected results and identifying alternative marketing mixes.

Marketing objectives and strategies

The purpose of setting marketing objectives and marketing strategies is to target the profit, revenue and market share necessary to satisfy the mission, and how an integrated marketing mix is to be devised to achieve the target for each segment. A **marketing objective** is a precise statement, which outlines what is to be accomplished by the service company's marketing activities; **marketing strategies** are the means by which marketing objectives are achieved.

It has been suggested that after a SWOT analysis and the explicit statement of assumptions about conditions affecting the business, the process of setting objectives should in theory be comparatively easy. However, this is not often the case, possibly because companies do not typically approach the task in a logical way. A logical sequence is as follows:

- **Level 1** – setting broad marketing objectives. The broad marketing objectives would be concerned with long-term profitability, and be related to the organizational objectives. By setting broad objectives, communications will be enhanced and the marketing personnel will be motivated by a set of expectations.

- **Level 2** – setting objectives for key result areas. Here the objectives are defined more precisely and specifically relating to different functions.

- **Level 3** – setting subobjectives to support the broad objectives. These objectives would be based on sales volume goals, geographic expansion, and service offering extension.

This approach closely follows that of management by objectives. Marketing objectives help us determine where we want to go and also provide yardsticks by which we can measure our performance. A marketing objective should meet several criteria, and should be:

- **Relevant** – the marketing objective should be relevant in relation to the corporate mission and objectives.
- **Specific** – it should focus on clear and identifiable goals.
- **Measurable** – the objective should be quantified.
- **Time bound** – it should have an achievement date attached to it.
- **Challenging** –objectives should be realizable, but should stretch people in achieving them.
- **Focused** – marketing objectives should focus on issues relating to both the markets, and products and services, which the company wishes to address.

The last point above is especially important. Many managers fail to differentiate between marketing objectives and marketing strategies when developing marketing plans. Marketing objectives relate to the target markets and are concerned with achieving sales of products and services to them. In Chapter 3 we discussed the four broad options in terms of markets, and product and services. These options, derived from the Ansoff matrix that was shown in Figure 3.2, were market penetration, market development, service development, and diversification. These four categories represent the domains to be considered in achieving the marketing objectives for the company's future development and growth.

Whilst some writers discuss marketing objectives in much broader terms, we support the view that it is only by selling something (a product or service) to someone (a market) that firms remain in business; thus marketing objectives should be solely about products and markets.[7] Other marketing elements such as pricing, advertising, site location, processes, etc., are marketing strategies that help in achieving these objectives. These are the marketing mix elements. Note that broad decisions about the overall services to be offered will be determined at the marketing objectives level, whilst specific decisions about individual products and services lines will be made at the marketing strategies level. The relationship between marketing objectives and marketing strategies for a service organization are shown in Figure 7.6.

Marketing objectives with respect to target markets will be covered within two areas:

● **Current users** – here the marketing strategy has two key tasks, the retention of existing customers, and obtaining additional business from existing customers.

● **New users** – for new users the marketing strategy is concerned with both increasing trial of the services offered, and then obtaining repeat usage of the services, after the initial trial, on an on-going basis.

We should recognize that it is, in general, far more profitable and less expensive to sell to existing customers than to sell to new customers. The issue of customer retention has particular strategic importance and will be discussed further in Chapter 8.

Marketing objectives are usually set in terms of expected achievement from the specific market segments to be addressed, as well as the total. They typically cover the following areas:

● Sales volume.
● Market share.
● Profit.
● Customer objectives.
● Marketing costs.

One very useful technique to help consider the difference between existing profit and sales performance, and the target required as a result of the process of objectives setting, is 'gap analysis'. This analysis is used to identify the extent to which existing marketing

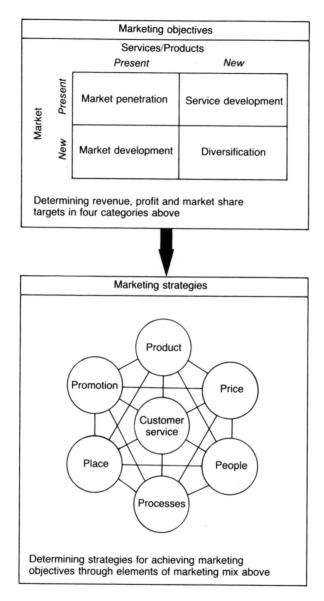

Figure 7.6 Marketing objectives and marketing strategies

strategies will fail to deliver the desired level of performance required by the service organization. Gap analysis is most commonly used to measure gaps in revenue and profitability but can be used for other measures such as earnings per share, return on investment, etc. Figure 7.7 shows a gap analysis, in this case between revenue objectives and a

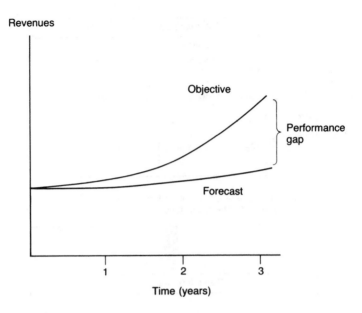

Figure 7.7　Gap analysis

forecast. This type of gap indicates the magnitude of the task to be achieved by the marketing strategies and its timing. Gap analysis stimulates the search for new marketing strategies to achieve objectives.

Marketing objectives and strategies to achieve the target include:

- **Increased productivity:**

    sales force effectiveness;
    more efficient distribution;
    pricing strategies; and
    improved customer service.

- **Increased revenues from:**

    market penetration;
    service development;
    market development; and
    diversification.

- **Decrease expenses:**

    scale related (experience curve benefits in operations or marketing); and
    non-scale related.

Each of these elements needs to be systematically investigated to determine its potential impact on reducing the identified gap.

The identification of appropriate marketing strategies will be helped by a consideration of the following:

- The Ansoff matrix.
- Gap analysis.
- Existing policies and capabilities.
- The service firm's distinctive competences.
- Portfolio analysis and associated generic strategies.

The marketing strategies will be made up of three elements: the means, the timetable and the resources necessary to ensure successful achievement of the objectives. Marketing strategies outline the broad plan of action to achieve marketing objectives through the marketing mix elements. These elements consist of the service product, price, service availability, promotion, people, processes and customer service. (The marketing mix was examined in detail in the previous chapter, so we will not repeat the discussion here.)

An integrated combination of elements is used to satisfy customers' needs. The thrust of the marketing mix involves creating the differential advantage which makes the service firm's offer different (in a way preferred by the segments that are targeted) from its competitor's offer. Differential advantage results from creating a marketing strategy that delivers the desired positioning, as discussed in Chapter 5.

Estimate expected results

The purpose of examining the expected results from the marketing strategies is to ensure that marketing strategies will actually deliver the desired marketing objectives. Once the strategies have been determined and decisions made about the marketing mix to be developed in each market segment, the financial implications of the strategies need to be evaluated. Estimating expected results involves the detailed review of sales revenues, cost of sales, marketing costs, operating expenses and overhead expenses. The financial analysis should show that the strategy will produce anticipated results. If it does not, the marketing strategies need to be examined further to see how they can be redeveloped to achieve the desired results. This, like all steps in the marketing plan, may be an interactive process.

Pro forma income statements are a useful tool to help in the estimation of expected results. Pro forma income statements are forecasts of both operating expenses and demand. When introducing new products, in times of economic difficulty or with increased competitive activity, demand levels may be less certain. It may therefore be appropriate to develop three alternative income statements based on pessimistic, most likely and optimistic levels of demands. Various forecasting techniques such as extrapolation, regression analysis, jury of executive opinion, test marketing and consumer surveys can be used to help identify likely demand patterns.

Forecasting in service businesses is a critical issue because of the perishability dimension discussed in Chapter 2. As services cannot be kept in inventory a number of variables need to be considered at this point. These include the capacity of the service company, costs in extending capacity, moving to multi-site locations, and changing demand patterns through differential pricing. Whilst demand and capacity planning is complicated in manufacturing businesses, the characteristics of services make it much more difficult in the services sector. Quantitative and qualitative market research and forecasting methods are helpful in making decisions regarding estimation of expected results.

Identify alternative mixes

The purpose of considering alternative mixes is to discover if more effective marketing strategy is available before the plan is implemented. A marketing manager may evaluate a number of mixes, using both analysis and trial and error, to find the best use of available resources before selecting the final marketing mix to be implemented as marketing programmes.

If the proposed marketing strategy is not likely to achieve the desired level of expected results other marketing strategies will need to be considered. However, even if the proposed marketing strategies will deliver the desired results, alternative marketing mixes should also be investigated to determine if they can deliver improved results. Thus several further sets of marketing strategies should be developed and evaluated.

It is at this point that plans should be formulated to cover anticipated lower or higher levels of demand. It should be noted that the response curves of different marketing mixes may vary considerably. Levels of demand and revenues, as well as availability of a marketing budget, need to be considered carefully. Some illustrative examples of response curves are shown in Figure 7.8.

At this point the development of contingency plans should be considered. Although it is not possible to establish a contingency plan for every eventuality, the impact of different sets of assumptions should be assessed and, where appropriate, broad contingency plans should be developed. Contingency plans are alternative plans that will need to be considered if certain situations arise. These can be divided

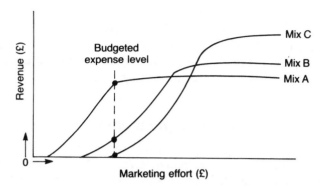

Figure 7.8 Response functions for three different services marketing mixes

into defensive reactions – reactions to threats which had not been anticipated; and offensive reactions – reactions to opportunities that had not been identified.

In spite of the best intentions, changed situations can force marketing strategies to be altered. Changes in economic conditions, the emergence of new competitors, events such as the Gulf War, the changes in the Eastern Bloc and natural disasters, can create the need to modify marketing plans. It is easy to be lulled into a sense of complacency when things are working well. Service managers need to discipline themselves to allow the necessary time to develop contingency plans.

It is especially important that responsibility for determining why variances have occurred, and for taking appropriate corrective action, is delegated to specific managers to ensure that plan objectives can be met by marshalling the necessary resources and by taking positive and timely action.

Resource allocation and monitoring

The last phase in the marketing planning process has now been reached, and involves two final steps: marketing programmes; and monitoring, control and review. It is at this point that we become more concerned with the one-year time horizon. For a three-year strategic marketing plan a fairly brief outline of the marketing budget supporting agreed strategies is included in this section. However, for a one-year operating marketing plan, we become involved in a detailed and more specific breakdown of subobjectives, schedules, budgets and resource allocation.

A one-year operational marketing plan has to be developed after the preparation of a three-year strategic marketing plan. A carefully constructed series of sequential one-year plans will assist management in developing the detailed programmes which support the marketing mix strategies needed to achieve marketing objectives.

Marketing programmes

The purpose of marketing programmes is to ensure that all firm's staff know what actions they are responsible for, and to determine how to allocate the physical and financial resources available to secure success in each market segment.

The programmes for a one-year marketing plan need to be detailed and cover such activities as the responsibility attached to personnel, schedules, budgets, forecasts, priorities and resource allocations and commitments. Each element of the marketing mix will have its own specific programme, which in turn will be linked to specific marketing objectives. Marketing programmes are similar to marketing objectives and strategies in that they should do the following:

- Have an established timetable and be able to be carried out within a defined period of time.
- Identify the resources needed to carry them out.
- Provide for monitoring and control of performance.

Programmes should clearly describe the resources needed to accomplish marketing strategies and the time horizon in which to achieve them. Programmes provide the opportunity for all members of the marketing team to work together in an integrated manner. It is this team work that will develop a spirit of cooperation between sales, marketing and other functional areas.

Programmes involve the development of a practical, fact-based, results-oriented approach which acts as a road map for management to implement marketing activities over the forthcoming year. A detailed marketing budget needs to be prepared at this point to ensure that the necessary budget allocations, reflecting projected costs, are available to carry out the programmes.

Although many companies base their programmes on last year's budget plus some percentage increase, this form of budget setting is not recommended. A zero-based approach, based on a clear understanding of objectives to be achieved and likely market conditions and opportunities, is advocated.

Marketing managers responsible for developing marketing plans need to develop skills in building programmes, and in identifying and defending the necessary marketing budgets to carry them out. Close liaison with the accounting function is essential to ensure that detailed monthly (or other desired frequency) data are available in a form that will permit meaningful review against targets on an on-going basis.

A further task within programmes is the development and prioritization of important marketing activities, subactivities and tactics. This involves the preparation of marketing programme timetables to help ensure that key tasks are accomplished on schedule. Regular exception reports or programme activity timetables should be used to ensure that progress in accomplishing tasks is on track. Regular monthly review meetings are an important mechanism for ensuring that programmes progress to schedule.

Programmes should be based on the following:

- Good communications to the various groups, inside and outside the company, who have existing or potential involvement in the implementation of the marketing plan is essential. This includes sales people, marketing staff, operations management, R&D as well as agents and intermediaries.

- Accurate market research to determine customer needs and service quality compared with competitors.

- Internal marketing to support the external marketing activity.

Marketing programmes need to be closely linked with the final stage of monitoring, control and review to ensure success.

Monitoring, control and review

The purpose of monitoring, controlling and reviewing the programmes and strategies is to ensure that the short-term strategies are working to bring the business consistently towards achieving its long-term objectives and mission. Some service companies are very weak at setting quantified marketing objectives; it is thus extremely difficult to monitor and control their achievement. By contrast other service firms are extremely rigorous in their monitoring and control procedures. One diversified service firm requires all business units to report detailed weekly results into an electronic mailbox so that performance and profitability is calculated on a weekly basis. Some retailers have similar performance details available at the close of each day!

One US study of seventy-five organizations in various services and manufacturing sectors illustrates the inadequate control systems in many firms. It found that:[8]

1. Smaller companies had poorer control procedures than larger ones. They made a poorer job of setting objectives and monitoring them.
2. Less than half the companies knew the profitability of individual products, and one-third had no system set up to identify weak products and services.
3. Almost half failed to analyze costs, evaluate advertising or sales force call reports, or compare their prices with competitors'.
4. Many companies had long delays – four to eight weeks – in obtaining control reports, and even then their reports were sometimes inaccurate.

Monitoring and control of marketing plans should be an integrated and natural part of the marketing planning process.

Clearly the level of detail and frequency of reporting will be determined by the type of service company and the sector in which it operates. Some service firms will want weekly or even daily performance figures, whilst others can control operations adequately with monthly or quarterly reports.

As the marketing plan is implemented, performance criteria for measuring the performance of marketing efforts will need to be determined. These will be derived from the longer-term marketing objectives as well as the more detailed shorter-term programmes. Typical performance measures to be monitored and controlled, by market segment where appropriate, include the following:

- Revenues.
- Market share.
- Marketing costs.
- Overhead costs.
- Profits.
- Return on investments.
- Consumer attitudes.
- Sales force productivity.
- Advertising effectiveness.
- Complaints.
- Customer retention.
- Etc.

Accurate, timely and appropriate control data do not arrive by accident. Information systems and reporting procedures need to be established to ensure that the right information is issued to the right person at the right time, and in a useful format. The essential element of monitoring and control is to ensure the development of information systems that meet the need of the marketing management charged with taking corrective action.

Marketing planning success comes from a willingness to learn and experiment and to adapt the planning system to the company and its circumstances. The ten-step marketing planning framework represents a practical and proven approach for developing and refining a services marketing plan.

Marketing planning and services

In the previous sections of this chapter we have reviewed the ten key steps in the marketing planning process. In this final section of the chapter we briefly review the available studies on the use of marketing planning by UK service companies and make some summary comments on usage and implementation of marketing planning by them.

The need for effective planning in the services sector has been recognized for a considerable time. For example, in 1975 Chisnall pointed to the growing services sector and emphasized that in planning services, whether in the commercial or public sector, greater attention should be given to input/output measurement to ensure that the resources used reflected their contribution to organizational output.[9] He described the relevance of marketing techniques such as marketing research, strategic planning and marketing control in helping to improve service orgaizations, but argued there was an institutionalized reluctance in service industries to develop a more realistic and market-oriented approach to marketing planning.

There is little evidence that service organizations in the UK have adopted marketing planning on a widespread and successful basis. Hooley and his colleagues found 43 per cent of their sample of 529 service firms claimed to have both one-year and long-range marketing plans but noted that their mailed surveys were skewed towards more successful companies.[10] No attempt was made to formally evaluate how comprehensive the marketing planning was.

Greenley examined marketing planning practices in fifty UK service companies from a number of industries including banking and insurance, freight forwarding and transport, management and market research consultancy, technical consultancy, catering, television entertainment, and the gas and electricity sector.[11] He compared the headings of the major sections of marketing plans of these service companies with typical lists of headings suggested in the marketing literature, which included situation analysis, objectives, strategy statements, action programmes, budgets and control. The study found that although 62 per cent of the companies claimed to have prepared a marketing plan, only 12 per cent disclosed a format considered to be comprehensive. (This represented 25 per cent of the total companies prepared to divulge the contents of marketing plan headings). Greenley concluded that marketing planning in service companies was not well developed.

The research on marketing planning in service organizations follows more general research on marketing planning. Despite the obvious and theoretically supported benefits of marketing planning, a review of empirical studies that have been carried out suggest that as little as 10 per cent of companies actually use a comprehensive marketing planning process and even the most optimistic of these studies only offered a figure of 25 per cent.[12] A further study of 385 medium and large firms in the UK found that just over half attempted to prepare marketing plans. Of these, 73 per cent were described 'as having a go at the entire marketing planning model whilst doing little of it comprehensively'.[13]

There has been a growing emphasis on and acceptance of marketing planning over the past ten years and an increasing body of literature focusing on the preparation of marketing plans has started to appear. However, it is true to say that development of marketing planning in UK industry appears to lag that in the USA.

Effective marketing is greatly enhanced by a well thought through and developed marketing plan. Such a plan helps bring all the service firm's marketing activities together in an integrated manner and helps create a positive future for the firm. However, a number of problems create barriers to the development and implementation of marketing planning. These include the following:[14]

1. Confusion between tactics and strategy.
2. Isolating the marketing function from operations.
3. Confusion between the marketing function and the marketing concept.
4. Organizational barriers.
5. Lack of in-depth analysis.
6. Confusion between process and output.
7. Lack of knowledge and skills.
8. Lack of a systematic approach to marketing planning.
9. Failure to prioritize objectives.
10. Hostile corporate cultures.

Several of these barriers including (2), (3), (4) and (10) relate to the need for a more marketing-oriented culture in service organizations. In our view two issues are critical to successfully implementing marketing in a service firm: firstly, the development of a comprehensive and integrated marketing plan; and secondly, the development of a marketing-oriented and customer-focused attitude throughout the service organization. The latter is the topic of our next and final chapter.

Notes

1. M. McDonald, *Marketing Plans: How to prepare them, how to use them,* Butterworth-Heinemann, oxford, 2nd edn., 1989.
2. P. Drucker, *The Practice of Management,* Harper and Row, 1957.
3. A. Wilson, *Marketing Audit Check Lists,* McGraw Hill, Maidenhead, 1982.
4. J. Naylor and A. Wood, *Practical Marketing Audits,* Associated Business Programmes, 1978.
5. M. McDonald and J. Leppard, *The Marketing Audit,* Butterworth-Heinemann, Oxford, 1991.
6. W.E. Sasser, R.P. Olsen and D.D. Wyckoff, *Management of Service Operations: Text, cases and readings,* Allyn and Bacon, Boston, Mass., 1978, pp. 534–66.
7. M. McDonald, *op. cit.,* pp. 118–19.
8. P. Kotler, *Marketing Management,* Prentice Hall, Englewood Cliffs, 7th edn., 1991, p. 709.
9. P. Chisnall, 'Marketing planning in a service economy', *Long Range Planning,* December 1975, pp. 43–52.
10. G.J. Hooley, C.J. West and J.E. Lyme, *Marketing in the UK: A Study of current practice and performance,* Institute of Marketing, Cookham, Berks, 1984.
11. G. Greenley, 'An overview of marketing planning in UK service companies', *Marketing Intelligence and Planning,* vol. 1, no. 3, 1983, pp. 55–68.
12. J.W. Leppard and M. McDonald, 'Marketing planning and corporate culture', *Journal of Marketing Management,* vol. 7, 1991, pp. 213–35.
13. L. Cousins, 'Marketing plans or marketing planning?', *Business Strategy Review,* Summer 1991, pp.35–54.
14. M. McDonald, 'Ten barriers to marketing planning', *Journal of Marketing Management,* vol. 5, no. 1, 1989, pp. 1–18.

8

The customer-focused service organization

Customer service, quality and marketing

Over the past five years we have asked over six hundred senior and middle level executives from large and medium sized service companies two questions. The first question is: 'Does your chief executive claim your organization is marketing driven, marketing oriented or customer focused?' Approximately 75 per cent of managers claim that these or similar terms are used by their chief executives. We then asked a second question: 'What percentage of the top 200 service organiations in this country are **really** customer focused?' The average response is between 10 and 20 per cent. It seems that there is an enormous gap in the services sector between those organizations that claim to be customer focused and those which actually are.

In this final chapter we address the issue of developing a customer-focused service organization. We commence by briefly discussing the relationship between customer service, quality and marketing. We then proceed with an examination of the nature of service quality. We then highlight the role of customer retention and explore several techniques for improving service quality. Finally, we examine an approach for developing a marketing orientation in service organizations.

The issue of improving customer focus concerns the relationship between the service organization and its customers. This involves consideration of the relationship marketing approach outlined in Chapter 2. The relationship marketing concept brings quality, customer service and marketing together.[1] The specific linkages between these elements are shown in Figure 8.1.

Just as many service companies have not been as successful as they

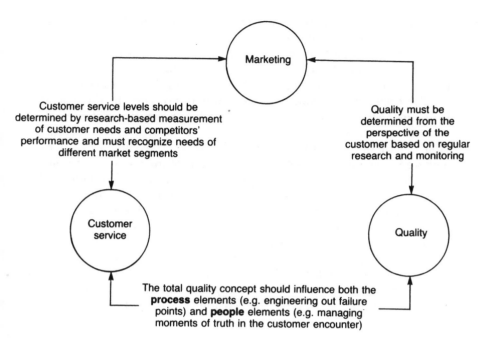

Figure 8.1 Linkages between quality, customer service and marketing

would have liked in achieving a customer focus through their marketing activities, so success has evaded many organizations in their quality and customer service initiatives. Despite the advent of total quality management, BS5750, ISO9000 and, in the USA, the Baldridge Awards, many service organizations continue to address quality primarily on the basis of an operations perspective concerned with conformance to specifications, rather than customer-perceived quality. Amongst many service companies there is also a frustration with their quality initiatives.

In the 1980s enormous attention was directed at the area of customer service. Customer service programmes have been embraced widely within the services sector, notably in financial services, airlines and the hospitality sectors, but also in many other service industries including public utilities. However, despite considerable efforts and expenditure the results have been slow to materialize in all but a small percentage of programmes. Research by consulting firm Bain & Company shows that whilst 92 per cent of chief executives agreed that customer service was extremely important and 77 per cent of service industry companies had customer service programmes in place, only 27 per cent of them had achieved significant results from these programmes.

Customer service initiatives *should* be closely related to quality initiatives; but this is not always the case. Our view is that this failure is attributable to a lack of company-wide alignment of purpose towards meeting customers' requirements. The traditional transactional approach towards marketing must bear much of the responsibility for this. Relationship marketing is concerned with bringing the three areas of customer service, quality and marketing into much closer alignment. In many service organizations there is little linkage and integrated management of these three crucial elements. The situation can be compared to three spotlights on a stage: each of the areas may receive attention, but on a separate individual basis. Thus three spotlights fall on the stage as shown in Figure 8.2. Relationship marketing is concerned with bringing all three elements much closer together as shown in Figure 8.3, where all the three spotlights are focused on, as nearly as possible, the same area.

Research supports the argument that customer-focused quality is a highly important strategic dimension. The PIMS (Profit Impact of Market Strategies research work) study undertaken by the Strategic Planning Institute shows relative customer-perceived quality as a

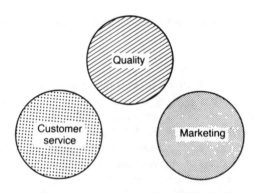

Figure 8.2   Unaligned marketing

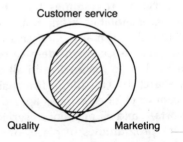

Figure 8.3   Integrated services marketing

critical variable in profitability. One study concluded: 'In the long run, the single most important factor affecting a business unit's performance is the quality of its products and services, relative to those of competitors.'[2]

Figure 8.4 shows the relationship between relative customer perceived quality, market share and profitability, measured as return on investment (ROI). The findings suggest that **relative perceived quality** is more positively related to a company's financial performance than such things as relative market share. While a combination of high relative market share and superior relative quality yield the highest ROI (38 per cent) it is possible to obtain good profitability (21 per cent ROI) with a low relative market share through high relative quality.

The research shown in Figure 8.4 refers to both products and services. More recent research which has focused on fifty high performers in the service industry confirms this relationship. The research showed that high-quality service providers earned an average return on investment of 8 percentage points above low-quality service providers.[3]

Quality can be viewed from two perspectives – internal and external. Internal quality is based on conformance to specifications. External quality is based on relative customer-perceived quality. The important point is that quality must be seen from the customer's viewpoint, not

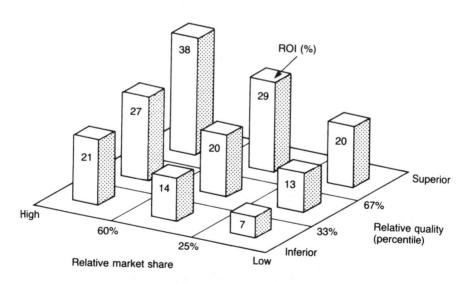

Source: R. D. Buzzell and B. T. Gale, *The PIMS Principles: Linking Strategy to Performance*, The Free Press, New York, 1987.

Figure 8.4 Impact of quality and market share on profitability

the company's. It is essential that quality is measured from the customer's perspective, not from what managers within a company think their customers' views are!

Several reasons have been identified as to why it is unsafe to rely on managerial opinions of customer perceptions. These include the following:

- Management may not know what specific purchase criteria users consider important. For example, customers frequently identify key purchase criteria not identified by management. Even when the criteria are correctly identified, management may misjudge the relative importance of individual criteria . . . sometimes by a factor of 3:1.

- Management may misjudge how users perceive the performance of competitive products on specific performance criteria. These differences in perception of performance may exist for the most basic of criteria.

- Management may fail to recognize that user needs have evolved in response to competitive product developments, technological advances, or other market or environmental influences.[4]

Service quality

A model has been developed by Parasuraman and his colleagues[5] which helps identify the gaps between the perceived service quality that customers receive and what they expect. The model identifies five gaps:

1. Consumer expectation – management perception gap.
2. Management perception – service quality expectation gap.
3. Service quality specifications – service delivery gap.
4. Service delivery – external communications to consumers gap.
5. Expected service - perceived service gap.

Gap 5 is the service quality shortfall as seen by the customers, and gaps 1–4 are shortfalls within the service organization. Thus gaps 1–4 contribute to gap 5. These gaps are shown in Figure 8.5 and will now be reviewed.

The first gap is the difference between consumer expectations and management perceptions of consumer expectations. Research shows that financial service organizations often treat issues of privacy and

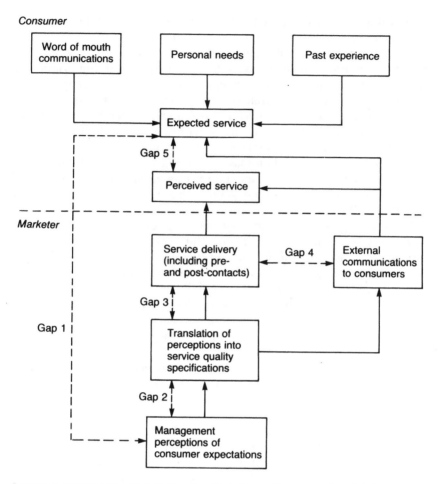

Source: A. Parasuraman, V. A. Zeithaml and L. L. Berry, 'A conceptual model of services quality and its implications for future research', *Journal of Marketing*, vol. 49, Autumn 1985.

Figure 8.5 The service quality gap model

confidentiality as relatively unimportant, whilst consumers considered them very important. In the UK we are poor at complaining when receiving bad service – instead we tend to take our custom elsewhere. If management does not receive feedback about poor service quality then it will believe that it is meeting customer expectations.

The second gap is the difference between the management perceptions of consumer expectations and service quality specifications. Managers will set specifications for service quality based on what they believe the consumer requires. However, this is not necessarily accurate. Hence many service companies have put much emphasis on technical quality, when in fact the quality issues associated with service delivery are perceived by clients as more important.

The third gap is the difference between service quality specification and the service actually delivered. This is of great importance to services where the delivery system relies heavily on people. It is extremely hard to ensure that quality specifications are met when a service involves immediate performance and delivery in the presence of the client. This is the case in many service industries: for example, a medical practice is dependent on all the administrative, clerical and medical staff performing their tasks according to certain standards. The practice may set a goal of a maximum fifteen-minute patient waiting time – however, a doctor who keeps a poor schedule will upset the system for all of the staff.

The fourth gap is the difference between service delivery intention and what is communicated about the service to customers. This establishes an expectation within the customer which may not be met. Often this is a result of inadequate communication by the service provider. An example from British Rail illustrates this gap. A timetable suggests to customers that trains will arrive at a fixed time; this is often not the case. Further, British Rail appears to only apologize to customers for late arrival of trains if they are seriously behind schedule, i.e. over five minutes late.

The fifth gap represents the difference between the actual performance and the customers' perception of the service. Subjective judgement of service quality will be affected by many factors, all of which may change the perception of the service which has been delivered. Thus a guest in a hotel may receive excellent service throughout his stay, apart from poor checking out facilities. But this last experience may damage his entire perception of the service, changing his overall estimation of the quality of the total service provided from good to poor.

The gap model outlined above provides a framework for developing a deeper understanding of the causes of service quality problems, identifying shortfalls in service quality and determining the appropriate means to close the gaps.

Service quality is concerned with the ability of an organization to meet or exceed customer expectations. The measure of performance is perceived service quality. It has been argued that the quality of a service has two important components:

- **Technical quality** – the outcome dimension of the service operations process.

- **Functional quality** – the process dimension in terms of the interaction between the customer and the service provider.

A question illustrates the difference between these two dimensions of quality. Ask someone who has just left hospital, or had their car serviced, 'Did you receive good service?' Provided the patient is well and the car runs smoothly it is difficult to judge the technical quality of the operation – will the patient continue to be well? – or the car service – was the differential oil changed and the oil filter replaced? Often a decision about quality is determined by the functional quality dimension – how the patient was treated in hospital or whether the garage staff were courteous, and the car clean and ready at the time promised.

These two dimensions of service quality highlight the subjective nature of quality assessments. Generally clients of professional service firms such as accounting and law firms have difficulty in distinguishing between good and outstanding technical quality of the service; thus judgements are often made on the subjective basis of how the client was treated.

Image also has a role to play here. Several writers suggest that technical and functional quality determine much of the corporate image which, in turn, can influence the customer's perceived service quality. In recent years research has been undertaken in an effort to understand the factors which influence service quality. Work by Berry and his colleagues has identified five key areas as follows:[6]

- **Tangibles** – the physical facilities, equipment, appearance of personnel.

- **Reliability** – the ability to perform the desired service dependably, accurately and consistently.

- **Responsiveness** – willingness to provide prompt service and help customers.

- **Assurance** – employees' knowledge, courtesy, and ability to convey trust and confidence.

- **Empathy** – caring, individualized attention to customers.

Table 8.1 provides details of the research on users of services in four service sectors: credit cards, repair and maintenance, long distance telephone and retail banking. Whilst the study showed all the above factors were important two findings were especially important. Firstly, tangibles have a relatively less important score than other dimensions. Secondly, reliability emerged as by far the most important dimension across all the services studied. Service recovery should also be included within the reliability dimension.

The message for the service provider seems clear. Above all, be reliable and deliver what is promised to the customer. Further, human performance plays a critical role in the customer's perception of service

Table 8.1　Importance of service quality dimensions in four service sectors

	Mean importance rating on 10-point scale*	Percentage of respondents indicating dimension is *most* important
Credit card customers (n = 187)		
Tangibles	7.43	0.6
Reliability	9.45	48.6
Responsiveness	9.37	19.8
Assurance	9.25	17.5
Empathy	9.09	13.6
Repair and maintenance customers (n = 183)		
Tangibles	8.48	1.2
Reliability	9.64	57.2
Responsiveness	9.54	19.9
Assurance	9.62	12.0
Empathy	9.30	9.6
Long-distance telephone customers (n = 184)		
Tangibles	7.14	0.6
Reliability	9.67	60.6
Responsiveness	9.57	16.0
Assurance	9.29	12.6
Empathy	9.25	10.3
Bank customers (n = 177)		
Tangibles	8.56	1.1
Reliability	9.44	42.1
Responsiveness	9.34	18.0
Assurance	9.18	13.6
Empathy	9.30	25.1

*Scale ranges from 1 (not at all important) to 10 (extremely important).
Source: L. L. Berry, A. Parasuraman and V. A. Zeithaml, 'The service-quality puzzle',
Business Horizons, September–October 1988, p. 37.

quality. Three of the five dimensions outlined above – assurance, empathy and response – result directly from human performance; and a fourth factor, reliability, is also largely dependent on human performance.[7]

Improving service quality

How do we improve service quality performance? A starting point is to consider the options for service quality improvement. Figure 8.6 suggests emphasis may be placed on structural, operational, visionary or strategic factors. This figure shows the emphasis placed on these

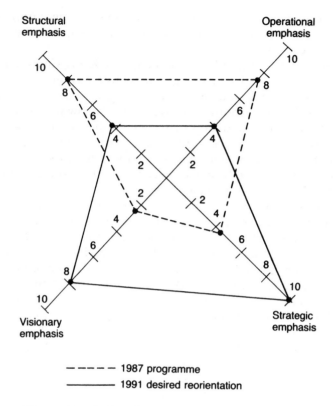

Figure 8.6 Options for service quality improvement

factors by a major British bank and an assessment of how emphasis should be changed. This framework is a useful one for considering where emphasis should be placed in a service quality improvement initiative.

A number of techniques can be used to help improve service quality. Some of these have been used in manufacturing, whilst others have been developed or refined in the context of the services sector. In this section we introduce two of the more important.

Benchmarking

In order to evaluate service quality it is important to establish a firm's performance relative to its competitors. Benchmarking involves looking for the best ways to achieve competitive advantage. It stems from the Japanese practice of *dantotsu* which means striving to be 'best of the best'. The company's products, service and practices are continually compared with the standards of the best competitors and identified industry leaders in other sectors. By observing and measuring the best within and outside the industry it is possible to improve the performance of the company.

An early firm to adopt benchmarking was Xerox Corporation who use it as a major tool in gaining competitive advantage. Xerox first started benchmarking in their manufacturing activities and focused on product quality and feature improvements. Following success in the manufacturing area, Xerox top management directed that benchmarking be performed by all cost centres and business units and by 1981 it was adopted company wide. A key feature of the process was a high level of employee involvement, which was the principal means by which benchmarking was implemented.

There was some initial difficulty in performing benchmarking in departments such as repair service, maintenance, invoicing and collection and distribution until it was recognized that the 'product' was, in fact, a process. It was this process which needed to be considered and compared with that of external organizations. By examining competitors' processes step by step and operation by operation, Xerox were able to identify the best methods and practices in use by their competitors. Benchmarking has now come to be recognized as appropriate for any area of a company's operations. Table 8.2 illustrates the wide range of areas where benchmarking can be undertaken.

At the start benchmarking activities were concentrated solely on competitors until it became clear that Xerox's objective in achieving superior performance in each business function was not being met by only looking at competitors' practices. The task of creating competitive advantage involves outperforming, rather than matching, the efforts of competitors. This, together with the obvious difficulties in gaining all the information required on competitors, and their internal systems and processes, led to the adoption of a broader perspective on benchmarking. Thus benchmarking was expanded from a focus solely on competitors to a wider, but selective, focus on the products and services of top performing companies regardless of their industry sector.

This broader perspective on benchmarking has been used as a major element in increasing both quality and productivity. Collaboration between firms in non-competing industries offers significant opportunity in this regards. For example, in the Xerox logistics and distribution unit annual productivity doubled as a result of benefits obtained from non-competitive collaborative benchmarking.

Xerox is now seen as a world role model for quality improvement with some 240 different functional areas of the company routinely involved in benchmarking against comparable areas. Service companies can identify improvement opportunities from a wide range of different industries, not just services.

Table 8.2   Potential areas for competitive benchmarking

You can create benchmarks for practically any part of your operation. This list of potential benchmarking categories can help measure your operations against your competitors'.

Advertising	**Marketing**
Expenditure	Product/brand strategy
Themes	Market share
	Pricing
Sales	
Terms	**Financials/costs**
Sales force	Profitability
• Size	Overhead
• Structure	Return on assets
• Training/experience	Return on equity
• Compensation	Net worth
• Number of calls	Margins
• Turnover rates	Cash flow
Sales literature	Debt
Proposals	Borrowing capacity
• Style	
• Structure	**Plant/facility**
• Pricing	• Size
Accountability	• Capacity
Cross-selling	• Utilization
	• Equipment costs
R&D	Capital investments
Patents	Integration level
Staff	Quality control
R&D dollar/sales	Fixed and variable costs
Government contracts	
	Organization
Customers/products	Structure
Sales/customer	Values
Breadth of product line	General goals
Product quality	Expected growth
Average customer size	Decision-making level
	Controls
Distribution	
Channels used	**Strategic plans**
Middlemen	Short term
	Long term
	Core business/expansion or stability
	Acquisitions

Source: Strategic Intelligence Checklist, Fuld & Co. Inc., Cambridge, MA.

The value chain concept described in Chapter 5 can be especially useful in benchmarking competitors. By systematically comparing processes within each element of the firm's value chain with those of competitors, areas for improvement can be identified. Such systematic comparisons can make transparent areas where competitive advantage can be secured. Benchmarking can be used to improve service quality or reduce cost. For example, it may show where competitors are subcontracting activities out to third parties at prices lower than it would cost them to perform the activities themselves.

Service blueprinting/process analysis

Service companies who wish to provide high levels of service quality and customer satisfaction need to understand all the factors which may influence customer perception. 'Blueprinting' or service process analysis is a concept which breaks down the basic systems and structures of an organization in order to develop a greater understanding of the service process. The approach requires the identification of all of the points of contact between the customer and the service provider. Possible breakdowns in the service encounter can then be identified. These can then be acted upon and improved, thereby improving service quality.

Several approaches to carrying out a blueprinting exercise have been suggested:[8]

1. **Blueprinting/cycle of service analysis.** The concept suggests that each contact with the customer is a 'moment of truth', each being an opportunity to either increase or decrease customer satisfaction. The customer's perception is a continuous stream of experiences which together determine the service quality. The company will very often not perceive the service in this way as their employees are constrained in their view by the particular part of the overall service with which they are involved. The blueprinting/cycle of service approach enables a service company to shift its employees' perception so that they have a better understanding of the customer's experience.

2. **Value chain analysis.** This important analytical tool was described earlier. It involves breaking down each of the activities of a firm into its various activities, and showing where value is added for its customers. Each activity can be analyzed to determine its contribution to customer satisfaction and service quality.

3. **Storyboarding.** This concept was developed by the Walt Disney organization in designing its theme parks in order to engineer the customer experience and ensure the greatest customer satisfaction. When a film is made, each scene is outlined in advance, using a

series of sketches arranged in a sequence known as a storyboard. Similarly, sketches of each contact a customer has with the service provider can be used to identify points for improvement in customer service. Scenes can be rearranged to improve the quality of the customer experience.

The best known methodology is the blueprinting approach suggested by Shostack. An example of a service blueprint is shown in Figure 8.7. Blueprinting involves flow charting the service delivery system of each aspect, including both front office and back office, of the service process, via the following steps:[9]

- The first step in blueprinting is to chart all the components of a service so that the service can be seen clearly and objectively.
- The next important task in blueprinting is the identification of fail points, i.e. the areas most likely to cause execution or consistency problems.
- Setting execution standards is the third critical part of the blueprint. These represent the main quality targets for the service. Execution standards not only define the costs of a service, they also define the performance criteria and tolerances for the completion of each service step.
- Finally, the manager must identify all of the evidence of the service that is available to the customer. Each item that is visible to the customer represents an encounter point where service interaction will occur.

Blueprinting involves identification and management of encounter points, pressure points, or moments of truth. 'Moments of truth' is a term used by Jan Carlzon of SAS to describe every interaction between the service provider and the customer. In the context of an airline these include the following:[10]

1. Customer calls the airline for information.
2. Customer books the flight with the airline representative.
3. Customer arrives at airport counter.
4. Customer waits in line.
5. Ticket agent invites customer to the counter.
6. Ticket agent processes payment and issues ticket.
7. Customer goes looking for the departure gate.
8. Gate agent welcomes customer to the flight, validates boarding pass.

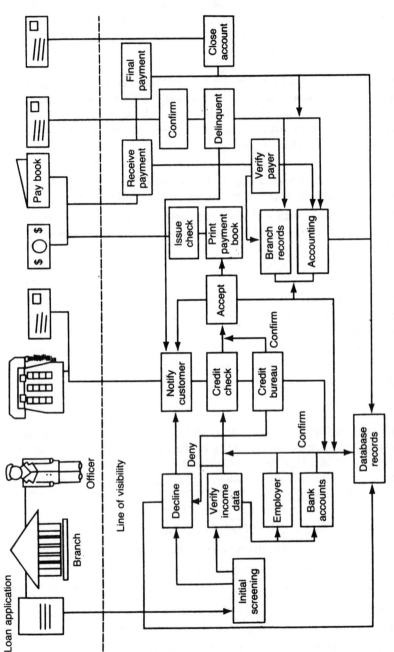

Figure 8.7 Service blueprint for instalment lending

Source: based on G. L. Shostack, 'Service positioning through structural change', *Journal of Marketing*, vol. 51, January 1987, pp. 34–43.

9. Customer waits in departure lounge for flight to depart.
10. Boarding agent takes customer's ticket and invites customer on board.
11. Customer boards aeroplane, is greeted by flight attendant.
12. Customer looks for his/her assigned seat.
13. Customer looks for a place to stow carry-on luggage.
14. Customer takes his/her seat.
15. Etc., etc.

Each moment of truth represents a point where the service provider demonstrates elements of both functional and technical quality in different proportions. Every individual moment of truth adds to or detracts from the overall image of the service provider. Every moment of truth reinforces the quality of service or lack of it.

British Airways has consciously adopted this approach in redesigning its products. When Club World – its Business Class – was relaunched, British Airways sought to **increase** the moments of truth. Following their customer service and quality initiatives their confidence in their quality performance was increased. Increasing customer contact could thus enhance customers' overall perception of service quality. For example, meals had previously been served on one large tray; now each course was served separately, and this increased the moments of truth.

The blueprint is a valuable tool in helping visualize the service process, understanding what can go wrong and setting performance standards for improvement in service quality. This helps not just with solving potential problems but also in designing ways to deal with service recovery. Many service companies are now becoming interested in using blueprinting methods to improve their service quality.

Customer retention

We introduced the relationship marketing ladder of customer loyalty in Chapter 2 and pointed out how many service companies place too much emphasis on winning new customers and too little on retaining existing customers. Service firms have, in the past, been very preoccupied with attempting to attract new customers. Advertising campaigns have been designed around the theme of 'Try us or you will miss out because we are better than the competition'. However, a body of recent research points to the strategic importance of customer retention. Companies are now starting to develop specific programmes in order to increase customer loyalty.

Research by consulting firm Bain & Co. suggests that there is a high correlation between customer retention and company profitability.[11] They have developed a formal approach to customer retention that points out the tremendous profit potential that can be unlocked. Customer retention improvement of just a few percentage points can have a dramatic impact on improvement of profitability. Figure 8.8 illustrates the profit impact of a 5 per cent increase in customer retention for a range of service businesses. These examples show improvement in profitability, in net present value terms, from 20 per cent to 85 per cent.

There are many reasons why retaining customers is so profitable. These include the following:

- Retained business.
- Sales, marketing and set up costs are amortised over a longer customer lifetime.
- Increased expenditure over time.
- Repeat customers often cost less to service.
- Satisfied customers provide referrals.
- Satisfied customers may be willing to pay a price premium.

All these reasons may not apply for a particular service business, but overall they represent a significant profit improvement opportunity for most service sector companies.

The ability to achieve an increase in customer retention is related to the existing level of retention. Bain & Co. have identified how average retention rates vary by industry in the USA:

- Credit cards – 92 per cent
- Financial services –83 per cent.
- Industrial distribution – 80 per cent.
- Auto services – 75 per cent.
- Mail order – 63 per cent.

Although it may not be easy to obtain a 5 per cent increase in retention in businesses such as credit cards, on the basis of the statistics in Figure 8.8, even a 1 per cent improvement in this area could yield a 15 per cent increase in profitability.

Probably the most important issue for companies to remember is that a customer who is lost through dissatisfaction with a service provider will be gained by a competitor. Keeping customers is therefore a key strategic issue for service companies to address. Customer retention

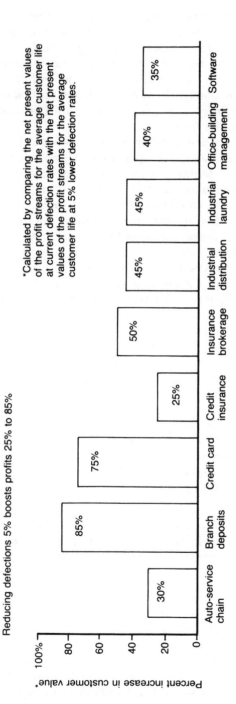

Reducing defections 5% boosts profits 25% to 85%

*Calculated by comparing the net present values of the profit streams for the average customer life at current defection rates with the net present values of the profit streams for the average customer life at 5% lower defection rates.

Percent increase in customer value*

Auto-service chain	Branch deposits	Credit card	Credit insurance	Insurance brokerage	Industrial distribution	Industrial laundry	Office-building management	Software
30%	85%	75%	25%	50%	45%	45%	40%	35%

Source: F. F. Reichheld and W. E. sasser, Jr., 'Zero defections: quality comes to services', *Harvard Business Review*, September–October 1990, pp. 105–11.

Figure 8.8 Profit impact of a 5 per cent increase in customer retention

helps predict the profitability of the company, and therefore provides an excellent management tool for considering the success of quality and customer service programmes. Retaining a customer allows a company to develop the relationship and encourages both repeated, and increasingly frequent, buying activity. Bain & Co. have found that there is a link between quality, client retention and profitability. This is not surprising – customers who are satisfied with the quality of the service will be loyal to the firm.

Marketing activity directed at retaining customers can be expensive, and needs to be closely evaluated against results. The most successful retention programmes segment customers into different levels of profitability, and this helps identify the type and frequency of marketing activity which should be directed at them. Obviously the most profitable customers are the most valuable, and these are the ones on whom the most resources should be spent.

In order to establish why clients defect, Bain & Co. use 'root cause of defection analysis'. The process involves looking behind the apparent reason for defection and establishing the real reason for a problem. Thus a long wait in the post office may be due to inadequate staffing, lack of training, lack of motivation of staff, complicated form filling, lack of administrative organization or a variety of other reasons. The end result is a dissatisfied customer who may see the problem as inadequate numbers of staff. The real cause, may, however, be very different. Root cause analysis gets to the real reasons for service quality failure.

An additional benefit of effective retention programmes is employee satisfaction. The quantified results of retaining customers can act as a great motivator to staff and increase their willingness to perform excellent customer service. A total quality management approach which strives to attain a service free of defects should be considered an essential part of a retention programme.

The relationship marketing programme

There are many excellent examples of firms which have used relationship marketing programmes to develop customer loyalty. One successful example is the air miles scheme. Consumers enrol in the programme, and manufacturing and service companies award Air Miles to programme members when they purchase specified products and services. When consumers earn enough mileage credit, they are able to obtain travel awards. The programme has been very successful in the United Kingdom, with over 3.5 million members joining since 1988 and over 120 sponsoring companies participating. It was launched in the USA in 1992. Sponsoring companies increase customer loyalty to their organization with this programme. The programme is heavily advertised by individual sponsors as they promote the programme to their customers. It permits Air Miles and its sponsors to have communication with customers – by bimonthly statements and a book of incentives of sponsors' offers. Sponsors can prospect for new customers through placing entries in the special offers book. The secret of the success of the programme is the interactive relationship between the sponsor and the customer.

American Express is one of the best examples of the success of relationship marketing. 'Membership has its privileges', sets the scene for the special nature of the relationship between the card holder and the company. The approach is not dissimilar to that of many business to business marketing programmes. American Express, however, has learned that the quality of customer service is essential to building a successful relationship with customers. Customers are considered a 'private audience', and any opportunity to offer special service and individual attention is acknowledged as producing added value in customers' eyes. Thus additional benefits to the card, such as 'Buyers Assurance' and 'Global Assist' (worldwide emergency assistance) and 'Special Events' (tickets for events blockbooked in advance and available only to card members) are important additional services offered to customers.

The shift to relationship marketing involves a focus away from one-off sales, which involve limited commitment to the customer. Relationship marketing recognizes the importance of repeat buying, and a high level of commitment to the buyer.

To attract the attention of front-line staff, as well as junior and middle management, we need to dramatize the importance of relationship marketing. Tom Peters has captured the importance of this in his phrase 'treat the customer as an appreciated asset'. He suggests that his US$1500 a month Federal Express account is worth US$360 000 in terms of future custom.[12] He points out that US$1500 per month is US$18 000 per year or US$180 000 over ten years – assuming a ten-year customer life time. Based on the concept of a satisfied customer becoming a supporter or an advocate (described in Chapter 2), he or she will generate considerable additional business through word of mouth recommendation. A conservative estimate of one referred acquaintance becoming a lifetime (ten-year) user of Federal Express increases the value of the current user from US$180 000 to US$360 000. Assuming that the Federal Express courier calls upon forty customers with a similar average sized sales this represents a customer portfolio of 40 × $360 000 or US$14 million of business to Federal Express!

Viewing customers as an appreciating asset with the monetary values described above, suggests that a different approach should be taken by front-line staff dealing with customers. It supports a much more serious approach to hiring, training and compensation of a staff member who is managing, say, a US$14 million portfolio of business.

Whether an organization is selling financial services, airline seats or pizza pies it should consider the role of customer retention as part of its relationship marketing strategy. Seen in this way customer retention changes from being a tactical issue, involving a marginal increase in sales for a salesperson during a given year, to an issue of strategic importance at board level. The way to deliver this, of course, is increased service quality from each customer's perspective.

Developing a marketing orientation

So far in this chapter we have discussed the importance of service quality and techniques for improving and bringing together quality, customer service and marketing activity. We now consider how to go about developing a marketing orientation within a service firm to encourage and sustain an improvement in service quality through a continuous focus on the customer.

By their nature service organizations are potentially closer to their customers than companies which manufacture and sell physical products. However, marketing has come relatively late to the services sector. Whilst it is now widely accepted that a marketing orientation is vital to competitive success, companies often find it hard to discover exactly how they should achieve it. Just what do you need to do to become a marketing-oriented service organization?

The process of changing to a market orientation can appear deceptively simple. However, it demands genuine and on-going commitment, especially at top management levels, if real change is to happen. A programme to increase marketing orientation involves the following:[13]

- An identification of the existing types of orientation that already exist within the organization – some of these, outlined shortly, may be a long way from the marketing ideal.
- An assessment of the present levels of marketing effectiveness within the business.
- The formulation and implementation of an action plan to improve the marketing orientation.

Identification of orientations

The full potential of marketing is not realized in many service sector firms because of their conflicting orientations. Marketing authors have argued that many organizations are not serving their markets adequately because management is product oriented. A product orientation is, however, not the only inappropriate form of orientation. A range of conflicting orientations and associated attitudes restrict the development of a market orientation.

How can we identify these orientations within a service firm? One approach is to organize a meeting with senior managers in the company in order to identify the varying orientations and their associated attitudes. After a discussion of their implications, members of the senior management can identify the extent to which they believe these views are held in their company. The results are then summarized and contrasted with the desired marketing orientation. Table 8.3 shows the results of such an exercise for a professional service firm.

These are not the only orientations in service organizations – they will vary according to the service industry sector and company. Once the orientations are identified, the extent to which the company (and its competitors) holds them can be considered. The results of such an exercise can be disturbing. For example, the summary of results listed below were obtained from the board of a large insurance company.

Orientation	Extent possessed in firm
Product	10%
Cost	10%
Capacity	10%
Erratic	40%
Marketing	30%

Table 8.3 Typical orientations in professional service firms

Type of orientation	Typical associated attitudes
Product orientation	The technical quality of our services sell themselves, clients will always need our services
Response orientation	We will respond to any inquiry
Profession orientation	We uphold the highest levels of professionalism thus clients will automatically be attracted to us
Self-orientation	The company exists for the sole benefit of the partners
Sheep orientation	We must follow what is happening in the market place
Marketing orientation	We set goals based upon our in-depth understanding of the market and of differing clients' needs and aspirations

This was based on an average of the directors' rating for each of five orientations identified within the firm (product, cost, capacity, erratic and marketing) and shows a very low level of marketing orientation.

The extent to which a company has potentially conflicting orientations is a function of a number of factors, including the firm's history, the background of the senior management group within the company, and the amount of power held by functional specialisms within the firm. The environment within the specific service sector is also relevant here. The examples shown above are not exhaustive but do convey the types of orientation typically found.

These orientations, once identified, can form a useful background for a discussion of the mission of the organization and the shared values that must be developed by top management if a marketing orientation is to be developed.

Identifying marketing effectiveness

Once a broadly based understanding has been gained of the different orientations in the company, it is then appropriate to try and gauge an understanding of the current level of marketing effectiveness within the firm. Philip Kotler has developed a marketing effectiveness audit which was designed primarily for companies which are manufacturing products.[14] This audit needs to be modified for services, and preferably for a specific service industry. We have modified it for use in professional service firms and will use it as an illustration here.

Kotler identified five attributes that can be used to audit the marketing effectiveness of the business organization. Modifying these to reflect a professional firm environment, they include:

1. **Customer philosophy** – to what extent does the senior partner acknowledge the importance of the market place and client needs and wants in shaping the firm's plan and activities?
2. **Integrated marketing organization** – to what extent is the firm staffed for market analysis, competitive analysis, planning, implementation and control?
3. **Adequate marketing information** – does management receive the kind and quality of information necessary to conduct an effective marketing programme?
4. **Strategic orientation** – does the firm management generate innovative marketing strategies and plans for long-term growth and profitability, and to what extent have these proved successful in the past?

5. **Operational efficiency** – does the firm have marketing plans which are implemented cost-effectively, and are the results monitored to ensure rapid action?

The audit rates the firm on each of these five attributes. The five sections of the audit each include three questions with a maximum score of 6 points being possible for each of the attributes. Each of the five attributes has several questions. For example under 'adequate marketing information' the following questions are asked:

- When were the last market research studies of clients, referrals sources, premises and their location and competitiveness conducted?

- How well does the firm's management know its sales potential and the profitability of different market segments, clients, territories, services and forms of marketing promotion?

- What effort is expended to measure the cost effectiveness of different marketing expenditures?

We have used this modified audit (and more sophisticated ones) with over twenty-five professional service firms. The results we have obtained suggest that most professional firms are operating well below their potential in terms of marketing effectiveness. The results for a number of professional service firms are shown in Figure 8.9 which shows each firm's ranking on the five attributes.

An audit such as this can be used in a number of ways:

- It can measure a service company's overall marketing effectiveness.
- It can measure the difference in marketing effectiveness in different divisions or subsidiaries.
- It can measure perceived differences in marketing effectiveness as seen by different functional executives in departments such as marketing, operations and finance.
- It can measure the perceived marketing effectiveness in different firms in the same service industry. (For example, we have used this approach to measure perceived differences in marketing effectiveness in fourteen chartered accounting firms.)

An audit's primary purpose is to find and communicate to senior executives the perceived level of marketing effectiveness within the firm. It provides useful evidence of the need for a programme to improve the firm's marketing orientation. These are its primary functions; it is not intended to replace the rigorous marketing audit that is carried out as part of the marketing planning process.

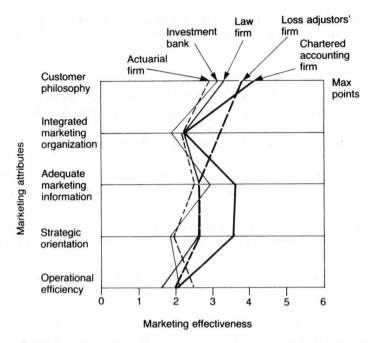

Figure 8.9   Marketing effectiveness ratings for five professional service firms

Planning a marketing orientation

An audit of this kind measures the perceived levels of marketing effectiveness within an organization either as a whole, at differing levels, or in comparison with other organizations. It is also very useful in convincing sceptics of the need to improve marketing effectiveness.

Assuming that the audit reveals a need for improvements in the marketing area – and an organization would be unusual if it did not – the next stage is to formulate a plan to realize them. That plan must involve the following steps:

- Understanding the organizational and cultural dimensions of change.
- Identifying a champion for marketing.
- Conducting a need analysis.
- Designing a training and development programme.
- Organizing key support activities.

Not all these steps should necessarily by followed by all service organizations; however, they should all be considered at this point.

The organizational dimension

Literature on corporate culture emphasizes that the shared values, common beliefs and behaviour of a company take a considerable amount of time and effort to change. To help identify the organizational and cultural dimensions of the problem, McKinsey & Co.'s '7 S' framework (see Figure 8.10) can be used to consider key elements required by an effective marketing-oriented services organization.

Figure 8.11 shows examples of aspects of these seven attributes that can be important in the transition to an effective marketing orientation. This is not intended to be a comprehensive list, but it is illustrative of the issues that emerge when using the '7 S' framework. This suggests that a strategy to develop a marketing orientation must be supported by a set of shared values, systems, management style, organizational structure, and of skills and staff (combined together in Figure 8.11).

This framework provides a means of viewing organizations as packages of key skills, or skill gaps. Hence, it can be used as a tool for analyzing organizational deficiencies, building on positive skills and identifying new skills needed. Tom Peters argues that there are three distinctive skills packages that are of prime importance in any organization, and says that these are evident in virtually all excellent companies. These skill packages are as follows:[15]

- A focus on total customer satisfaction.
- A focus of continuous innovation.

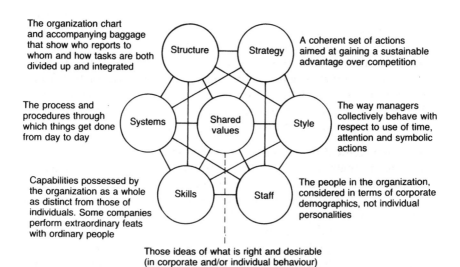

Figure 8.10 The McKinsey 7S framework

- A recognition that the above two factors are achieved by a concerted effort by all people within the organization.

Recognition of each of these cultural, organizational and skill requirements is an essential task in installing a marketing orientation. Management must also be prepared to change parts of the organization to meet these requirements.

A champion for marketing

The attitude of the chief executive can be the determining factor in the success or failure of the plan to change to a marketing orientation. Ideally, the chief executive should champion the adoption of a marketing orientation. The development of a fully marketing-oriented organization requires intense effort to shift existing attitudes and requires a leader with imagination, energy and persistence. Without this person, the programme can fail or degenerate into a token management-training exercise. Of particular importance is this champion's behaviour. The ways in which senior managers can communicate or fail to communicate the importance of their commitment to what they are saying are especially important.

Conducting a needs analysis

A management development needs analysis is the third step. Management development can be defined as an 'attempt to improve current or future managerial performance by imparting information, conditioning attitudes or increasing skills'. The needs analysis is a thorough examination of the competitive and marketing environment in which the company is placed and will identify the knowledge, skills and attitudes that need to be developed. The needs analysis should be based on interviews with appropriate managers within the firm. It should be conducted by someone with a good understanding of the knowledge, attitudes, and skills appropriate to the development of a marketing orientation in that type of organization.

The management development programme

The needs analysis can form the basis for a management development programme aimed at improving marketing effectiveness. While several options exist, one effective method is to design and run a series of courses involving marketing staff and executives from all other functions within the organization. While the content will vary according to the company's situation, in general it will cover the knowledge, skills and attitudes necessary to develop a marketing-driven organization. The objective is to demonstrate to all executives that marketing is a function to which every member of the organization has the potential to make some contribution, as well as to identify how this can be done.

Shared values
- We will become a fully customer-driven organization
- Customers come first
- Marketing expenditures are an investment
- Service is paramount

Style
- Top management support for marketing through symbolic actions and commitment of time to marketing and customer-related activities
- Open communications between all functional groups and marketing staff
- Recognition and reward of customer/market-oriented behaviour

Strategy
- Integrated plan for development of marketing orientation
- Formalized definitions of markets and mission
- Detailed specification of marketing objectives
- Commitment to implementation

Systems
- Customer intelligence reports
- Competitor intelligence reports
- Marketing planning and control systems
- Remuneration and performance appraisal systems geared to support marketing orientation
- Financial reporting systems reflecting product line contribution and profitability

Structure
- Simple structure based on markets/geography
- Key account sales structure to service most important customers
- Decentralized marketing staff to provide close and fast support to customers
- Staff rotation of non-marketing staff through customer contact positions

Skills/staffing
- Recruitment of an adequate number of people with requisite marketing skills
- Marketing training programmes and facilities
- Knowledge of market
- Analytical skills in segmenting markets and identifying decision-making units

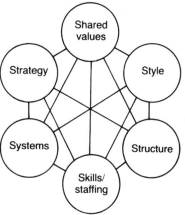

Figure 8.11   Developing a marketing-oriented service organization

A workshop approach, where a series of sessions are designed to immediately apply the newly acquired knowledge and skills to marketing problems in the organization, works particularly well. In such a programme emphasis should be placed not only on knowledge but also on the identification and development of relevant skills. The development of skills and changes in attitude are far more important than the transfer of information.

Key support activities

Once the management development programme has been initiated, a number of further tasks must be completed to ensure the successful installation of a marketing orientation. While the requirements of individual services companies will vary, the following ten key activities should be considered as part of the plan:

1. **Establish a marketing task force.** A marketing task force comprising an inter-functional group of senior managers within the company should be set up with the objective of overseeing the development of marketing activities.

2. **Organize for marketing.** It is now generally accepted that successful companies organise themselves around their markets and deliberately restrict the size of sales and service operations to maintain close contact with customers. An appropriate organizational structure should be used to support the firm's marketing activities.

3. **Acquire marketing talent.** A programme should be put in place to ensure that suitable marketing talent is hired. This will involve external recruitment and internal development of staff.

4. **Use external consultants.** Relatively few companies have the necessary in-house skills in advertising, public relations, marketing, market research and management training to be able to satisfy an organization's needs. Consultants should be used where appropriate. However, the consultants should also be used to help build in-house skills among the company's own staff.

5. **Promote market-oriented executives.** By recognizing the importance of marketing in performance review and promotion systems, management can send a message throughout the organization that marketing is important, and that managers recognizing this will be rewarded. Development of such systems will help ensure success.

6. **Maximize the impact of management development.** The management development programme discussed earlier can be augmented by a series of on-going, problem-oriented seminars designed to stimulate problem solving within the organization. Careful attention to designing these marketing workshops and seminars should help transfer learning from the seminar room to the business.

7. **Develop a marketing information system.** Successful marketing depends on accurate information, yet few organizations have developed a system that satisfactorily collects all the required marketing data from all relevant personnel. Such a system should recognize that everybody in the organization, from the sales force and technical staff to the board of directors, can make a contribution to marketing intelligence.

8. **Install an effective marketing-planning system.** As discussed in Chapter 7, many service firms have poorly developed marketing-planning systems. A coherent, comprehensive, and externally oriented marketing plan should be established and updated on a regular basis.

9. **Recognize the long-term nature of the task.** The development of a marketing orientation where it has not previously existed will require a major change in attitudes and a fundamental shift in shared values. One major company set up a marketing orientation programme in which all senior managers were involved. Continuous activity lasting five years was necessary before a marketing orientation was achieved. It can take from three to six years before a real marketing orientation is developed.

10. **Ensure commitment.** It has become clear from studies of excellent companies that abnormal effort, total commitment and possibly dysfunctional behaviour are necessary to achieve success. The committed champion for marketing will need to be obsessive in his role over several years.

Summary

The transition to a marketing orientation is a considerable challenge for management of service-sector organizations. There is increasing evidence that marketing will be an important competitive edge in many industries not traditionally seen as marketing oriented. In the past, many service businesses have been able to prosper and still rank low in marketing effectiveness! This has been possible because other competitors in the industry have ranked even worse in marketing effectiveness! However, with the increasing complexity of competition and an increasing recognition of the importance of such factors as 'closeness to the customer' in marketing success, this will not be the case in the future.

Companies need to recognize the difference between the marketing activity and the marketing process. Marketing activities consist of advertising, market research, product planning, selling and so forth, and are principally undertaken in the marketing department. Marketing processes involve the whole company, as processes are the means by which the company continuously maintains a match between its products and its customers' needs. They are at the core of all business activity, and responsibility for them crosses functional lines. Achievement of a marketing orientation is a question of establishing processes rather than activities.

There is no such thing as a quick path to market orientation. No one appointment, reorganization or pronouncement will make an organization marketing driven. The change requires a long-term view of customers and competition and a recognition that development of a marketing capability will require years of continuous work. Such effort should be looked upon as an investment by top management.

The importance of a marketing orientation in achieving success is reinforced by the work undertaken by McKinsey & Co. on excellent companies. Out of a sample of seventy-five excellent companies tracked by McKinsey & Co., five are resource based. Of the remaining seventy, sixty-five of the firms position themselves as service companies, even though most make physical products. Their success comes from quality, service, reliability or supplying higher-value products tailored for specific market niches. It is clear that these excellent companies are marketing driven, in that they provide superior service and quality.

Whilst such strategies are not prerequisites for success in every business today, and some of the excellent companies have lost their leadership position, it seems likely that the competitive dynamics of virtually all markets will compel companies to adopt customer-focused cultures in the future. Those service sector companies who take the initiative to position themselves as truly marketing oriented will be those who will be the winners in the 1990s and beyond.

While such a process of moving towards market effectiveness may seem relatively simple and straightforward, it is not easy. Nor can it be rapid, or amenable to 'quick fix' solutions. The programme outlined above involves a substantial change to the whole ethos of an organization. And it must involve the *whole* organization, for marketing in service organizations is too important to be left to just the marketing department.

But the rewards can be great. Indeed, the very survival of the organization may be at stake if it does not make such changes. The 1990s will be the decade of effective relationship marketing – especially for the service sector. No company will be able to survive on the basis that its competitors are even worse at marketing. Companies will increasingly adopt a customer-focused culture as they come to view relationship marketing as a key success factor in what looks like being a continuing difficult economic climate. Any organization that does not do the same is courting disaster.

Notes

1. M. Christopher, A. Payne and D. Ballantyne, *Relationship Marketing: Bringing quality, customer service and marketing together*, Butterworth-Heinemann, Oxford, 1991.
2. R.D. Buzzell and B.T. Gale, *The PIMS Principles: Linking strategy to performance*, The Free Press, New York, 1987.
3. R.J. Allio and J.M. Patten, 'The market share/excellence equation', *Planning Review*, September/October 1991, p. 15.
4. P. Thompson, G. De Souza and B.T. Gale, *The Strategic Management of Service Quality*, Pimsletter No. 33, The Strategic Planning Institute, 1985.
5. V.A. Zeithaml, A. Parasuraman and L.L. Berry, *Delivering Quality Service*, The Free Press, New York, 1990.
6. L.L. Berry, A. Parasuraman and V.A. Zeithaml, 'The service-quality puzzle', *Business Horizons*, September–October 1988, p. 37.
7. *op. cit.*
8. W. Band, 'Blueprint your organisation to create satisfied customers', *Sales & Marketing in Canada*, April 1989, pp. 6–8.
9. G.L. Shostack, 'Planning the service encounter' in J.A. Czepiel, (ed.) *The Service Encounter*, Lexington Books, Lexington, Mass., 1985.
10. K. Albrecht, *At America's Service*, Dow Jones-Irwin, Homewood, Illinois, 1988, pp. 26–7.
11. F.F. Reichheld and W.E. Sasser Jr., 'Zero defections: quality comes to services', *Harvard Business Review*, September-October 1990, pp. 105–11.
12. T. Peters, *Thriving on Chaos*, MacMillan, London, 1988.
13. Parts of this section are based on A.F.T. Payne, 'Developing a marketing-oriented organization', *Business Horizons*, May–June 1988, pp. 46–53.
14. P. Kotler, 'From sales obsession to marketing effectiveness', *Harvard Business Review*, November–December 1977, pp. 67–75.
15. T. Peters, 'Strategy follows structure: developing distinctive skills', *California Management Review*, vol. 26, no. 3, 1984, pp. 111–25.

Further reading

K. Albrecht and R. Zemke, *Service America: Doing business in the new economy*, Dow Jones-Irwin, Homewood, Illinois, 1985.

K. Albrecht, *At America's Service*, Dow Jones-Irwin, Homewood, Illinois, 1988.

K. Albrecht, *Service Within*, Dow Jones-Irwin, Homewood, Illinois, 1990.

K. Albrecht and L.J. Bradford, *The Service Advantage*, Dow Jones-Irwin, Homewood, Illinois, 1990.

K. Andrew, *The Bank Marketing Handbook*, Woodhead-Faulkner, Cambridge, 1986.

J. Bateson, *Managing Services Marketing: Text and readings*, Dryden, Chicago, 1989.

L.L. Berry, C.M. Futrell and M.R. Bowers, *Bankers Who Sell: Improving selling effectiveness in banking*, Dow Jones-Irwin, Homewood, Illinois, 1985.

L.L. Berry, D.R. Bennett and C.W. Brown, *Service Quality: A profit strategy for financial institutions*, Dow Jones-Irwin, Homewood, Illinois, 1989.

L.L. Berry and A. Parasuraman, *Marketing Services: Competing through quality*, The Free Press, New York, 1991.

S.W. Brown, E. Gummesson, B. Edvardsson and B.O. Gustavsson, (eds.), *Service Quality: Multidisciplinary and multi-national perspectives*, Lexington Books, Lexington, Mass., 1990.

J. Carlzon, *Moments of Truth*, Ballinger, Cambridge, Mass., 1987.

D.F. Channon, *The Service Industries*, Macmillan, London, 1978.

D.F. Channon, *Bank Strategic Management and Marketing*, Wiley, Chichester, 1986.

M. Christopher, A. Payne and D. Ballantyne, *Relationship Marketing: Bringing customer service, quality and marketing together*, Butterworth-Heinemann, Oxford, 1991.

L.L. Coffman, *Public Sector Marketing*, Wiley, New York, 1986.

C.A. Congram and M.L. Friedman, *The AMA Handbook of Marketing for the Service Industries*, Amacom, New York, 1991.

D. Cowell, *The Marketing of Services*, Heinemann, London, 1984.

E. Coxe, *Marketing Architectural and Engineering Services*, Van Nostrand Reinhold, New York, 1983.

J.A. Czepiel, M.R. Solomon and C.F. Surprenant, *The Service Encounter: Managing employee/customer interaction in service businesses*, Lexington Book, Lexington, Mass., 1985.

A. De Primio, *Quality Assurance in Service Organizations*, Chilton Book Co., 1987.

J.H. Donnely, L.L. Berry and T.W. Thompson, *Marketing Financial Services: A strategic vision*, Dow Jones-Irwin, Homewood, Illinois, 1985.

R.P. Fisk and P.S. Tansuhaj, *Service Marketing: An annotated bibliography*, American Marketing Association, Chicago, 1986.

G. Foxall (ed.), *Marketing in the Services Industries*, Special Issue of the Services Industries Journal, vol. 4, no. 3, November 1984.

C.C. Gilson, L.C. Cawley and W.R. Schmidt, *How to Market Your Law Practice*, Aspen Systems Corporation, Germantown, Maryland, 1979.

C. Grönroos, *Services Marketing and Management*, Lexington Books, Lexington, Mass., 1990.

B.R. Guile and J.B. Quinn, *Managing Innovation: Cases from the services industries*, National Academy Press, Washington, D.C., 1988.

J.L. Heskett, *Managing in the Service Economy*, Harvard Business School Press, Boston, 1986.

J.L. Heskett, W.E. Sasser Jr. and C.W.L. Hart, *Service Breakthroughs*, The Free Press, New York, 1990.

E.M. Johnson, E.E. Scheuing and H.A. Gaida, *Profitable Services Marketing*, Dow Jones-Irwin, Homewood, Illinois, 1986.

P. Jones (ed.), *Management in Service Industries*, Pitman, London, 1989.

P. Kotler and P.N. Bloom, *Marketing Professional Services*, Prentice Hall, Englewood Cliffs, 1984.

P. Kotler and K.F.A Fox, *Strategic Marketing for Educational Institutions*, Prentice Hall, Englewood Cliffs, 1985.

C. Lovelock, *Services Marketing*, Prentice Hall, Englewood Cliffs, 1984.

C. Lovelock, *Managing Services: Marketing, operations and human resources*, Prentice Hall, Englewood Cliffs, 1988.

A. Meidan, *Bank Marketing Management*, MacMillan, London, 1984.

B. Moores (ed.), *Are They Being Served?: Quality consciousness in service industries*, Philip Allan, Oxford, 1986.

K. Newman, *Financial Marketing and Communications*, Holt, Rinehart and Winston, Eastbourne, 1984.

R. Normann, *Service Management: Strategy and leadership in service businesses*, Wiley, Chichester, 1984.

J.M. Rathmell, *Marketing in the Service Sector*, Winthrop Publishing, Cambridge, Mass., 1974.

D.I. Riddle, *Service-Led Growth*, Praeger, New York, 1986.

B. Scanlon, *Marketing of Engineering Services*, Thomas Telford, London, 1988.

K.E. Sveiby and T. Lloyd, *Managing Knowhow*, Bloomsbury, London, 1987.

P.L. Townsend, *Commit to Quality*, Wiley, Chichester, 1986.

T. Watkins and M. Wright, *Marketing Financial Services*, Butterworths, London, 1986.

A. Wilson, *Practice Development for Professional Firms*, McGraw Hill, London, 1984.

V.A. Zeithaml, A. Parasuraman and L.L. Berry, *Delivering Quality Service: Balancing customer perceptions and expectations*, The Free Press, New York, 1990.

R. Zemke, *The Service Edge: 101 companies that profit from customer care*, NAL Books, New York, 1989.

Index